The Political Economy of Africa

The Political Economy of Africa

Edited by Richard Harris

Schenkman Publishing Company Inc.

Halsted Press Division

John Wiley and Sons
New York London Sydney Toronto

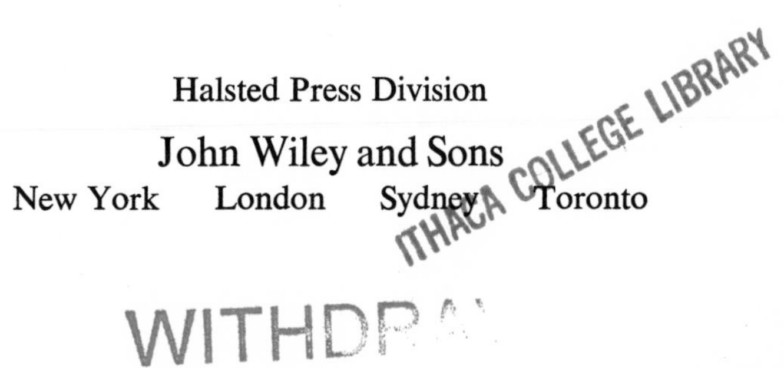

Distributed solely by Halsted Press, a Division
of John Wiley & Sons, Inc., New York

Library of Congress Cataloging in Publication Data
Main entry under title:

The Political Economy of Africa

1. Africa, Sub-Saharan—Economic Conditions—
Addresses, essays, lectures. 2. Africa,
Sub-Saharan—Politics and government—
Addresses, essays, lectures. 3. Africa,
Sub-Saharan—Social Conditions—Addresses,
essays, lectures. I. Harris, Richard, 1939–

HC502.P57 330.9'67 75-29391

CLOTH—ISBN 0-470-35420-8
PAPER—ISBN 0-470-35421-6

CONTENTS

AFRICA
POLITICAL DIVISIONS
Boundary Representation is not necessarily authorative
• Capital
0 miles 500 1000
0 500 1000 kilometers
MOROCCO
Rabat
Algiers
Tunis
TUNISIA
Tripoli
Benghazi
ALGERIA
LIBYA
Cairo
EGYPT
SPANISH SAHARA
Villa Cisneros
MAURITANIA
Nouakchott
MALI
NIGER
CHAD
Khartoum
SUDAN
CAPE VERDE IS.
Dakar
SENEGAL
THE GAMBIA
Banjul
GUINEA-BISSAU
Bissau
Freetown
SIERRA LEONE
Monrovia
LIBERIA
GUINEA
Conakry
UPPER VOLTA
Bamako
Ougadougou
Niamey
IVORY COAST
Abidjan
GHANA
Accra
DAHOMEY
Porto Novo
Lagos
NIGERIA
Fort Lamy
CENTRAL AFRICAN REPUBLIC
Bangui
CAMEROUN
Yaounde
Lome
TOGO
EQUATORIAL GUINEA
Bata
Libreville
GABON
CONGO
Brazzaville
Kinshasa
ZAIRE
RWANDA
Kigali
Bujumbura
BURUNDI
UGANDA
Kampala
KENYA
Nairobi
TANZANIA
ZANZIBAR
Dar es Salaam
F.T.A.I.
Djibouti
ETHOPIA
Addis Ababa
SOMALIA
Mogadishu
Luanda
ANGOLA
ZAMBIA
Lusaka
MALAWI
Zomba
Salisbury
RHODESIA
MOZAMBIQUE
NAMIBIA
Windhoek
BOTSWANA
Gaberones
Pretoria
SOUTH AFRICA
Lourenco Marques
SWAZILAND
Mbabane
LESOTHO
Maseru
SEYCHELLES IS.
COMORO IS.
MALAGASY REPUBLIC
Tananarive
MAURITIUS

PREFACE

This volume is not just another academic publication on Africa. It has been written as a protest and hopefully as an alternative to the conventional Western social science literature on Africa. It is the result of the contributors' general dissatisfaction with this literature and our rejection of the "conventional wisdom" held by Western scholars and experts on the so-called developing areas. The contributors to this volume believe that the foundations of this conventional wisdom are largely fallacious. We hold that an understanding of contemporary Africa and the underdeveloped areas in general can only be advanced by making a radical departure from the assumptions and modes of analyses associated with this conventional wisdom.

We have therefore attempted to provide the reader with an analytical perspective on contemporary Africa which is less biased and closer to the reality of the African people. We have proceeded on the basis of different assumptions, adopted different foci of analysis, and utilized different analytical concepts and modes of analysis. In contrast to the proponents of academic specialization in the Western social sciences, we firmly believe that a genuine understanding of the problems of development in Africa requires an analytical perspective that transcends the disciplinary boundaries of the Western social sciences—particularly those boundaries that divide the study of politics from the study of economics and *vice versa*. Thus all the contributors to this volume are concerned with the interrelationship of political and economic factors. Indeed, this is the predominant focus of the volume and it justifies to some extent our adoption of the term "political economy" in the title. However, by no means do we wish to convey the idea that we are following a classical political economics approach.

Unlike our more conventional counterparts, we not only find it impossible to separate the study of politics from the study of economics, but we believe it is the nexus between what is conventionally considered politics and what is considered economics that requires our primary attention. Only by studying this nexus can we understand in any meaningful sense the causes of underdevelopment and the prerequisites for development in Africa.

In the same vein, it is our contention that the political and economic life of the African states cannot be adequately understood if we restrict our analysis to internal or domestic factors within the individual states.

What is required is a global perspective that brings into focus the interrelationship of external and internal factors, particularly the extent to which the dynamics of the international politico-economic system affect the continued underdevelopment of the continent. Thus, in contrast to the conventional literature which tends to focus on domestic or internal factors, the contributors to this volume have attempted to introduce a more holistic and global perspective which gives attention to the external conditions (both historical and contemporary) that have influenced and continue to shape the political economy of Africa. Indeed, we do not see how the conditions of underdevelopment and the barriers to development can be analyzed without giving important consideration to the external factors influencing the economic, political, and social life of the African people.

Another important difference between the studies in this volume and many of those found in the existing literature of the Western social sciences is the extent to which all of these studies are concerned with the *effects* of the present political economy of Africa on the aspirations and welfare of the African people. In other words, we are not interested in studying the political economy of Africa for the purpose of amassing data on this subject for Western social scientists. On the contrary, we are concerned with the interests and welfare of the African people and wish to contribute in some small way to the advancement of their interests; we hope to throw some light on the structures that impinge directly on African interests and affect the quality and destiny of African lives. We wish to avoid the tendency which too often seems characteristic of Western social science inquiry: the study of processes or structures of society without any consideration of their effects on people's lives. To abstain willfully from this kind of consideration under the pretext of value-free analysis and the need to maintain objectivity is not only intellectually dishonest, it is also inhumane. Our common humanity with the African people requires that we be intellectually and morally concerned with their interests and welfare.

The contributors to this volume on the political economy of Africa are relatively young scholars who have recently been engaged in field research. Our essays depart in varying degrees from the conventional wisdom; this variation is only to be expected within any group of scholars experimenting with new modes of analysis and attempting to cover new ground. The individual essays are not intended to be comprehensive studies of the political economy of the countries in question. Some of the essays in this volume focus on one particular aspect, while other essays are more general in scope and attempt to touch upon the major characteristics of the political economy of the country or countries concerned. While states from West, East, Central, and Southern Africa are included, there is little on the North African and French-speaking West African states. Thus, this volume is restricted in its coverage to sub-Saharan Africa and has a bias in favor of the Anglo-phone states. However, a fairly broad sampling of countries of varying size and cultural diversity are dealt with in this volume. And since this volume is more concerned with introducing a different perspective on African affairs than with providing a comprehensive coverage of the continent's multitude of states, we feel that the imbalance in geographic coverage should be acceptable.

The concept of "political economy" reflects the general perspective of the contributors. We are all concerned with the interrelationship between "the political" and "the economic" in contemporary Africa, and wish to emphasize the *inter-connectedness* of what are conventionally considered as separate dimensions of social reality. Indeed, we are prepared to argue that the conventional separation of "politics" from "economics" is misleading and invalid upon careful empirical analysis. Thus, we speak of the political economy of a given country, meaning the interrelated structure of its political and economic life.

Since the contributors to this volume regard their efforts as a preliminary departure from the conventional and familiar areas of inquiry, it is hoped that this volume will be considered as the first step in the direction of developing a different analytical perspective rather than the final, perfected result of the application of such a perspective. We seek to develop a more valid framework of analysis for understanding the contemporary reality of Africa through the act of inquiry rather than through arm-chair "theorizing" or "conceptualizing."

R. L. Harris

THE POLITICAL ECONOMY OF AFRICA: UNDERDEVELOPMENT OR REVOLUTION

by

Richard L. Harris

Introduction

For the most part, the study of Africa in Western academic circles has been hopelessly biased by the influence of government funding on academic research, grants from the large private foundations, the bureaucratization of knowledge by disciplines, the prevailing social and political ideologies, and the general ethnocentricism of Western scholars, experts, and policy-makers. To correct the distortions resulting from this situation, a great deal of intellectual effort and research needs to be concentrated on the real barriers to development in Africa and the manner in which these barriers can be overcome. This means that Africa's economic dependence and subordination to foreign interests must be openly acknowledged and, along with the failings and shortcomings of the present regimes, analyzed in depth. In addition, attention must be focused on those strategies of development and configurations of power which will lead to a political economy of "rapid, self-sustained expansion, controlled and directed by and for the African people themselves." [1]

The political economy of the individual African states and their strategies for development cannot be examined in isolation, since the failure heretofore to evolve an effective strategy of development is, as Giovanni Ar-

[1] This quote is taken from one of the more notable exceptions to the prevailing orientation in Western studies on Africa, i.e., Reginald Green and Ann Seidman's *Unity or Poverty? The Economics of PanAfricanism* (Baltimore: Penguin, 1969), p. 21.

righi argues, "rooted in the political economy of Africa itself, namely the power base of the African governments." [2]

This essay seeks to outline the basic features of the political economy of Africa—particularly the conditions and structure of underdevelopment in Africa. It also attempts to provide some perspective on the prospects for meaningful development in Africa and the necessity for arriving at a relevant strategy for development of the continent and its peoples. In order to pursue these objectives it is first necessary to critique the conventional wisdom on underdevelopment and development, and introduce an alternative conceptual framework more appropriate to examining the social realities of contemporary Africa.

The Conventional Wisdom on Underdevelopment and Development

Andre Gunder Frank, a noted Latin American scholar, has laid bare the fallacies of the conventional wisdom on underdevelopment and development.[3] This conventional wisdom, which can more appropriately be labelled the "Western ideology of development," has been exported to the underdeveloped areas as an "objective" and "scientifically valid" framework for analyzing and solving the problems of these areas. Frank convincingly argues that the bulk of this conventional wisdom is invalid when confronted with the empirical reality of these areas; and ineffective if not detrimental as an intellectual basis upon which to develop policies aimed at promoting their development.

Frank points out that underlying the various "theories" of development and "analyses" of the problems of the underdeveloped areas are certain prevailing assumptions which reoccur throughout the literature of the Western social sciences. Foremost among these fundamental assumptions is the belief that the primary task of the underdeveloped countries is to undergo the process of "modernization." Although there are variations in the definition of this concept, in general modernization is used as a euphemism for "Westernization" and implies the transformation of the underdeveloped countries in the image of the developed countries of the Western world. The following definition of modernization by S. N. Eisenstadt is a good example:

[2] Giovanni Arrighi, "International Corporations, Labor Aristocracies, and Economic Development in Africa," in Robert T. Rhodes, ed., *Imperialism and Underdevelopment* (New York: Monthly Review Press, 1970), p. 255.

[3] "The Sociology of Development and the Underdevelopment of Sociology," in Andre Gunder Frank, *Latin America: Underdevelopment or Revolution?* (New York: Monthly Review Press, 1969), pp. 21–94.

Historically, modernization is the process of change towards those types of social, economic, and political systems that have developed in Western Europe and North America from the seventeenth century to the nineteenth and have then spread to other European countries and in the nineteenth and twentieth centuries to the South American, Asian, and African continents.[4]

The second basic assumption is that while the modernization of the underdeveloped countries has been stimulated and supported by the developed countries, it has been impeded by a variety of obstacles and conditions *within* each of the underdeveloped countries. This is revealed in the following excerpt from C. E. Black's, *The Dynamics of Modernization*:

Societies in the process of modernization must therefore be considered both as independent entities, the traditional institutions of which are being adapted to modern functions, and also as societies under the influence of many outside forces. Indeed, the outside influences are so powerful that modernization is sometimes thought of primarily as acculturation—the adoption of the culture traits of another society . . . . The models adopted by modernizing leaders, except in the societies that were first to modernize, are always derived in a considerable degree from outside their own society. The problems they face, however, are domestic and in essential ways unique.[5]

The list of domestic obstacles to modernization according to the proponents of the conventional wisdom is almost endless. However, a number of obstacles are repeatedly singled out, namely: "traditionalism," capital scarcity, a low level of technology, rapid population growth, lack of social integration, political instability, etc. Take, for example, the two following quotes, the first from an article by J. J. Spengler and the second from an essay by Milton J. Esman:

. . . . in the underdeveloped world, per-capita income, capital equipment, and capital formation are very low; inferior technologies predominate; enterprise is lacking; accessible natural resources are badly exploited; natality and (usually) natural increase are relatively high . . .[6]

In virtually all these societies, the stability of political authority is impaired by a limited capacity to provide satisfactions or outputs demanded by the impatient elites themselves or by other mobilized groups. This disproportion between expectation and performance is aggravated by (1) clashes of interest

[4] S. N. Eisenstadt, *Modernization: Protest and Change* (Englewood Cliffs: Prentice-Hall, 1966), p. 1.

[5] C. E. Black, *The Dynamics of Modernization* (New York: Harper & Row, 1966), p. 50.

[6] J. J. Spengler, "Economic Development: Political Preconditions and the Political Consequences of Economic Development," *Journal of Politics*, Vol. 22 (August, 1960), p. 387.

beyond the capacities of the elites to resolve; (2) shortages of physical and financial resources and of technical and managerial skills; and (3) the persistence of ethnic, sectional, or kinship loyalties and power structures and the absence of substitute institutions which can perform the integrative functions essential to the effective performance of tasks to which the governing elites are increasingly committed.[7]

Thus, it is largely argued that the continued underdevelopment of the African, Asian, and Latin American countries is the result of their internal economic, political, and cultural deficiencies.

Frank deals with each of the aforementioned assumptions, showing how fallacious they are when applied to the reality of the underdeveloped countries. First, he refutes the conventional wisdom on the grounds that it is hopelessly ethnocentric and based on an unilinear conception of developments which has no historical foundation.

"It is generally held that economic development occurs in a succession of capitalist stages and that today's underdeveloped countries are still in a stage, sometimes depicted as an original stage, of history through which the now developed countries passed long ago. Yet even a modest acquaintance with history shows that underdevelopment is not original or traditional and that neither the past nor the present of the underdeveloped countries resembles in any important respect the past of the now developed countries. The now developed countries were never *under*developed, though they may have been undeveloped.[8]

In contrast to the conventional wisdom, Frank attributes the underdevelopment of the Third World countries to their incorporation as dependent satellites within the international capitalist system. Their underdevelopment, therefore, is the result of their subordinate role in this system and the continuing contribution they have made to the development of the advanced capitalist societies. To quote Frank:

"In reality, the now underdeveloped countries have long since been incorporated and integrated into the single world embracing capitalist system, to whose development they contributed and still contribute with cheap labor, raw materials or, in a word, with investible surplus capital. In this process—that is, in the process of capitalist development and of the economic development of the capitalist metropolis in Europe and North America—the social physiology of Africa, Asia, and Latin America has been totally and uniformly changed into what it is today, the structure of underdevelopment which was

[7] Milton J. Esman, "The Politics of Development Administration" from *Approach to Development,* edited by John D. Montgomery and William J. Siffin (New York: McGraw-Hill, 1968), p. 71.

[8] Frank, op. cit., p. 4.

> . . . created by and still is consolidated by the development and structure of the world capitalist system.[9]

Frank continues:

> It is in capitalism then, and not in population growth or inertia and traditionalism, that the fundamental cause of underdevelopment resides. This is equally true of Africa, Asia, and Latin America, which are distinguished by the remarkable uniformity of their structure of underdevelopment rather than by differences of nationhood, fatalism, and institutions.[10]

Frank argues that the structure and causes of underdevelopment in Africa, Asia and Latin America are distinguished by their "remarkable uniformity." In other words, Frank sees the underdevelopment of all of these countries as resulting from the same cause, their incorporation in the world capitalist system as dependent satellites of Western Europe and North America.

Furthermore, Frank emphasizes the price paid by the underdeveloped countries as a result of their incorporation into the international capitalist system.

> "This process has resulted in a truly incalculable number of corpses—physical, cultural, and spiritual—in Africa, Asia, and Latin America. Entire civilizations have been wiped out, cultures destroyed, and countless millions have met an untimely death which liberated them from miseries that were previously unknown.[11]

Elsewhere, Frank gives specific examples of how the now developed countries "underdeveloped" (here used as a transitive verb) Africa, Asia, and Latin America. For instance, he discusses the de-industrialization of India under British colonialism, the disruption of African society by first the slave trade and then colonialism, and the total destruction of the high civilizations of the Incas and Aztecs in Latin America by the Spanish conquistadores.[12] Frank attributes the underdevelopment of the Third World countries not only to the manner of their past incorporation into the capitalist system but also to the fact that their continued participation in this system maintains and even aggravates their underdevelopment. On this score, he refutes the prevailing belief that the developed countries diffuse capital to the underdeveloped countries by demonstrating facts that indicate the reverse; i.e., that there has been a diffusion of capital *from* the underdeveloped to the developed countries. He cites U.S. De-

[9] Ibid., p. 128.
[10] Ibid.
[11] Ibid.
[12] Ibid., pp. 41–42.

partment of Commerce figures which indicate that between 1950 and 1965 there was a capital flow of $25.6 billion into the U.S. from the underdeveloped countries, in return for an outflow of capital investment to the underdeveloped areas of only $9. billion.[13] In fact, the statistics understate the actual amount of capital obtained from the underdeveloped countries by the developed ones, since they do not include the larger outflow of capital from underdeveloped to the developed countries in the form of debt service, transportation and insurance costs, transfer of funds, etc. In sum, capital badly needed for the development of the underdeveloped countries is taken out of these countries by the advanced capitalist nations. This leads Frank to conclude that the development of the underdeveloped areas is *not* dependent upon the diffusion of capital, institutions and values from the advanced capitalist nations; rather their development "can now occur only *independently* of most of these relations of diffusion." [14]

An Alternative Analytical Framework:

In view of the biases and inadequacies of the conventional wisdom, it is clear that an alternative theoretical analysis must be utilized to examine the reality of the present structure of underdevelopment and the prospects for development in Africa, Asia, and Latin America. Frank's analytical framework appears to offer such an alternative. According to Frank, any valid examination of the reality of the underdeveloped countries must be based on: 1. a holistic conception of their dependent satellite relationship to the developed capitalist metropoles; 2. their internal class and socio-cultural structure (which has been determined by their past and present economic exploitation and political domination); and 3. the prospects for their genuine liberation and development through the destruction of the present external and internal structural configuration and the pursuit of an effective strategy of development. [15]

The conventional wisdom is invalid because it does not, in Frank's words, "identify the determinant social whole." It does not direct our attention to the relations between the underdeveloped countries and the developed ones, to the historical process and world system which have made the former underdeveloped and the latter developed. Frank offers us a framework for focusing on the relationships between the developed and underdeveloped countries which have caused the underdevelopment of the latter. These relationships are seen as the product of the historical

[13] Ibid., p. 49.
[14] Ibid., p. 4.
[15] Ibid., pp. 371–372.

development of an entire social system, i.e., international capitalism. According to Frank, it is only in terms of the world capitalist system and the relations between its developed and underdeveloped parts that we can understand and explain the reality of underdevelopment.

Frank offers us a holistic model of the international capitalist system. This model consists of two parts—metropoles and satellites—connected by a structure of relationships which result in the development of the former and the underdevelopment of the latter. The international capitalist system, if we follow this model, consists of a series of constellations of metropoles and satellites. On the international level, the United States and the other major capitalist nations are the metropoles for numerous satellite countries which provide capital, resources, and labor to the metropoles. In this schema, any given satellite may be within the orbit of more than one metropole, and countries such as Spain and Portugal are satellites to other more developed countries as well as metropoles to their colonies. Moreover, Frank sees this structural relationship extending into the hinterlands of each underdeveloped country. Thus, the national capital or major urban center of each satellite country serves as a metropole with respect to the productive sectors and population of the interior. The provincial and regional centers are satellites to the national metropole and the world metropole beyond. Moreover, the provincial and regional centers each have their own local orbit of satellites. According to Frank, this heirarchical structure of metropoles and satellites was imposed on the underdeveloped countries during the course of the expansion of the world capitalist system. It is a system of monopolistic and exploitative relationships which has promoted the development of the advanced capitalist nations and the enrichment of their ruling classes at the expense of the resources and capital needed for the development of the now underdeveloped areas.[16]

Within each of the underdeveloped countries the internal structure is the product of the historical development of the world capitalist system which has "effectively and entirely penetrated even the apparently most isolated sectors of the underdeveloped world." He rejects the "dual society" thesis and insists that:

> . . . The contemporary underdeveloped institutions of the so-called backward or feudal domestic areas of an underdeveloped country are no less the product of the single historical process of capitalist development than are the so-called capitalist institutions of the supposedly more progressive areas.

He backs this contention up with evidence from Latin America which indicates that even the most remote and backward areas are linked eco-

[16] Ibid., pp. 4–6.

nomically with the more developed centers as a result of past or present instances of capitalist penetration and exploitation.[17]

Frank's analytical framework places emphasis on the class structure of the underdeveloped countries and the relationship of this structure to the system of exploitation and domination imposed on these countries by the developed ones. Speaking of Latin America, he states:

> The Latin American class structure was formed and transformed by the development of the colonial structure of international capitalism, from mercantilism to imperialism. Through this colonial structure, the consecutive metropoles of Spain, Britain, and North America have subjected Latin America to an economic exploitation and political domination which determined its present class and socio-cultural structure. The same colonial structure extends throughout Latin America, where national metropoles subject their provincial centers, and these the local centers, to a similar internal colonialism. Since these structures are completely interpenetrated, the determination of the Latin American class structure by the colonial structure does not prevent the fundamental contradictions of Latin America from being "internal." The same is true for Asia and Africa.[18]

By "colonial structure," Frank means the continued economic and political dependency of the underdeveloped countries on the major advanced capitalist powers. Although most of these countries are no longer formal colonies of the major capitalist powers, Frank considers their economic and political relations with these powers to be essentially colonial or neo-colonial in nature. Moreover, he conceives of the internal structure of these societies as reflecting similar relationships of domination and exploitation at the domestic level. In fact, he argues that popular mobilization against the "internal" contradictions and the local ruling class is the appropriate manner of confronting the imperialist system. In other words, although "imperialism is the principal enemy, it must be fought through immediate struggle against the class enemy at home."[19]

Who is the "class enemy at home," and what is the class structure that has been produced by imperialism in the underdeveloped areas? According to Frank, the underdeveloped countries are ruled by a local bourgeoisie who serve as the junior partners or executors of the bourgeoisie in the metropoles. The following quote indicates this:

> It seems legitimate to ask—and in the case of contemporary Africa there can be little question—to what extent national states in the classical sense have

[17] Ibid., pp. 5–8; see also Frank's *Capitalism and Underdevelopment in Latin America* (New York: Monthly Review Press, 1969).

[18] Ibid., p. 371.

[19] Ibid., p. 373.

existed in Latin America since Independence, and to what extent the state machinery has been at most times since then an instrument of a coalition between the metropolitan bourgeoisie and the major sectors of the Latin American bourgeoisies, who have always been the junior partners or even the executors of imperialism. Military governments have been installed to manage state affairs for these interests when civilian governments were unable to do so.[20]

Frank's words have particular meaning for the student of contemporary African society. Indeed, there is little question about the extent to which "national" states exist in Africa today. With few exceptions, they simply do not exist. Moreover, the rash of military *coup d'états* in Africa suggests that military governments have been installed to manage state affairs for the interests of the local bourgeoisie in coalition with the metropolitan bourgeoisie.

In terms of the specific character of the internal class structure of the underdeveloped countries, Frank argues that much research needs to be done on this question, since it has been largely neglected by Western and Western-trained social scientists. In general, however, he conceives of the class structure as one dominated by a small and venal local bourgeoisie composed of bureaucratic, comprador, national and land-owning elements (the exact mix naturally varies from country to country)—all of whom tend to be tied to, or dependent upon, foreign financial and business interests in one or more of the capitalist metropoles. Beneath the local bourgeoisie, are a small but politically important petty bourgeoisie of merchants, owners of medium-sized farms, and white-collar employees, plus a small and relatively privileged urban proletariat, a large and growing marginal population of unemployed town dwellers, an agricultural proletariat (which in certain countries is fairly large and of potential political importance), and a large and as yet politically inert peasantry. According to Frank, until the political mobilization of the subordinate classes against the present class structure dominated by the local bourgeoisie takes place, no meaningful breakaway from the present structure of underdevelopment and neo-colonial domination can be anticipated. On this score, Frank states with regard to Latin America:

. . . neo-imperialism and monopoly capitalist development in Latin America are drawing and driving the entire Latin American bourgeois class—including its comprador, bureaucratic, and national segments—into ever closer economic and political alliance with and dependence on the imperialist metropoles. The road of national or state capitalism to economic development is already foreclosed to them by neo-imperialist development today. The political task of

[20] Ibid., p. 393.

> reversing the development of Latin American underdevelopment therefore falls to the people themselves.[21]

How the political mobilization of the subordinate classes will take place, or what elements will provide the initiative for this process, remain open questions which Frank believes can only be answered by further analysis and practice.

In general, Frank's conceptual framework of underdevelopment, which encompasses its international and domestic aspects, its causes, and the means whereby it can be overcome, offers a framework for analysis far more compatible with the social, economic, and political reality of contemporary Africa than any of the supposedly "objective" and "scientific" theories and methodological approaches in current favor among Western social scientists and policy advisors. Frank's analytical framework, with certain modifications, can be reconciled with the works of Frantz Fanon, Amilcar Cabral, and Kwame Nkrumah, as well as the studies of Giovanni Arrighi, John Saul, Samir Amin, Reginald Green, Ann Seidman, Basil Davidson, René Dumont, and others. The remainder of this essay will draw upon these works and, with the aid of Frank's holistic conceptual framework, analyze the political economy of underdevelopment and the prospects for meaningful development in Africa.

The Structure of Underdevelopment in Africa:

The present structure of underdevelopment in Africa stems from the incorporation of the continent into the expanding capitalist system over a period of some four centuries. This process of incorporation had its beginnings in the sixteenth century when the mercantile phase of capitalist expansion brought European explorers and traders to the coasts of Africa. However, during this phase, Africa was not colonized and it did not attract any sizeable number of European settlers. Thus what took place during this same period in the New World of North and South America did not occur in Africa until a much later date. It was not until the nineteenth and early twentieth centuries that the incorporation of Africa into the international capitalist system was completed with the colonial partition of the continent. Moreover, this took place under the imperialist expansionism of industrial rather than mercantile capitalism and at a time when the capitalist system was characterized by a number of competing industrial powers. Consequently, the continent was fragmented like a patch-work quilt into a number of separate colonial units under the various capitalist metropoles of Western Europe.

Under colonialism, the basic features of the present political economy

[21] Ibid., p. 396.

of Africa took form. Colonialism provided the context within which "the development of underdevelopment," to use Frank's phrase, took place in Africa. The colonial authorities of the respective imperialist metropoles made the continent "safe for capitalism," or more precisely, safe for British, French, German, Belgium, Portuguese, and Italian capitalism—depending upon the colonial territory involved. Each colonial metropole appropriated a portion of the African continent and proceeded to impose exclusive trading rights on the hapless inhabitants. This entailed restricting the trade of the colonial population to the merchants and companies of the Colonial metropole, as well as eliminating all independent local merchants and traders who had previously performed as middlemen and traders between the Europeans and the uncolonized peoples of the interior. In this way colonialism prevented the development of a viable indigenous capitalist class and made each colony a trading monopoly of the companies and merchants of the colonial metropole. A fairly accurate account of how this process took place can be found in historical studies such as Crowder's *A Short History of Nigeria* and G. I. Jones' *The Trading States of the Old Rivers.* The classic case of Jaja, King of Opobo, who had built a powerful trading kingdom on the Niger Delta and had to be removed by the British to make way for metropolitan trading interests, was but one of a countless number of instances in which European colonial authorities eliminated indigenous merchants and traders in order to secure unhindered exploitation of the economic benefits of the colonial territory for the commercial interests of the metropole.[22]

In the colonial period the traditional pattern of economic relationships in Africa were largely destroyed and in their place were created satellite economies whose primary function was the production of one or a few cash crops or raw materials for export to the colonial mother country. It has been argued that many of the colonies did not "pay for themselves" in that the costs of their administration were higher than the revenues derived from their economic exploitation. This argument overlooks the fact that colonialism was very profitable for the relatively few European companies and capitalists who operated in these colonies. In fact, colonialism can best be viewed as serving the economic interests of a handful of companies and capitalists in the colonial metropole at the expense of both the population of the colonies as well as the home population of the metropole (whose taxes helped pay the costs of maintaining the colonial empire).

[22] See Michael Crowder, *A Short History of Nigeria* (New York: Praeger, 1966), pp. 150–209.

> The economic principle of colonial rule dictated government in what was believed to be the best interests of metropolitan capital, in short the operation of the colony as if it were a subsidiary company. As a result, the modern sectors of African economies are export biased in a way which distorts even short-term comparative advantage.[23]

Trading firms such as the United Africa Company (the largest African affiliate of Unilever), The Compagnie Française de l'Afrique Occidentale (CFAO), and the Societé Commerciale de l'Ouest Africaine (SCOA) made fortunes from their domination of the export-import trade in the colonies to which they were given privileged access. Take for example, the French trading firm CFAO.

> The Compagnie Française de l'Afrique Occidentale (CFAO), associated with banks, steamship lines, and industry in Marseille and Bordeaux, built up its business around the export of French West African produce and the import of French manufactured goods. It achieved control of French West African river transport, extended its operation into British West Africa, and worked together with the French West African Central Bank. Before the Second World War, CFAO's profits reached as high as 90 percent of its nominal capital and only in the poorest depression years fell below 25 percent.[24]

Today, these same firms continue to play a major role in the export-import trade of the now "independent" states which were formerly their colonial preserves. They have been frequently criticized for their practice of paying low prices for the cash-crops they export to Europe while setting high prices for the consumer goods they import for sale in Africa, and for sending the major share of their profits back to their home countries rather than investing in the African economies where they make these profits.

As a result of their colonial legacy, the present day economies of the African countries are characterized by a lop-sided dependence on the export of raw materials, and the import of manufactured goods from the former colonial metropoles, with the United States increasingly assuming a major role in both exports and imports. According to Green and Seidman,

> Over three-fourths of Africa's total exports are shipped to the industrialized countries of the world. However, a significant shift in trade since before the Second World War, when about three-fourths of Africa's exports went to Western Europe, is that the United States has increased its share from less than 4 percent (1938) to over 10 percent (1962).[25]

[23] Green and Seidman, op. cit., p. 127.
[24] Ibid., p. 112.
[25] Ibid., p. 38.

The structural imbalance in these economies resulting from their over-dependence on the export of one or a few primary products makes these economies extremely vulnerable to external factors and seriously hinders their internal development. Based upon their analysis of this situation, Green and Seidman conclude:

> An economy limited to specializing in the production of a few primary products for export is, by the definition of economic independence here used, highly *dependent.* Loss of markets can be catastrophic and sharp falls in the price of exports only a little less so. The national rate of growth will be no higher than the rate of growth in export receipts.[26]

In sum, the deformed development that took place under colonialism has rendered the economies of the present day states of Africa highly dependent on external economic interests and made their balanced development extremely difficult.

This structural imbalance and dependence on exports has been responsible during the last decade or so for most of the countries incurring a chronic trade deficit. This has arisen largely as a result of the declining prices of Africa's exports and the rising prices of imports from Western Europe and North America. René Dumont has estimated that between 1955 and 1959 alone the decline in export prices entailed a loss to Tropical Africa of some $600 million or twice the annual amount of foreign aid to the continent as a whole. [27] Coming at a time of increasing imports of manufactured goods for development purposes, this decline in export prices relative to import prices has, as Green and Seidman put it, caught the new states of Africa in a "giant price scissors."

> The newly independent states of Africa, like the rest of the underdeveloped world, have been caught in a giant price scissors. While the prices for Africa's exports have fallen in recent years, the prices of imported manufactured goods purchased from industrial nations tended to remain stable or even rise. As export earnings have slackened and goods have remained stable or increased, efforts by independent states to accelerate growth by importing capital machinery as well as fuels and materials, have led to growing deficits in the balance of trade.[28]

As a result of balance of trade deficits, the African countries have been forced to finance imports as well as their development programs through borrowing from foreign sources. This in turn has led to their increased dependence on foreign capital and "foreign aid" from Western governments. As Green and Seidman note, no country can expect to pursue

[26] Ibid., pp. 79–80.
[27] René Dumont, *False Start in Africa* (New York: Praeger, 1969), p. 123.
[28] Green and Seidman, op. cit., p. 42.

policies designed to achieve economic independence under such circumstances.[29]

Under colonialism, Africa was opened up to foreign investors anxious to make quick profits on their investment. As a result, foreign investment is today an important feature of the economies of all the states of Africa. Of course, the largest share of current foreign investment goes to South Africa, where net profit return averages 15 per cent per annum —one of the highest rates anywhere in the world.[30] Nevertheless, foreign investment has a great impact on all the economies of Africa, even though the amount that goes to each country may represent only a very small percentage of the total foreign investment of any given foreign firm or developed country. Unfortunately, the impact of this investment, with the exception of Rhodesia and South Africa, has not led to the industrial development of the African countries but to continued structural imbalance and external dependence of their economies. As under colonialism, most foreign investment continues to be concentrated in the export sector, with mining and petroleum extraction accounting for the largest share of such investment. Outside of mineral extraction, investment has been largely in the processing of primary products for export or in import substitution of such items as soap, beverages, textiles, shoes, furniture, and other light industry consumer goods. Foreign capital has consistently refrained from investing in heavy industry (with the exception of white-ruled Rhodesia and South Africa) or other enterprises which would compete with metropolitan manufacturers operating in the African market. Investment in economic infrastructure (roads, transportation, communication, etc.) is now undertaken exclusively by the new states to attract foreign investment. The governments of these states have had to indebt themselves increasingly to foreign lending agencies (public and private) in order to finance such infrastructure development.[31]

The natural tendency of foreign investors in Africa, as elsewhere in the underdeveloped world, has been to invest only in the high profit sectors of the African economies. The lucrative profits which they make from these sectors are immediately sent back to metropolitan banks and/or their home offices. This practice prevents domestic capital formation and results in a net outflow of capital from the African economies to the developed capitalist economies in the form of repatriated profits, royalties, interest, etc. Thus, Green and Seidman conclude that,

[29] Ibid., p. 43.
[30] *Wall Street Journal,* December 11, 1969.
[31] See Arrighi, loc. cit., pp. 225–226.

> On the whole, the post-war level of interest and profit remittance has been extremely high in relation to capital invested, to the value of production by foreign firms, and to taxes paid. To profits, moreover, must be added the interest on loans for the infrastructure in support of foreign investment and the cost of government services provided to the import-export, plantation, extractive, and consumer goods manufacturing sectors . . . . It has been estimated that profits, interests, and personal remittances exported from Africa total as much as one quarter of the continent's gross annual income.[32]

Not only does foreign investment prevent domestic capital formation in most of the African countries, it also results in a drain on their valuable foreign exchange earnings. The transfer of profits and remittances to the metropolitan countries requires that the African countries give up for this purpose the foreign exchange earned from the sale of their exports and needed for the purchase of their essential imports.

Giovanni Arrighi has called attention to the fact that a new pattern of foreign investment in Tropical Africa has been emerging in recent years as result of changes in the structure of the metropolitan economies themselves. This new pattern is characterized by: (1) a relative decline of foreign investment in Africa and (2) the growing relative importance of direct investment by large oligopolistic corporations and consortia. This pattern reflects the decline of competitive capitalism in the industrial metropoles and the growing predominance of conglomerates and multinational corporations.

> "The upshot of these changes has been the emergence of a new pattern of foreign investment in which financial and merchanting interests and small-scale capital (mainly in agriculture but also in secondary and tertiary industries) have declined in importance relative to large scale manufacturing and vertically integrated mining concerns. The typical expatriate firm operating in Tropical Africa is more and more what has been called the multinational corporation or the "great territorial unit," i.e., an organized ensemble of means of production subject to a small policy-making center which controls establishments situated in several different national territories.[33]

According to Arrighi, the investment policies of these multinational corporations are biased *against* the development of capital-goods industries in Africa and the other underdeveloped areas, and biased *in favor* of the use of capital-intensive techniques in their extractive and export-oriented undertakings in these countries. Both of these biases hinder the balanced development of the African economies. Capital intensive techniques require less labor per level of output than labor-intensive techniques. They

[32] Green and Seidman, op. cit., pp. 128–129.
[33] Arrighi, loc. cit., p. 225.

also require a small labor force composed of specialized management personnel and semi-skilled workers whereas labor intensive techniques tend to require a much larger labor force composed largely of skilled and unskilled workers. Thus, Arrighi argues that the multinational corporations are creating a small, but a relatively privileged "labor aristocracy" of well-paid employees while restricting the growth of wage employment opportunities in the modern sector of the economy for the large number of unemployed or underemployed urban migrants.[34]

The bias against development of the capital goods sector prevents a balanced growth of the internal market and, along with the use of capital-intensive techniques, increases the dependence of the African economies on the importation of specialized machinery and other capital goods from the metropolitan countries. The latter aggravates the balance of payments problem experienced by most of these countries and further integrates the modern sectors of their economies into the economies of the industrialized metropolitan countries. In sum, the new pattern of investment which Arrighi sees emerging in Tropical Africa is incompatible with both the attainment of economic independence and any significant improvement in the living standards of the African people.

Moreover, the governments of the African countries are no match for the multinational corporations. Consequently, their efforts to bargain with, and regulate the operations of, these giant corporations are largely ineffectual, particularly when the corporations are backed by the governments of their home countries. Green and Seidman note that "the individual African states are often smaller in terms of revenues and reserves than the firms whose policies they seek to control" and the dependence of these countries upon foreign investment and foreign aid "results in the determination of 'national' economic policy and even the limitation of domestic investment resources by foreign public and private interests."[35]

In fact, foreign investors and their governments tend to work together to exact as favorable conditions as possible from the African states. According to Green and Seidman:

> "The resulting pattern is one of joint investor and government pressure on the African states. High rates of profits are a usual symptom, and a drain on capital needed for economic reconstruction. But probably the most crippling results are the determination of structural change, the warping of economic plans to suit foreign investors or governments, and the thwarting or blocking of policies designed to secure African control over African economies.[36]

[34] Ibid., p. 240.
[35] Green and Seidman, op. cit., p. 81.
[36] Ibid., p. 131.

Under such circumstances, the individual states find it next to impossible to formulate and execute development plans which do not have the approval of the foreign private interests involved in their economies. In other words, foreign interests tend to exercise a veto over the development planning of the African states. Moreover, it is obvious that under these conditions, foreign financial pressures can be used to coerce these states to pursue domestic and foreign policies compatible with foreign interests.

The detrimental effects of foreign investment upon the economies and development efforts of the underdeveloped countries are increasingly being recognized by these countries. For example: Octaviano Campos Salas, former minister of industry of Mexico, has summarized the effects of foreign investment as follows:

> A) Private foreign capital takes over high profit sectors permanently, expelling or not permitting the entry of domestic capital, by relying on the ample financial resources of its home office and on the political power which it sometimes exercises. B) The permanent takeover of important sectors of economic activity impedes domestic capital formation and creates problems of balance of payments instability. C) Private direct foreign investment interferes with anti-cyclical monetary and fiscal policy—it comes when there are expansions and withdraws during depressions. D) The demands by private foreign investors for concessions to form a 'favorable climate' for investment in the receiving countries are unlimited and excessive. E) It is much cheaper and more consistent with the underdeveloped countries' aspirations to economic independence to hire foreign technicians and to pay royalties for the use of patents than to accept the permanent control of their economies by powerful consortia. F) Foreign private capital does not adapt itself to development planning.[37]

As the above quote indicates, the unfavorable effects of foreign investment are numerous and pose serious obstacles to the development of the underdeveloped countries. In Africa, as elsewhere in the underdeveloped world, efforts to maintain a "favorable climate" for foreign capital continue to make it possible for foreign investors and firms to monopolize the high profit areas of the economy, to subordinate or absorb weaker national firms, to impede domestic capital formation, make excessive profits which are sent abroad rather than reinvested in the domestic economy, to exercise what amounts to a veto over development planning, and to interfere in the social and political life of the African states. The reason this situation continues to prevail and the individual states have done little to change this situation is to be found in the nature of their

[37] Quoted in Frank, op. cit., p. 53.

class structures and political regimes. However, before going on to analyze their class and power structures, let us conclude this discussion of underdevelopment in Africa by listing the main determinants of underdevelopment effecting the individual African states:

(1) The economies of the African states are largely colonial creations and as such they are characterized by a lop-sided dependence upon the export of a few primary products to one or a few advanced capitalist states.
(2) The high profit sectors of these economies tend to be controlled either directly or indirectly by foreign interests. This impedes domestic capital formation and results in a heavy outflow of capital abroad in the form of repatriated profits, royalties, interests, etc.
(3) The major share of investment in these economies tends to be direct foreign investment, and this investment is concentrated in the extractive and export-oriented sectors rather than in the production of capital goods or heavy manufacturing. As a result, investment policy is largely in the hands of foreign interests and the development of these economies continues to be distorted and imbalanced.
(4) Due to unfavorable terms of trade and the heavy outflow of capital, the economies of the African states tend to suffer from chronic balance of payments deficits. This forces them to borrow increasingly from foreign lending agencies in order to purchase essential imports of capital goods and pay their rising foreign debts.
(5) Because of their dependency upon a few foreign markets for the sale of their exports and the predominance of foreign investment and firms in their economies, the economic policies and development plans of the African states tend to be influenced and even determined by foreign private interests and governments.
(6) The resulting structural pattern is one in which the African economies serve as dependent satellites tied to one or more metropoles which extract their major resources and investible surplus capital. This structural pattern prevents balanced development and economic independence.

Class Structure and Political Power in Africa:

Frank's thesis that the internal class and socio-political structure of the underdeveloped countries is the product of their incorporation within the world capitalist system is supported by the African experience. Although antagonistic social differences had already emerged in Africa before European contact, the impact of European trade followed by colonial rule greatly transformed the fabric of African society and produced new and more accentuated social cleavages. Thus, Samir Amin, in an article on the class struggle in Africa, concludes that:

> The complete colonisation of West Africa had two principal social effects: The acceleration of the decadence of the primitive community and the reinforcement of traditional class difference on the one hand, the introduction and development of new class differences linked to the capitalist exploitation of the country on the other hand.[38]

In other words, colonialism created a class structure in Africa in which certain traditional strata were reinforced and new strata were developed as a result of the capitalist exploitation fostered by colonial rule. Where possible, the colonizers recruited their local agents from the traditional ruling classes, and as Amin notes, they even tried to introduce traditional class relationships from the more "feudal societies" into less differentiated societies where no previous foundation for such relationships existed.

> The artificial creation of 'district chiefs' in the French colonies, and 'headmen' in the English colonies derived from the desire to create an auxiliary class of privileged people to exploit the peasants.[39]

The descendents of the traditional elements favored under colonialism today constitute a segment of the privileged sectors of the contemporary African states (e.g. the traditional aristocrats in Northern Nigeria and Uganda).

However, the emergence of a series of new classes stemming from the capitalist transformation of African society was by far the most important development during the colonial period. As Nkrumah states in his last published work, the colonial period gave rise to the development of "capitalist social structures" in Africa.

> . . . Although feudal relics remained, the colonial period ushered in capitalist social structures. The period was characterized by the rise of the petty-bourgeoisie consisting in the main of intellectuals, civil servants, members of the professions, and of officers in the armed forces and police. There was a marked absence of capitalists among the bourgeoisie, since local business enterprise was on the whole discouraged by the colonial power. Anyone wishing to achieve wealth and status under colonialism was therefore likely to choose a career in the professions, the civil service or the armed forces, because there were so few business opportunities. Foreigners controlled mining, industrial enterprises, banks, wholesale trade and large-scale farming.[40]

[38] Samir Amin, "The Class Struggle in Africa," *Revolution,* Vol. I, no. 9 (reprinted as a pamphlet by the Africa Research Group), p. 36.

[39] Ibid.

[40] Kwame Nkrumah, *Class Struggle in Africa* (New York: International Publishers, 1970), pp. 55–56.

As Nkrumah indicates, the class structure which emerged during the colonial period was composed of: a ruling class of European colonial officials and businessmen; a petty bourgeoisie of non-European functionaries, professionals, merchants, and (in some cases) large farmers; a small or insignificant proletariat of dockworkers, railway workers, miners, etc.; and a huge peasantry.

The urban petty bourgeoisie, largely composed of functionaries in the colonial administration and large European firms, has been singled out as the single most important element in the movement for independence. Amin calls this element of colonial society "the social class begotten by colonialism which had the mission of liquidating its domination." [41] In the absence of a proletariat and a politically conscious peasantry, this was the only group that developed an anti-colonialist conscience and seriously challenged the colonial regime. Largely confined to the role of commercial middlemen or minor functionaries in the colonial administration, this element mobilized against colonial rule because its members found that their material and status aspirations were blocked by the exclusively European colonial ruling class. However, as Romano Ledda argues, the movement for national independence throughout Africa was predominantly petty bourgeois in composition and aspirations and was its greatest weakness. [42] This is because the interests of this class were such that they were content to fill the positions vacated by their colonial masters on the terms set by the latter and without regard for the interests of the great mass of their countrymen. Thus, Amin concludes in his study of the Maghreb (Algeria, Tunisia, and Morocco) that the urban petty bourgeoisie determined the extent of decolonization that took place and "became the new *de facto* elite, which alone gained significant benefits from independence." [43]

Frantz Fanon condemns the "national middle class" or "national bourgeoisie" of the African countries for compromising the goals of the national liberation movements and permitting a process of "false decolonization" to take place. According to Fanon, the mission of the national bourgeoisie "has nothing to do with transforming the nation;" it is content with playing "the role of the Western bourgeoisie's business agent" and serving as the local instrument of neo-colonialism.[44] In fact, what

[41] Amin, op. cit., pp. 38–39.

[42] Romano Ledda, "Social Classes and Political Struggle in Africa," *International Socialist Journal* (August, 1967), p. 563.

[43] Samir Amin, *The Maghreb in the Modern World* (Baltimore: Penguin, 1970), p. 179.

[44] Frantz Fanon, *The Wretched of the Earth* (New York: Grove Press, 1963), pp. 152–153.

Fanon refers to as the national bourgeoisie are the same petty bourgeoisie elements discussed above. He characterizes this strata as an "underdeveloped middle class" since it has little or no independent economic power and no capability or inclination to play the historical role performed by the bourgeoisie in Western society. Thus, he states that the national bourgeoisie:

> . . . lacks something essential to a bourgeoisie: money. The bourgeoisie of an underdeveloped country is a bourgeoisie in spirit only . . . . Consequently it remains at the beginning and for a long time afterward a bourgeoisie of the civil service . . . . it will always reveal itself incapable of giving birth to an authentic bourgeois society with all the economic and industrial consequences which this entails.[45]

In other words, Fanon perceives what Ledda, Amin, Nkrumah, and others have correctly perceived—that this new ruling class has no independent economic existence apart from its control of the state apparatus and its ties to foreign capital. It cannot, therefore, be accurately described as a *national* bourgeoisie, since it is dependent for its privileged positions upon the intermediary role which it plays in the neo-colonial framework.

That the post-independence structure of African society is best described as neo-colonial cannot be adequately disputed, for the concept of "neo-colonialism," as Thomas Hodgkin has so cogently argued, aptly describes the nature of the relationship that exists between the African states and the major centers of Western capitalism.

> . . . 'neo-colonialism' tends to be regarded as something of a dirty word, to be used—if at all—in inverted commas, reflecting the shocking lack of gratitude of the former colonial peoples for the benefits which they continue to receive from the former colonial powers, and from the West in general. But in fact it is an entirely necessary way of describing the situations arising out of 'false decolonization'—the preservation of the basic relationship of Western dominance and African dependence by other means, after the transfer of formal power. This is evident not only in the field of economic relations . . . but in the military, diplomatic, cultural, educational and all other fields.[46]

This neo-colonial relationship is the product of the transfer of formal political power to a class created by, and dependent upon Western capitalism.

It is important to dispell the myth that political independence was "won" by the Africans from their former colonial powers. The granting of formal political independence by the colonial powers to their erstwhile

[45] Ibid., pp. 178–179.

[46] From Thomas Hodgkin's foreword to Green and Seidman's *Unity or Poverty?*, op. cit., p. 14.

colonies was not (with few exceptions) the achievement of popular based national liberation movements, but rather the result of a compromise reached between the former colonial powers and the almost minuscule African bourgeoisie they created—a compromise aimed at continuing the dependent-satellite status of the colonies on a new basis and in the face of growing challenges to the international capitalist system. The real character of decolonization and the context within which it has taken place is accurately described by Amilcar Cabral—one of Africa's foremost revolutionary intellectuals and leaders—in his essay "The Struggle in Guinea":

> . . . we think there is something wrong with the simple interpretation of the national liberation movement as a revolutionary trend. The objective of the imperialist countries was to prevent the enlargement of the socialist camp, to liberate the reactionary forces in our countries which were being stiffled by colonialism, and to enable these forces to ally themselves with the international bourgeoisie. The fundamental objective was to create a bourgeoisie where one did not exist in order specifically to strengthen the imperialist and the capitalist camp. The rise of the bourgeoisie in the new countries, far from being anything surprising, should be considered absolutely normal, it is something that has to be faced by all those struggling against imperialism.[47]

According to Cabral, decolonization has given Western imperialism a new lease on life by permitting the continued economic exploitation of the underdeveloped countries through indirect means. In other words, decolonization has made possible an alliance between the local bourgeoisie and the bourgeoisie of the capitalist metropoles—an alliance which permits on the one hand the local bourgeoisie to share in the benefits derived from the continued exploitation of their countries by Western capitalism and on the other hand frees the capitalist metropoles from the onus of direct domination of these countries.

Since formal political independence was granted to the new states of Africa, transformations in the social structure of these countries have been taking place. The process of social differentiation initiated during the colonial period has been accelerated by a process of rapid urbanization, by the "Africanization" of the government bureaucracy and many positions in the foreign-owned firms, and by the expansion of public education. Further differentiation of the local bourgeoisie has taken place to the point where it is possible to identify, as Ledda has done, various distinct components of this class: (1) a *comprador* element (present during

[47] Amilcar Cabral, "The Struggle in Guinea," first published in the *International Socialist Journal* (And reprinted as a pamphlet by the Africa Research Group), p. 442.

the colonial period) which serve as middlemen for the foreign import-export firms; (2) local entrepreneurs who are either associated with foreign capital or involved in housing, internal transportation, contracting, etc.; (3) the bureaucratic bourgeoisie composed of top administrative and military officials as well as government ministers, members of parliament, judges, etc.; and (4) rural bourgeois elements such as local planters, feudal landlords, and large farmers who are involved in the production of cash crops for export.[48] All of these groups—comprador, entrepreneurial, bureaucratic, and rural bourgeoisie—are, to use Ledda's phrasing, "tied body and soul to foreign capital" upon whom their privileges and livelihood are dependent. Moreover, their position is founded upon the "increasing impoverishment of the popular masses and on the general economic stagnation of the economy."[49]

In addition to the changing character of the local bourgeoisie, the nature of the alliance between this class and foreign capital has been changing. Nkrumah notes that the alliance has been further consolidated by the increased "participation" of the African bourgeoisie in the local operations of the giant, multi-national corporations.

> The Alliance between the indigenous bourgeoisie and international monopoly finance capital is being further cemented by the growing trend towards partnership between individual African governments, or regional economic organizations, and giant, imperialist, multinational corporations. African governments, some of whom claim to be pursuing a socialist path of development and "nationalizing" key industries, are in fact merely "participating" in them. They are combining with collective imperialism in the continuing exploitation of African workers and rural proletariat. The African government shields the corporations from the resistance of the working class, and bans strikes or becomes a strike-breaker; while the corporations strengthen their stranglehold of the African economy, secure in the knowledge that they hold government protection. In fact, the African governments have become the policemen of imperialist, multinational corporations. There thus develops a common front to halt socialist advance.[50]

In this regard, Arrighi forsees the possibility of a "lumpen bourgeoisie" developing around the operations of the multi-national corporations in Africa. According to Arrighi, "it is not inconceivable . . . that investment by multinational corporations in Tropical Africa will encourage the growth of a satellite, small-scale national bourgeoisie."[51] This bourgeoisie would be a bourgeoisie of small businessmen in service and retail

[48] Ledda, op. cit., p. 565.
[49] Ibid., pp. 567–568.
[50] Nkrumah, op. cit., p. 63.
[51] Arrighi, op. cit., p. 242.

industries dependent upon subcontracts and orders from the large multinational corporations. Arrighi borrows the term "lumper bourgeoisie" from C. Wright Mills to describe this stratum because of their analogy to the multitude of owners of small firms with a high death rate, existing on subcontracts from the big corporations in the advanced capitalist countries.

However, the segment of the bourgeoisie which continues to be the most important in Africa is the bureaucratic bourgeoisie. This element has assumed a central role in the neo-colonial structure and has begun to consolidate its economic relationship with the other segments of the bourgeoisie. Although it is by nature a parasitic and unproductive element, many of its members have become involved in urban land speculation, various types of commercial ventures, and even agrarian investments. Thus, Ledda concludes that the bureaucratic bourgeoisie has developed strong ties with the other elements of the local bourgeoisie. [52] These activities, however, have not provided the bureaucratic bourgeoisie with any real economic base, and they continue to be, in Nkrumah's words, "the most devoted of the indigenous agents of neo-colonialism." Their educational backgrounds, their elitist orientation, their identification with the values and life-styles of the international bourgeoisie, their privileged position within the neo-colonial state structure, and their close association with foreign bureaucrats and capitalists, all make them one of the strongest supporters of the existing neo-colonial character of their societies. [53]

The extent to which the bureaucratic bourgeoisie support the continued domination of Africa by Western capitalism is masked to some degree by the lip service they give to socialist goals and ideas. This tendency of the officials and politicians to superficially support "socialism" while serving Western capitalism and maintaining a privileged position in the neo-colonial set-up is one of the contradictions most characteristic of the new states in Africa. Amin calls attention to this phenomenon and concludes:

> Bureaucracy always puts on the "socialist" label because by the nature of things it puts a high value on the development of the State. But the development of the public sector is not necessarily either "socialism" or even a "system preparing the way for socialism." Bureaucracy can become the wealthy class and behind the mask of public property exploit the masses. The historic conditions of its arrival in power in Africa, the international conditions which

[52] Ledda, op. cit., p. 566.
[53] Nkrumah, op. cit., p. 62.

> permit it to obtain important external aid, favorize to a certain point latent tendencies of the bureaucracy to become a privileged caste.[54]

Thus, the bureaucratic bourgeoisie consolidates its privileged position and serves as the instrument of neo-colonialism in the name of "socialism" and "public property." Indeed, there is some analogy here to the state capitalist societies of the Soviet Union and Eastern Europe which are ruled by a "new class" of state and party bureaucrats. [55]

Beneath the uppermost strata of bureaucrats, compradors, entrepreneurs, and the rural bourgeoisie is a growing petty bourgeoisie of small merchants, traders, artisans, students, and salaried employees. This class can be regarded as an important variable affecting the future development of African society. There is increasing dissatisfaction among this class with the present social order and the more privileged elements above them. This new petty bourgeoisie of the post-independence period has found it increasingly difficult to gain access to the system of privileges enjoyed by the bureaucratic and comprador elements above it. Moreover, they are increasingly threatened by the competition of the large foreign companies, inflation, the rising cost of living, and decreasing opportunities for advancement in the civil service and commercial firms. As a result, Ledda notes that the petty bourgeoisie in the new states "today finds itself increasingly pushed to the margins of political and social life," and "therefore it has concrete reasons for opposing the rule of the privileged groups." [56]

More will be said about the revolutionary potential of the petty bourgeosie. However, it should be noted here that this strata is of much greater potential and social importance in Africa that it is in the advanced capitalist societies of the West.

Below the petty bourgeoisie is a small proletariat. In general, it consists of an urban and a rural component. The urban proletariat includes dock workers, transport workers, miners, and wage laborers in both the public and private sectors. The rural proletariat is composed of plantation workers, migrant farm laborers, and landless peasants reduced to a serf-like status. The urban working class is generally a rather weak economic and political force, but in certain countries (such as Ghana, Nigeria, Senegal, Congo-Brazzaville, and Dahomey) the workers are organized into trade unions and they have at times acted in a militant manner. The rural proletariat, on the other hand, is not organized and as a result is exposed to some of the worst forms of exploitation. [57]

[54] Amin, op. cit., p. 45.
[55] See Milovan Djilas, *The New Class* (New York: Praeger, 1957).
[56] Ledda, op. cit., p. 571.
[57] Ibid., p. 572.

There is considerable dispute over whether or not the urban proletariat, due to its relatively privileged position *vis-à-vis* the great mass of the population, constitutes a "labor aristocracy." Fanon argues that the urban working class in the former colonial territories is a source of support for the neo-colonial system since the workers are economically better off than the majority of the population living in the rural areas.[58] For this reason, he believes a radical transformation of African society must be carried out by the rural masses. Ledda on the other hand argues that this conception is "completely abritrary and shortsighted," and contends that the African proletariat will be "one of the decisive forces in the struggle against neo-colonialism." [59] According to Ledda, the poor living conditions suffered by the proletariat make it impossible for this strata of society to remain content with the present social order. He notes that due to the present state of agricultural production in Africa, roughly two-thirds of a working class income go toward the purchase of food alone, and that housing in the big cities and towns is both costly and miserable. [60] This, plus the fact that the workers tend to be willing to organize for the improvement of their conditions, would suggest that in the long-run they will increasingly oppose the existing order. Ledda acknowledges the fact that the proletariat does not yet possess a strong sense of class consciousness. However, he argues: "the fact that it is generally concentrated in the cities, along with the petty bourgeoisie, further increases the proletariat's potential as a revolutionary force." [61] He bases this contention on the developing consciousness of the subordinate classes which he predicts will result from the pressures of urbanization and their continued confrontation with the glaring contradictions of neo-colonial society in the cities.

Failure to take into consideration both the heterogeneity as well as the stratification of the salary and wage-working class in Africa can lead to faulty conclusions about the present and future role of this segment of African society. In this regard, Giovanni Arrighi makes an important distinction between wage-earners in terms of their *proletarianization.* By proletarianization, he means a complete dependence upon wage employment for subsistence and the severance of reciprocal obligations with the extended family in the traditional, agricultural sector of the economy. [62] A large proportion of the labor force, according to Arrighi, are only *semi-proletarianized.* That is to say, they are employed for temporary periods and receive such low wages that they are forced to return to their tradi-

[58] Fanon, op. cit., p. 108.
[59] Ledda, op. cit., p. 572.
[60] Ledda, op. cit., p. 572.
[61] Ibid., p. 573.
[62] Arrighi, loc. cit., p. 235.

tional villages from time to time to engage in subsistence farming and/or continue their reciprocal obligations with their extended family. As a result, they are neither committed to, nor dependent upon, wage-employment. On the other hand, the *proletariat proper* is composed largely of semi-skilled workers employed by the large foreign companies utilizing capital-intensive production techniques (which require specialized semi-skilled workers as opposed to either skilled or unskilled workers). This segment of the labor force has received favorable treatment from both the government and foreign firms in the form of rising wages and relatively stabilized employment. The large European firms and the multinational corporations have been willing to pay sufficiently high wages to stabilize the semi-skilled section of the work force because capital-intensity production makes wages a small proportion of total production costs and requires labor stability. The bourgeois elite in control of the public sector has also been willing to pay rising wages and pad the government payrolls as a means of coopting the small, but potentially powerful, proletariat. The policies of both the government and the large corporations, according to Arrighi, tend to produce "a situation of rising productivity and living standards in a limited and shrinking modern sector" for the semi-skilled proletariat "while the wage employment opportunities in that sector for the unskilled, semi-proletarianized peasantry . . . are reduced."[63]

Because the proletariat proper holds a relatively privileged position in African-society as a component of the "labor aristocracy,'" Arrighi argues that the interests of this class conflict with the needs of the African states to disengage from international capitalism and curtail their present expenditure of investible surplus on non-essential consumption.

> The 'labor aristocracy' . . . owes its very existence and consolidation to a pattern of investment in which the international corporations play a leading role. The displacement costs involved in the disengagement from international capitalism have to be borne mainly by the 'labor aristocracy' itself. The most important consideration, however, concerns the reallocation of the surplus that is necessary for the mobilization of the disguised saving potential of Tropical Africa. Such a reallocation directly hits the 'labor aristocracy,' which has most benefited from the present pattern of growth without development, and whose consumption therefore has to be significantly curtailed.[64]

Arrighi contends that there is a conflict of interests between the semi-proletarianized peasantry and the labor aristocracy of fully proletarianized wage-earners in Africa. He argues that failure to consider the "time dimension" of class interests can lead to faulty assumptions about the

[63] Ibid., p. 239.
[64] Ibid., p. 256.

compatibility of the class interests of Africa's semi-skilled proletariat with the transformation of the present socio-economic order. According to Arrighi, "disregard of the time dimension may lead both to a kind of 'proletarian messianism' and unrealistic assumptions concerning the class interests that can be attributed to international capitalism." [65]

Closely associated with Arrighi's semi-proletarianized peasantry is that segment of urban African society which Ledda, Cabral, Nkrumah, and others refer to as the *lumpen-proletariat.* This lumpen proletariat consists of *déclassés:* the permanent unemployed, large numbers of young migrants to the cities, beggars, prostitutes, and other social outcasts. Ledda contends that if this segment of African society is properly led, it can play an important role in the overthrow of the present order. [66] However, Cabral indicates that "the really déclassé people—the permanent layabouts, the prostitutes, and so on—have been a great help to the Portuguese police" who have utilized them as informers against the liberation movement in Guine-Bissau. [67]

On the other hand, Cabral notes that young migrants to the urban areas have been an important source of recruits to the liberation movement in Guine-Bissau. He attributes this to the fact that they are in a position to make the comparison between the standards of living of their own families in the rural areas and the standard of living of the Portuguese in the urban areas, and as a result they become aware of the inequities in the present society. In fact, Cabral argues that the urban experience contributes to the individual's *prise de conscience* (awakening of critical consciousness). [68]

This discussion so far has concerned itself almost exclusively with the urban class structure of African society. However, no examination of the class structure in Africa could possibly overlook the social stratification of the rural areas, which contain some 70–80 percent of Africa's total population. The fact that the class structure of rural Africa has received little attention has contributed to the false assumption that Africa's rural population is a relatively undifferentiated mass of peasants engaged in subsistence agriculture. However, this is definitely not the case. At least four distinct strata can be found throughout the rural areas of much of Africa today. These are: (1) plantation owners and traditional feudal landlords; (2) cash-crop farmers; (3) peasants; and (4) agricultural wage-earners.

[65] Ibid., p. 257.
[66] Ledda, op. cit., p. 573.
[67] Cabral, op. cit., pp. 434–435.
[68] Ibid., p. 435.

Nkrumah identifies six strata in agrarian society which he groups into two categories—the exploiters and the exploited. The exploiting strata are: (1) plantation owners; (2) 'absentee' landlords; (3) large farmers; and (4) petty farmers. The exploited strata are: (1) the peasants, and (2) the rural proletariat. About these classes Nkrumah says the following:

> At the top of the class stucture in the rural areas are the traditional feudal landlords who live on the exploitation of the peasants; and the capitalist landlords—many of whom are absentee—who are dependent on the exploitation of wage labor. Among the latter—who form part of the rural bourgeoisie—are the clergy of various sects and religions who live on the feudal and capitalist exploitation of peasants. The rural bourgeoisie own relatively large farms. They own capital, exploit wage labor, and for the most part specialize in export or 'cash' crops. The small farmers, who may be classed as petty rural bourgeoisie, possess little capital and cultivate land which they either own or rent. They employ members of their family or clan and/or wage labour . . . . Below the petty rural bourgeoisie in the rural strata are the peasants, those who cultivate negligible areas of land, and are often forced to sell their labour power to become seasonal workers. Finally there are the agricultural labourers, the rural proletariat, who own nothing but their labour.[69]

Nkrumah contends that the exploited rural strata—the peasants and rural proletariat—are "potentially the main force for socialist revolution" in Africa, and that they must be politically awakened and led by their "natural class allies—the [urban] proletariat and the revolutionary intelligentsia."[70]

Ledda notes that in West Africa about 60% of the rural population consists of peasants with medium-sized farms of between two and ten hectares.[71] However, he distinguished between those peasants with holdings between five and ten hectares and those with holdings between two and five hectares. The first group of peasants tends to operate family farms which produce export crops and they frequently dabble in trade and money lending, while the second group tends to earn an income which only satisfies their basic needs and keeps them only one step above the poor peasantry. The poor peasantry, according to Ledda, account for approximately 30% of the rural population and have farm holdings of less than two hectares. These holdings belong to the local community or to feudal lords. Frequently they are forced to seek wage employment on a seasonal basis or migrate to the cities in an attempt to escape the "process of progressive impoverishment" which this strata of rural society suffers.

[69] Nkrumah, op. cit., p. 75.
[70] Ibid.
[71] Ledda, op. cit., p. 574.

In this latter category, Ledda also places agricultural wage-earners whose numbers are on the increase in export-crop producing countries such as Nigeria, Ghana, the Ivory Coast, etc. He contends that this segment of the rural population is subjected to the most degrading forms of exploitation.

As far as revolutionary potential of the peasantry is concerned, Ledda argues that this strata of African society is at present providing passive support for the existing social order. He attributes their support largely to the influence of their traditional leaders. However, he does not dismiss the peasantry as a major revolutionary force. Rather, he rejects the possibility of the peasantry becoming an *autonomous* revolutionary force. He looks to elements *outside* the rural areas to perform the absolutely essential role of mobilizing and organizing the peasantry against the established order. Thus, the peasantry can in no sense be looked to as a revolutionary vanguard, and only an outside force can mobilize their revolutionary potential. But the task of mobilizing the peasantry, according to Ledda, is made easier by the fact that there is rising discontent within this strata of the population resulting from the increasing disregard shown them by the ruling elites.[72]

The State Structure:

Increasingly, the widening gulf between the progressively impoverished masses and the privileged few is generating an explosive social crisis in African society, and it is in this context that both the present character of the existing regimes and recent political developments—such as the military coups—can best be understood. The present ruling elements inherited a state structure, created by their colonial predecessors, which they have maintained largely intact. To quote Nkrumah:

> At the end of the colonial period there was in most African states a highly developed state machine and a veneer of parliamentary democracy concealing a coercive state run by an elite of bureaucrats with practically unlimited power . . . a professional army and a police force with an officer corps largely trained in Western military academies; and a chieftaincy used to administering at the local level in behalf of the colonial government.[73]

This state structure has served as the main instrument by which the African bourgeoisie have imposed their domination on the subordinate classes and secured their privileged position in the present neo-colonial system.

No one has done a better job of accurately describing the character of

[72] Ibid., pp. 574–575.
[73] Nkrumah, op. cit., p. 16.

the present regimes in Africa than Franz Fanon. His contribution is all the more remarkable because his observations were made in the late fifties before most of the present states of Africa had yet gained their formal independence. What Fanon saw then has since become more manifest; namely, that "the dictatorship of the bourgeoisie" has been established under the guise of "single party rule," and failing that, it has been secured by the military.

Fanon predicted that the African bourgeoisie, who led the national independence movements, would increasingly turn their backs on the masses and ally themselves with foreign interests. They are forced to collaborate with foreign capital and erect an authoritarian regime around a popular leader because they lack the economic power to secure their domination in any other way. As Fanon states:

> The bourgeoisie turns it back more and more on the interior and on the real facts of its underdeveloped country, and tends to look toward the former mother country and the foreign capitalists who count on its obligating compliance. As it does not share its profits with the people, and in no way allows them to enjoy any of the dues that are paid to it by the big foreign companies, it will discover the need for a popular leader to whom will fall the dual role of stabilizing the regime and of perpetuating the domination of the bourgeoisie.[74]

Without an economic power base of its own, the bourgeoisie has no choice but to become the willing accomplice of neo-colonialism and to rely upon an authoritarian dictatorship to maintain its domination and privileges.

Having established themselves as a ruling class, the bourgeoisie genarally enriched themselves at the public's expense through public graft and corruption as well as deals with foreign capital. Fanon prosaically describes this situation in the following words:

> By dint of yearly loans, concessions are snatched up by foreigners; scandals are numerous, ministers grow rich, their wives doll themselves up, the members of parliament feather their nests and there is not a soul down to the simple policeman or the customs officer who does not join in the great procession of corruption.[75]

As a result, the bourgeoisie have become increasingly obligated to foreign interests who are only too glad to offer loans, grants, and credits which will place the bourgeoisie in debt to them. Thus, in order to finance their conspicuous consumption, the bourgeoisie have mortgaged both the local economy and the state to foreign capital. Today, the operating budgets of many of the African states are totally dependent upon loans and grants

[74] Fanon, op. cit., pp. 165–166.
[75] Ibid., p. 172.

from one or more of the major Western powers, while local entrepreneurs and businessmen are dependent upon loans and credits from foreign banks and firms to finance their operations. The end result is a neo-colonial society tied in a multiplicity of ways to foreign capital.

As the corruption and profiteering of the ruling bourgeoisie have become more blatant and the stagnation of the African economies have reached the point of national bankruptcy, popular discontent has become widespread in Africa. As a result, many of the African regimes have dropped their previous popular facade and become openly repressive. This in turn has set the stage for military *coup d'états*. As Fanon has stated, when the discontent of the masses grows and the regime is forced to resort to harsher measures of rule, "it is the army that becomes the arbiter . . ." [76] Under such conditions, the military—whose officers are an important segment of the local bourgeoisie—enter the center of the political arena in order to replace the discredited nationalist politicians and prevent the mobilization of the discontented masses.

Not only do the military assume power to preserve the continued dominance of the local bourgeoisie, they also do so to protect the neo-colonial interests of the former mother country and international capitalism. Thus, Fanon states:

> The ranks of the decked-out profiteers whose grasping hands scrape up the bank notes from a poverty-stricken country will sooner or later be men of straw in the hands of the army cleverly handled by foreign experts. In this way, the former mother country practices indirect government, both by the bourgeoisie that it upholds and also by the national army led by its experts, an army that pins the people down, immobilizing and terrorizing them.[77]

Nothing really changes with the establishment of a military regime. The neo-colonial and class structure of the society remain intact—only the faces in the uppermost reaches of the state apparatus change.

The nationalist parties were useful organizational forms which allowed the colonial petty bourgeonsie to unite the rest of the colonial population behind them in a limited anti-colonial struggle that brought the petty-bourgeoisie to power. Following independence, these parties became an adjunct of the inherited state structure (under the guise of "single-party rule") with the purpose of maintaining popular support for the new ruling class and masking the continuing contradictions and inequalities in African society. In some countries, these parties still continue to perform these two functions. However, increasing social differentiation has been

[76] Ibid., p. 174.
[77] Ibid.

taking place in most of Africa since independence and there is growing awareness on the part of the masess of the corruption and self-seeking behavior of the ruling elites. As a result, the nationalist parties and "single-party rule" are rapidly becoming obsolete forms for ensuring the domination of the local bourgeoisie and the protection of the interests of international capitalism.[78]

Coincident with the decline of the party as an instrument of popular support has been the decline of the nationalist leader. In an excellent article on militarism in Africa, Roger Murray attributes this phenomenon to the deplorable economic conditions in these countries and the growing political cynicism of the people. He argues that there has been a significant decline in attachment to the "heroes and charlatans of the independence struggle" as a direct result of the effects of economic stagnation, urban inflation, the ossification of the nationalist parties, and the profiteering of the ruling elements. These have all served to create public cynicism and popular disregard for both the institutions and personnel of these regimes.[79] If these conditions are allowed to develop they can cause a radicalization of the exploited strata and a potential revolutionary situation. In order to prevent such a situation from developing, both the bourgeoisie and foreign interests have increasingly turned to the military.

As Murray points out, most of the post-colonial regimes have been unable to deal with the growing contradictions in their societies and have had difficulty legitimizing their authority among the population at large. Consequently, both foreign as well as internal pressures have provoked changes in the ruling personnel of the African states. The corruption, incompetence, and ineffectiveness of the nationalist politicians have increased the "fringe costs" of foreign investment and economic activity in these states, and undermined the function of these regimes as "political holding companies for foreign capital."[80] The military, on the other hand, have offered a more effective alternative to foreign capital and to the local bourgeoisie not directly implicated in the discredited regimes.

The military have come to power on the crest of rising public discontent over the corruption and decadence of the political leaders who inherited state power from the colonial rulers. They have turned the moral outrage of the people to their advantage and justified their seizure of power on the basis of the corruption and inefficiency of the nationalist politicians. The military are not associated with the excesses of the old regime because of their relatively spartan life in barracks and remote

[78] See Ledda, op. cit., pp. 577–578 for an analysis of the obsolescence of the party.

[79] Roger Murray, "Militarism in Africa," in *New Left Review,* Vol. 38 (July–August, 1966), p. 50.

[80] Ibid., p. 48.

military installations, and they are able to present themselves as the only national force that can restore national dignity and govern the country honestly and efficiently. However, their intervention is in reality aimed at protecting their class interests and the interests of foreign capital.

Nkrumah—himself a victim of a military *coup d'état* for the very reasons outlined above—has accurately observed that the reasons given by the military for their seizure of power (e.g., tribalism, corruption, economic 'chaos,' etc.) mask their true motivations and the class nature of their action. As Nkrumah states, most Western analyses of military coups in Africa ignore "the part played by bourgeois class interests and neo-colonialist pressures," and they gloss over the "repressive nature" of these coups as well as "the total non-participation of the vast majority of the population" in them. [81] The military officer corps of these countries have close ties with the other segments of the local bourgeoisie and with foreign interests. Most have been trained in the former colonial army or in the military academies of one of the Western powers, and they are generally closely allied with their Western-trained counterparts in the civil service with whom they share pro-capitalist and pro-Western attitudes. [82]

The counter-revolutionary and neo-colonial character of the numerous military regimes established in Africa in recent years is evident if the observer is willing to look beyond the "reformist" and in some cases "socialist" rhetoric which they use in an attempt to legitimize themselves and mask their true purpose. In practice these regimes have instituted few, if any, new domestic programs and in nearly every case they have gone out of their way to establish a favorable climate for foreign investment and reassure the major Western powers of their pro-Western "non-alignment." As Murray states; "it is unnecessary to posit that a foreign government or agency is behind every coup which occurs" since the neo-colonial orientations of the military are the product of their training, their dependence upon Western military aid and equipment, and their close ties with Western military advisors and institutions. In certain cases, Western intelligence agents may assist or encourage the coup-makers (this appears to have been the case in the Congo), but involvement of this sort by Western governments is rare and usually the coup is locally improvised. The need for clandestinity on the part of the coup-makers generally leads them to exclude their Western friends from the plotting. However, as Murray indicates, "a few swift reassuring gestures—an address to the local chamber of commerce, a ritual expulsion or denunciation of the

[81] Nkrumah, op. cit., pp. 47–48.

[82] See Ruth First, *Power in Africa* (New York: Pantheon, 1970) for an excellent discussion of the military-bureaucratic alliance in Africa.

Chinese, affirmation of a rightwing non-alignment policy, etc." serve to convince the appropriate Western governments and foreign investors that the new regime is compatible with their interests. [83]

While there hasn't been any mass participation in any of the recent military coups there hasn't been any popular resistance either. This is understandable in view of the political cynicism, alienation, and traditional passivity of much of the population. Ledda's comments on this are very much to the point. He states:

> Perhaps the most striking aspect of the recent events has been the absence of the masses and the lack of popular reaction to the military coups. This can be explained in various ways: the indifference of the masses towards a political system in which they played no part and an independence that has done nothing to better their lot; discontent with rapidly increasing corruption, seen by the masses more as a sign of moral degeneration of the political class than as an outcome of the established social system (the military has been quick to turn this attitude to its own advantage); the traditional passivity and alienation of large segments of the population to the problems of national politics, particularly in the rural areas.[84]

Because of their lack of identification with the post-colonial regimes and their more general alienation from the bourgeoisie-dominated political life of their societies, it is understandable why the masses have remained relatively unmoved by the transition from single-party to military rule.

However, the military regimes appear even less capable of winning popular support than the previous single-party regimes, and in order to preserve their interests as well as those of international capitalism they are forced to resort to repressive measures or to relinquish power to a new set of civilian politicians in order to prevent popular discontent from reaching the insurrectionary level. In either event, the military have unwillingly set in motion a vicious circle of coups and counter-coups and helped to bring into clearer focus the social and political crisis of neocolonial society. This crisis stems from the fact that the small, local bourgeoisie (including its military component) have neither the economic power nor the support of other social strata to stabilize their position of domination and privilege in African society. Consequently, they are increasingly forced to rely upon the support of the neo-colonial interests whom they serve, thereby revealing the true nature of their class interests. This advances both the critical consciousness of the subordinate classes and the polarization of African society.

[83] Murray, op. cit., p. 55.
[84] Ledda, op. cit., p. 576.

Tribalism and Racism in Africa

The "classless" nature of African society is a myth which serves no purpose other than to cover up the privileged position of the ruling bourgeoisie and the growing social contradictions in post-colonial African society. Another myth of this nature is that the major cleavages in African society are those between different ethnic ("tribal") or racial groups. Let us examine whether this is in fact the case.

To begin with, we need to clarify who has been responsible for the major social, political, and economic divisions in Africa today. Africa is today "balkanized" into a large number of states because the European imperial powers divided up the continent without any reference to the pre-colonial ethnic, political, or economic relationships of the indigenous population. Furthermore, the colonial partition of Africa and the imposition of colonial rule by a variety of European colonial powers introduced new factors—cultural, linguistic, and economic—which have since served to divide and fragment the African people. For example, one of the most obvious of these divisions is the linguistic one dividing "French-speaking" Africa from "English-speaking" Africa. Colonialism is also responsible for having created racially stratified societies in those areas—particularly southern Africa—where large numbers of European settlers were allowed or encouraged to immigrate. Finally, the fact that the economies of the individual African states tend to be competitive rather than complementary is due to the underdevelopment of Africa by the colonial powers. That is to say, the colonial powers divided the continent into a multiplicity of export-oriented, satellite economies dependent upon exporting the same or similar products to one or more of the industrialized capitalist countries of Western Europe and North America. For this reason, there is relatively little trade today among the African countries.

Western writers tend to detract attention away from the divisions in African society caused by colonialism by arguing that colonialism actually served to "integrate" the many petty states and tribes of pre-colonial Africa into larger political and economic units. This argument can be refuted by pointing out that there is historical evidence which indicates that large-scale societies such as the Sokoto and Segu empires were increasingly becoming the pattern in Africa before the intrusion of European colonialism interrupted this trend. Moreover, as Thomas Hodgkin has so ably put it:

> In any case, what those who regard the West as having a large responsibility for the balkanization of Africa have in mind is: (1) the way in which colonial policies tended to foster regional and ethnic particularism (as in Nigeria and the Sudan); (2) the tendency of the colonial powers (particularly France and

Belgium), during the transfer of formal political power, to permit the breakup of relatively large political systems (such as the French West African Federation) or to encourage separatist movements (as in the Congo); (3) the fact that the present political configuration of Africa, as a mosaic of petty states extremely vulnerable to external pressures, clearly accords with the general interests of the Western powers.[85]

As Hodgkin notes, the "integrative" contribution of the colonial powers on closer examination turns out to be no contribution at all.

The French governed their colonial territories in sub-Saharan Africa as two large units, but as the pressures for independence grew they split these two units (French West Africa and French Equitorial Africa) into a number of small and economically unviable states. Meanwhile, the British encouraged regionalism and feudalism in the decolonization of their colonies, thereby undermining the chances for political unity and viable economic development in these territories after independence. Nigeria is a perfect case in point. The British bequeathed the Nigerians a regionalized polity subdivided along ethnic lines. As a result, the regional ruling classes found themselves counterposed against each other and in a situation where the temptation to resort to ethnic conflict, in order to consolidate their positions, was overwhelming.

There has been a great deal written and said about "tribalism" in Africa and the importance of ethnic loyalties in general. However, it is important to note that tribalism or tribal politics is a recent phenomenon in Africa which owes its origin to colonialism and the colonial policy of "divide and rule." Under colonialism certain ethnic groups were given more favorable treatment than others and different ethnic groups were played off against one another. Moreover, the "economic development" of each colony was always geographically uneven, and as a result the people in certain areas have benefited more than those in other areas from this development. This has given rise to regional and/or ethnic animosity over differential access to education and public employment. In the post-colonial period, these differences, and ethnic identity in general, have been exploited by bourgeois politicians anxious to obscure the class differences in African society and direct the discontent of the masses away from themselves as a privileged and exploiting class.

The extent to which tribalism is a product of class exploitation and neo-colonial domination is noted by Nkrumah in his work on the class struggle in Africa. He writes:

In the era of neo-colonialism, tribalism is exploited by the bourgeois ruling classes as an instrument of power politics, and as a useful outlet for the dis-

[85] In Green and Seidman, op. cit., pp. 13–14.

> content of the masses. Many of the so-called tribal conflicts in modern Africa are in reality class forces brought into conflict by the transition from colonialism to neo-colonialism. Tribalism is the result, not the cause of underdevelopment. In the majority of "tribal" conflicts, the source is the exploiting bourgeois or feudal minority in co-operation with imperialists and neo-colonialists seeking to promote their joint class interests.[86]

As Nkrumah indicates, it is the ruling bourgeoisie who incite feelings of ethnic animosity to further their own ends. In certain cases, such as Nigeria, this practice has been carried to the extreme and has resulted in violent ethnic conflict. However, it needs to be emphasized that this conflict is a product of the structure of neo-colonial society. Such conflict does *not* take place spontaneously or as a result of popular initiative. On the contrary, it is initiated and manipulated by bourgeois and/or feudal elements anxious to promote their own interests through tribalism. The same is true in the case of the victimization of 'alien' or immigrant African workers in countries such as Ghana, The Ivory Coast, and Senegal. The ruling elites of these countries have aroused mass feelings against the immigrant workers from other African countries by claiming that the latter are responsible for the widespread unemployment and scarcity of urban housing that characterize the countries in question. [87]

Racial conflict, particularly as it applies to the Republic of South Africa and Rhodesia is a source of even greater misunderstanding. According to the conventional wisdom, the inequities and racial discrimination which characterize these societies are the result of cultural and psychological factors such as White attitudes of racial superiority and fears of miscegenation. The economic motives behind the system of racial stratification and oppression in South Africa and Rhodesia are at times acknowledged but never given sufficient emphasis. However, economic factors are largely responsible for the repressive and racist character of South African and Rhodesian society.

As the essay on South Africa in this volume clearly reveals, the capitalist economies of South Africa and Rhodesia are based on a system of forced labor which is rationalized by racist ideology and enforced by a racist power structure. As a result, it is impossible to separate race relations from the exploitative class structure of these societies. The African populations of both countries have been "underdeveloped" at the expense of the development of the European enclaves. First slavery and then coerced cheap labor have been relied upon by European capitalists to exploit the natural resources of these countries. Today, an explicit

[86] Nkrumah, op. cit., pp. 59–60.
[87] Ibid., p. 66.

hierarchy of racial differentiations coincides with the class differentiations in both societies. Class differences within the different racial groupings are muted by the class differences between them. The "non-European" racial groupings have been exclusively relegated to the lower strata of the society by the European bourgeoisie, while the small lower strata of the European population (e.g., skilled workers and petty bourgeois elements) have been coopted by the bourgeoisie and constitute a privileged labor aristocracy *vis-à-vis* the exploited African, Colored, and Asian populations. These groups hold the lowest-paying and least skilled positions in the economy. The African population, in particular, has been turned into a huge pool of cheap labor to be drawn upon at will by the industries and mines of international capitalism and the farms of the local Europeans. Indeed, the non-European racial groups constitute "internal colonies" whose cheap labor is exploited by the industrial enclaves of both the local European bourgeoisie and international capitalism.

A genuine national bourgeoisie has developed in both South Africa and Rhodesia alongside the mines and firms of international capitalism. This bourgeoisie is the product of a sizeable European settlement in both areas and the development of local economic power through commercial agriculture, state capitalism, and a massive use of forced labor. Racist ideology and racial discrimination have made it possible for the national bourgeoisie in both countries to develop a highly exploitative class structure which is masked by racial overtones. Since the racial differentiations in these societies closely parallel the class differentiations, the latter tend to be overlooked. However, there is a large proletariat of African urban and rural wage-earners; a sizeable petty bourgeoisie of Asians, Coloreds, and some Africans; and a large mass of African petty farmers and peasants who exist on a bare subsistence basis in the Bantustans and reserves. As Legassick indicates in the essay on South Africa in this volume, the racist class structure of this kind of society is maintained by a degree of repressive state control which is "unparalleled in all but the most totalitarian phases of Nazi Germany and Stalinist Russia."

The Liberation and Development of Africa

In view of what has already been said about the structure of underdevelopment and neo-colonialsim in Africa, it should be clear that the peoples of Africa cannot hope to achieve both genuine independence from foreign control and meaningful socio-economic development without a radical transformation of the present structure of their societies. In other words, the liberation and development of Africa is contingent upon a comprehensive social revolution which will replace the present social order with a new order based on totally different political and economic relationships. In the words of Thomas Hodgkin, "The basic problem of the African peoples cannot be solved by self-seeking bourgeois regimes, supported by neo-colonialist interests, within a framework of petty states."[88] What is needed is a new structural configuration serving the basic interests and needs of the African people, rather than the special interests of a privileged few and the needs of international capitalism. A new structural configuration of this sort must be based on Africa's disengagement from international capitalism and the elimination of the present class structure and political regimes which presently divide and oppress the African people.

Writing in a relatively recent issue of the *Journal of Modern African Studies,* Giovanni Arrighi and Jolin Saul set the problem of Africa's development in clear focus. They state that Africa must disengage from international capitalism for two basic reasons: (1) because of the capital drain which the present dependency on foreign capital engenders; and (2) because of the distorted "growth" which foreign investment encourages by its choice of capital intensive techniques and its concentration in the export and extractive sectors of the African economies. Moreover, they further argue that disengagement from international capitalism must be accomplished by a change in the power base of the existing African states:

> . . . The emergence of a labor aristocracy, with considerable political power, was brought about not only by the pattern of foreign investment but also by the acceptance of a colonial salary structure on the part of independent African governments. The labor aristocracy will therefore continue to use its power in a state-controlled modern sector in order to appropriate a considerable share of the surplus in the form of increasing discretionary consumption. Under these conditions 'perverse growth' would continue notwithstanding state ownership of the means of production. In order to achieve 'real' long-term development, disengagement from international capitalism will have to be accompanied by a change in the power base of the African governments.[89]

It will be recalled, that the concept of "labor aristocracy" is used to refer to the ruling "bourgeoisie" as well as the privileged salaried and wage-earning elements in the new states of Tropical Africa. It is this combination of strata that Arrighi and Saul identify as the present power base of the new states.

In so far as Africa's disengagement from international capitalism is concerned, the question naturally arises as to whether Africa can realis-

[88] In Green and Seidman, op. cit., p. 18.

[89] Giovanni Arrighi and Jolin Saul, "Socialism and Economic Development in Africa," *Journal of Modern African Studies,* Vol. VI, no. 2 (1968), p. 151.

tically hope to develop without the capital and "aid" of the Western capitalist nations. According to Frank, the development of both the Soviet Union and Japan indicates that development can take place through disengagement from the international capitalist system and isolation from foreign investment and control. Frank states:

> . . . Japan is the crucial example among the capitalist economies, as the Soviet Union is among the socialist, of a country which, in order to achieve the take-off into economic development in a world of already industrialized and imperialist countries, began by isolating itself substantially from foreign trade and totally from investment and control. Neither country found it necessary, let it be noted, to permit such foreign investment in order to take advantage of the technology of the industrially more advanced countries. Only *after* they had forged an economic structure and their own control of it, which permitted them to take advantage of more intimate economic ties with already advanced countries, did Japan and the Soviet Union enter into such relations.[90]

Frank is not suggesting that the underdeveloped countries of Africa, Asia, and Latin America follow the Soviet or Japanese roads to development. Rather, he is suggesting that the general experience of these two countries indicates that an underdeveloped society can isolate itself from foreign investment and direct foreign involvement in its economy and achieve the take-off into self-sustained economic development. The question remains, however, whether any one of the African states is sufficiently *large enough* to build a modern economy on the basis of its own human and material resources, assuming that it successfully isolates itself from foreign investment and control.

Green and Seidman, in their excellent analysis of the obstacles of Africa's development and the steps that must be taken to overcome these obstacles, conclude that the economic unification of the continent is absolutely essential if Africa is to break free of its present dependency on Western capitalism and satisfy the material aspirations and needs of its peoples. This conclusion is based on the simple but inescapable fact that individually the states of Africa are not viable economic units.

> No African state is economically large enough to construct a modern economy alone. Africa as a whole has the resources for industrialization, but it is split among more than forty African territories. Africa as a whole could provide markets able to support large-scale, efficient industrial complexes; but no single African state nor existing sub-regional economic union can do so.[91]

An integrated modern economy requires large markets so that economies of scale in production can be attained. It requires a wide array of natural

[90] Frank, op. cit., p. 159.
[91] Green and Seidman, op. cit., p. 22.

resources and diversified production. Moreover, in order to justify the costs of industrial production, there must be a sufficient market for the goods produced from this production.

Green and Seidman estimate that given Africa's average per capita income of $100 per annum, a national product of some $40 billion and a population of some 400 million would be necessary in order to provide the optimal market conditions for modern industrial development (these figures approximate the size of India's economy). Due to the fact that the average per capita income and markets of the individual African states are so small, it will take the population and the market size of the entire continent to provide the minimum conditions for industrial production. Because of its rich endowment in natural resources, Green and Seidman estimate that the minimum size for rapid economic growth in Africa would be a market of 200 million persons and a national product of $25 billion (at the time of their writing all of independent Africa had a population of almost 300 million and a total continental product of some $40 billion).[92] Thus, none of the Balkanized African states are of sufficient economic size, but the continent as a whole offers between the minimum and optimal conditions for the development of a modern industrial economy.

However, as Green and Seidman indicate: "African economic unity is a revolutionary concept." Economic unification cannot be achieved without political unification, and in view of the neo-colonial character of the present regimes, political union can only come about through revolutionary means. Moreover, the economic unification and development of Africa can only be organized and carried out under socialism. Capitalism has proved incapable of contributing to the development of Africa and is responsible for the present underdevelopment and economic backwardness of the continent. As Nkrumah so aptly put it, capitalism has had "its turn" in Africa for over 100 years, and it has failed dismally. Private ownership of the means of production and distribution only serves the interests of a privileged few while it impoverishes the vast majority of the African population.

Neo-colonialism and the venal nature of the African bourgeoisie have precluded any other route to development than socialist revolution. Half-way attempts at building socialism or following a "mixed economy" strategy of development have proven as useless as bourgeois capitalism. Nkrumah's comments on this score are particularly appropriate since he and his regime were victims of following a half-way strategy. He states:

> A "non-capitalist road," pursued by a "united front of progressive forces," as some suggest, is not even practical politics in contemporary Africa . . . . Either

[92] Ibid., pp. 59–60.

> it must remain under imperialist domination via capitalism and neo-colonialism; or it must pursue a socialist path by adopting the principles of scientific socialism. It is unrealistic to assert that because industrialization is in its infancy, and a strong proletariat is only beginning to emerge, that it is not possible to establish a socialist state. History has shown how a relatively small proletariat, if it is well organized and led, can awaken the peasantry and trigger off socialist revolution. In a neo-colonial situation, there is no half-way to socialism. Only politics of all-out socialism can end capitalist-imperialist exploitation.[93]

Nkrumah, like Fanon and others, perceives that the indigenous bourgeoisie is the immediate enemy of the African people. Therefore, he concludes that this class must be deposed from power by the workers and peasants, mobilized and led by a vanguard revolutionary socialist party.

> In Africa, the internal enemy—the reactionary bourgeoisie—must be exposed as exploiters and parasites, and as collaborators with imperialists and neo-colonialists on whom they largely depend for the maintenance of their positions of power and privilege. The African bourgeoisie provides a bridge for continued imperialist and neo-colonialist domination and exploitation. The bridge must be destroyed. This can be done by worker-peasant solidarity organized and directed by a vanguard socialist revolutionary party.[94]

Nkrumah's analysis coincides with Frank's analytical framework in that both perceive the indigenous bourgeoisie to be the immediate enemy of the impoverished masses and therefore the primary target of their struggle for genuine liberation and material well-being.

The foregoing discussion raises two fundamental questions: (1) who will bring about the armed struggle to liberate and unify Africa? and (2) how this struggle will take place? In essence, the answers to these questions constitute a revolutionary strategy for the liberation and unification of Africa.

In general, most of the writers concerned with a radical restructuring of existing political and economic relationships in Africa agree that this can only be accomplished through an armed struggle that overthrows the present social order and replaces it with a socialist society. Nkrumah, for example, states that "the privileged will not, unless compelled, surrender power" and that, as a result, "they can only be overthrown by violent revolutionary action." [95] However, there is much disagreement over which elements will set the revolutionary process in motion and carry it to a successful conclusion. As previously mentioned, there are those, such as

[93] Nkrumah, op. cit., p. 84.
[94] Ibid., pp. 84–85.
[95] Ibid., p. 80.

Fanon and Arrighi, who argue that the African proletariat are a privileged strata within the present system and as a result they cannot be counted as a revolutionary force. On the other hand, there are those such as Nkrumah and Ledda, who contend that the proletariat will form the backbone of the revolutionary struggle. Who are we to believe? Why is there such disagreement over which strata of African society are potential revolutionary forces? It seems clear that much of the confusion stems from the shortage of systematic studies on the class structure of African society. As a result, those who write about this subject are forced to make speculations based upon very little evidence.

In view of what is known about the existing structure of most of Africa, it seems safe to conclude that the revolutionary overthrow of the present social order will require a combination of different class elements. The writings of Cabral on the experience of the liberation struggle in Guine-Bissau are perhaps the most instructive in this regard. In that country, an impressive revolutionary movement has been built on a combination of elements from different strata in Guinean society. The leadership of the movement is largely petty-bourgeois in origin. The vanguard elements consist of *déclassé* migrants from the rural areas, wage-earners from the urban and rural areas, and some peasants. One thousand of these individuals were trained for two years outside of the country as revolutionary cadres. According to Cabral they were given a "working-class mentality" and sent into the rural areas of Guine-Bissau to mobilize the peasantry against Portuguese colonial rule. To quote Cabral:

> We realized that we needed to have people with a mentality which could transcend the context of the national liberation struggle, and so we prepared a number of cadres . . . so that they could acquire what you might call a working class mentality. You may think this is absurd—in any case it is difficult; in order for there to be a working class mentality the material conditions of the working class should exist. In fact we managed to inculcate these ideas into a large number of people—the kind of ideas, that is, there would be if there were a working class. . . . When these cadres returned to the rural areas they inculcated a certain mentality into the peasants and it is among these cadres that we choose the people who are now leading the struggle.[96]

It is clear from the above quote that it was a combination of urban elements initiating the struggle in Guine-Bissau and that they have taken the struggle to the rural areas, where they have aroused the consciousness of the peasantry and gained their support for armed struggle against the Portuguese.

The objection may be raised that the armed struggle in Guine-Bissau

[96] Cabral, op. cit., pp. 438–439.

as well as those in Angola, Mozambique, Rhodesia, South Africa and South West Africa are really "national independence" struggles directed against foreign or non-African elements rather than genuine revolutionary movements bent on radically restructuring these societies. However, Cabral makes it clear that his movement is a revolutionary movement committed to reconstructuring Guinean society from the bottom up. They are not interested in liberating it from colonial rule only to give power to a petty bourgeoisie that would soon ally itself with foreign interests in a vain attempt to transform itself into a national bourgeoisie.

Cabral's analysis of the petty bourgeoisie and its potential revolutionary role in neo-colonial societies is extremely relevant to the question of what elements will bring about a social revolution in Africa. He argues that the petty bourgeoisie in the neo-colonial situation has as decisive a role to play as the petty bourgeoisie under colonial rule. It has the function, along with the better educated members of the proletariat and certain alienated members of the bourgeoisie (e.g. revolutionary intellectuals), of leading the revolutionary struggle against what he calls the "native or national psuedo-bourgeoisie" and neo-colonialism. He states:

> The neo-colonial situation, which demands the elimination of the native pseudo-bourgeoisie so that national liberation can be attained, also offers the petty bourgeoisie the chance of playing a role of major and even decisive importance in the struggle for the elimination of foreign domination. But in this case, by virtue of the progress made in the social structure, the function of leading a struggle is shared (to a greater or lesser extent) with the more educated sectors of the working class and even with some elements of the national pseudo-bourgeoisie who are inspired by patriotic sentiments. The role of the petty bourgeoisie that participates in leading the struggle is all important since it is a fact that in the neo-colonial situation it is the most suitable sector to assume these functions, both because of the economic and cultural limitations of the working masses, and because of the complexes and limitations of an ideological nature which characterize the sector of the national pseudo-bourgeoisie which supports the struggle.[97]

Cabral goes on to state that in order to fullfill its vanguard function, the petty bourgeoisie must attain a high degree of revolutionary consciousness and commit "class suicide" by giving up their bourgeois aspirations and totally identifying with the workers and peasants.

As Ledda correctly points out, the formation of a revolutionary consciousness among the subordinate classes is in reality the decisive factor.[98] Any successful revolutionary movement in Africa must have the support

[97] Amilcar Cabral, *Revolution in Guinea* (New York: *Monthly Review* Press, 1969), p. 109.

[98] Ledda, op. cit., p. 500.

of the peasantry and large numbers of the less privileged elements in the urban areas. The importance of the petty bourgeoisie lies in the fact that the members of this class are both enlightened enough to perceive the contradictions in the present system as well as capable of influencing the consciousness of the proletariat and peasantry. If they reject their natural predilection toward absorbtion into the bourgeoisie and identify with the interests of the workers and peasants they will be committing class suicide but performing a critical role in the revolution. It is the task, therefore, of any effective revolutionary organization to radicalize the petty bourgeoisie and enlist them in mobilizing the workers and peasants against the present social order. These three elements can bring into being a genuine workers' and peasants' state based on a structure of decentralized, popular socialism.

Cabral cites Cuba as a case where petty bourgeois elements have succeeded in divorcing themselves from their class interests and have served as the vanguard of the socialist revolution based upon the popular support of the workers and peasants. He attributes this to the revolutionary consciousness of the petty bourgeoisie and the honesty and morality of the revolutionary leadership. It goes without saying that the character of the revolutionary movement itself—the extent to which it identifies with the masses and incorporates them into the struggle—is of crucial importance in determining the outcome of any revolutionary effort.

If we assess the prospects for a socialist revolution in Africa today along the lines of that described by Cabral, it is important to note that the trend toward military rule and more repressive regimes seems destined to alienate in increasing numbers the petty bourgeoisie of students, small merchants, traders, artisans, and clerks who can see that the realization of their aspirations is totally blocked by the venality of the ruling bourgeoisie and the inherent limitations of neo-colonial society. Add to this the increasing disaffection of intellectuals from the ruling bourgeoisie plus the example set by the advancing liberation movements in Guine-Bissau and southern Africa, and it would seem to be but a matter of time before viable revolutionary movements begin emerging in neo-colonial Africa. Indeed, the key to this development seems to be in the liberation movements struggling against racist rule and imperialism in Portuguese and White-settler Africa. As their struggle advances and ultimately succeeds, they may well serve as a catalyst and a source of support for the extension of the armed struggle for liberation and development to the rest of Africa. Moreover, states such as Guinea, Congo-Brazzaville and Tanzania may succeed in building socialist enclaves which can advance and support this process.

In the meantime, the African situation is likely to resemble increasingly the Latin American pattern with coups and counter-coups becoming commonplace, as the different segments of the bourgeoisie take their turn at alternately raiding the public treasury and trying to stop the deterioration of their position as a ruling class. In time, this pattern will serve to alienate all support for the bourgeoisie and preservation of the system will necessitate the direct intervention of the neo-colonialist powers to protect their interests. At this point, the contradictions in African society will be made clear for all to see and the present system of exploitative dependency and neo-colonialism will have no hope of continuing in the face of rising popular demands for an independent, united, and socialist Africa.

Ghana

THE POLITICAL ECONOMY OF GHANA

by

Emily Card

If you want to send your children to school, it is cocoa,
If you want to build your house, it is cocoa,
If you want to marry, it is cocoa,
If you want to buy cloth, it is cocoa,
If you want to buy a lorry, it is cocoa,
Whatever you want to do in this world,
It is with cocoa money that you do it.[1]

Background

On February 24, 1966, the fifteen-year rule of Kwame Nkrumah and his Convention People's Party (CPP) was ended by a military coup. Nkrumah's self-pronounced radical economic and foreign policy stance had irritated the military as well as other middle-class Ghanaians, and his excessive attacks on his political opposition had weakened his claim to "democratic" government, but it was his inability to control external economic relations which precipitated his demise. Nkrumah and the CPP had achieved political independence from the British in 1957, but the dependence of the economy upon the export of cocoa and other primary products had continued. Six months before the coup, the world cocoa price fell to half of what it had been the previous year. The resulting drop in export earnings meant that Ghana was unable to obtain necessary imports, the country's foreign exchange reserves having almost disappeared.

[1] A highlife song, quoted in Dennis Austin, *Politics in Ghana* (London: Oxford University Press, 1964), p. 275.

On January 13, 1972, the government of Prime Minister K. A. Busia was likewise toppled by the Ghanaian military. Busia's Progress Party (PP) had come to power in September, 1969, after three years of military rule. The institution of the Busia regime under a constitution closely guarded by entrenched clauses designed to prevent the excesses of the Nkrumah period was hailed in the Ghanaian press and Western press alike as a victory for democracy in Africa. Yet, almost before Busia took office, his party had begun maneuverings designed to limit the role of the opposition. Later a variety of laws were enacted which made Busia's "democracy" more nearly resemble a comic opera. Following Ghana's second coup in six years, an editorial in the government-owned *Ghanaian Times* proclaimed: "For the second time, the armed forces have had to come in to take over the reins of government to save the country from maladministration and corruption of politicians, and to save the nation from total economic collapse." [2]

In the month before the second coup, the price of cocoa had reached a five-year low. The fall in cocoa prices occurred simultaneously with a 44 percent devaluation of the Ghanaian currency in the same month. The devaluation was part of Busia's austerity program, necessitated by the continued dependence on export earnings and the consequent need to curb imports and limit private consumption. Once again cocoa prices and the import-export sector had coalesced to produce political instability in Ghana, but in both cases, it was instability born of continued colonial economic relations rather than instability derived from the birth of a new order.

The history of Ghanaian politics can be understood only in the context of Ghana's colonial past. The colonial situation created a condition of economic dependence which plagued Nkrumah's developmental plans, and the colonial legacy continues to ensnare the new regimes which have succeeded him. Political patterns growing out of the experience of anti-colonial nationalism also persist, as do the effects of Ghana's six-year dyarchy or period of shared rule with the British, 1951–57.

Despite political independence gained in 1957, Ghana exhibits continuing, albeit modified, colonial economic relationships. Nkrumah denounced neo-colonialism and pursued some socialist programs in an effort to free political and economic relationships from their colonial inheritance; yet his efforts suffered from contradictions inherent in any attempt to achieve economic independence while remaining almost completely dependent upon the same foreign, capitalist nations to which the country was attached before independence.

[2] The *New York Times,* January 15, 1972.

Nkrumah's answer to the problem of development was twofold. In the *economic* sphere, agricultural productivity was to be achieved through large-scale mechanized farming rather than through increased outputs of small-scale peasant agriculture. But, development was to center primarily around industrialization rather than agriculture[3] and state enterprises were considered essential to guarantee rapid and significant results. Both in agriculture and industry, development would be based upon direct state investment in the means of productions. The ultimate goal was a socialist economy freed from control by external forces, but, during a preceding transitional period, the economy was to be mixed. Paradoxically, while Nkrumah denounced the forces of Western imperialism, he envisioned that new investment capital for the development of Ghana would be obtained from Western public and private sources.

The *political* component of the development effort was guided by the realization that with Ghana's continued economic dependency on the West, the identification of the people with the socialist goals of the state was imperative. Furthermore, the government was opposed to the growth of a class of Ghanaian entrepreneurs who could potentially undermine socialist plans through their own identification and cooperation with external economic interests. "Nkrumah opposed on ideological and personal political grounds the accumulation of substantial economic power in the hands of Ghanaians."[4] In fact, the presence of external capital did militate against the rise of a national bourgeoisie. However, the continued presence of foreign influence undermined Ghana's transition from a capitalist to a socialist economy. In theory, the development effort was to have been guided by the single party, the CPP, through its auxiliaries, which were to provide a means of control over key sectors of the economy and, theoretically, build support for the government's development policy. The objective was to reorganize the whole life of the nation based on improvements in all sectors.[5]

In actuality, the party consumed much of its energy in an attempt to consolidate its own position of power, particularly through establishing party wings. Wings or auxiliaries in four sectors were to have played key

[3] Cuba's new revolutionary regime also attempted to follow a policy of forced industrialization which they had to modify drastically in favor of a more modest shift away from a primarily agricultural economy. Either program would have been possible only with massive trade commitments from one or both of the two communist "super powers." See Lee Lockwood, *Castro's Cuba, Cuba's Fidel* (New York: Vintage Books, 1969), pp. 87–104.

[4] John D. Esseks, "Indigenous Private Enterprise in Ghana," *Journal of Modern African Studies* 9 (May, 1971): 21.

[5] Roger Genoud, *Nationalism and Economic Development in Ghana* (New York: Frederick A. Praeger, 1969), p. 73.

roles in organizing the population—trade unions, farmers' cooperatives, and women and youth groups. Partly as a result of the predominance of political over economic priorities, Nkrumah succeeded in achieving neither. Preserving party power became an end in itself rather than a means to socialist development. As the CPP struggled with massive economic tasks, the opposition parties attacked it from the sidelines. The CPP itself seethed internally as various factions disputed the proper role of the party in political and economic development. The political contradiction which characterized the creation and deterioration of the CPP auxiliaries was to a great extent only the manifestation of the more fundamental economic contradiction: the attempt to achieve economic independence while relying upon foreign private capital, which in itself imposed grave political and economic constraints.

The necessity for rapid economic development was manifest. Political independence brought with it rising expectations on the part of the population which the nationalist government was increasingly hard-pressed to fulfill. Steady, rapid growth meant providing more consumer goods for the population at the same time that the government needed its scarce foreign exchange to support its increasing share of capital investment. A study for potential foreign investors noted in 1959 that "such steady development is counted on to support the political ascendency of the CPP."[6] The party's survival became tied to the growth of the economy, which reinforced the emphasis on the necessity for a concentration of power in the party. The successful military coup in February, 1966—which occurred when consumer prices were rising rapidly and shortages of consumer goods were critical—only provides the final example of the extent of the party's dependence upon its ability to deliver the economic "goods."

In order to understand the developmental challenge which faced Nkrumah, it is necessary to understand the conditions under which he and his party came to power. The central factor was that the CPP won independence not by prolonged struggle but through a period of electoral politics which extended over a six-year dyarchy.[7] In this period, 1951 to 1957, Nkrumah's government shared power with the British, and to a great extent both the party and Nkrumah were dependent on the British

[6] *The Ghana Report* (New York: G. H. Wittman, Inc., International Economic Consultants, 1959), p. 9.

[7] Frantz Fanon in *The Wretched of the Earth* (New York: Grove Press, 1963) describes the effects of the dyarchy in general terms; Immanuel Wallerstein, *Road to Independence* (Paris: Mouton, 1964), pp. 54–70, specifically for Ghanaian politics. See also Genoud, *Nationalism and Economic Development*, pp. 86–94; and Austin's *Politics in Ghana*, a study centered on the independence elections.

for their continued power. The fundamental economic and political decisions made during the dyarchy continued to impose their parameters upon Nkrumah's action long after nominal political independence was achieved. These decisions were made mostly by the British themselves, either directly or indirectly. The economic decisions determined the direction of the developmental effort; and the CPP's political reliance upon elections, and, later, legal control, deprived the party of any potential organizational base for an effective national challenge to continuing economic imperialism.

"The Political Kingdom"

On Sunday, June 14, 1949, Kwame Nkrumah announced the formation of the Convention People's Party;[8] less than two years later the CPP won the first national election in the then British colony of the Gold Coast. As soon as the results of the February 8, 1951 election became clear, the colonial government released Nkrumah from prison where he had been confined following the 1950 political disturbances. The governor general of the Gold Coast, recognizing that only Nkrumah would be able to form a government in the newly-elected assembly, invited him to do so. "The nationalists were in office; the election was over. The total cost of this first trial of strength had been £50,000." [9] Men who had been in prison for agitation against the colonial government and men who had been in the villages arguing for "self-government now" were suddenly faced with *being* the government. Although "the permanence of a revolution which had been accomplished so easily" [10] might have been questioned, the CPP followed Nkrumah's precept, "Seek ye first the political kingdom" for unless the CPP accepted office, notwithstanding the limitations of the 1950 constitution, a chance would be lost that might not be easily regained.[11]

Two difficult problems confronted the new CPP government. With the assistance of the British, the so-called "verandah boys" (who having no houses slept on Accra verandahs) had to formulate economic and governmental policies which would determine Ghana's future. Simultaneously, the party had to prevent its recently won victory and control from

[8] Austin, *Politics in Ghana,* p. 86.

[9] Ibid., p. 151.

[10] Ibid., p. 152.

[11] Ibid., p. 150. The dyarchy period in Ghana demonstrates many parallels with the same British strategy in Guiana. In terms of governmental power, the fates of Nkrumah and Cheddi Jagan were identical, for much the same reasons. Cf. Ibid, p. 170.

slipping through its fingers as it began to face challenges both from within the party and from without.

The CPP as a Nationalist Party

Nkrumah was a nationalist working for political independence; he was not a revolutionary socialist. Rather than coming to power through a revolutionary struggle, the CPP won a general election. The effects of this history upon the party were lasting, yet in later years as the party became steeped in socialist rhetoric, Nkrumah and other party leaders often appeared to have forgotten that they were not leading a revolutionary party. The British had defined the nationalist situation, and the CPP accepted parliamentary politics as the legitimate arena of conflict. Moreover, Nkrumah and his Ghanaian opponents restricted their pre-independence efforts to removal of the foreign political and administrative superstructure; all assumed at least a temporary continuance of the basic economic structures.[12]

The struggle within the context of electoral politics meant that more attention was focused on the CPP's electoral power than upon real, deep-rooted mass support or political mobilization. During the years of the nationalist struggle, the CPP made important compromises with the colonial administration and paid lip service to capitalist-oriented, middle-class interests in order not to alienate this sector of the electorate. This compromising meant that, far from forming an effective grassroots movement that could be used to mobilize the masses, the party was limited to rhetorical appeal to anti-colonial nationalism which began to lose its galvanizing effect once nominal national independence had been obtained.

The acceptance of the conditions imposed by the British during the dyarchy precluded fundamental challenges to the existing order. From 1951, when Nkrumah became leader of government business, to 1957, when Ghana became the first black African nation to gain its political independence, Nkrumah was, in fact, completely dependent on the British for his power and that of his party.

This sharing of power during the dyarchy served the British in several ways: they could "assist" in the determination of major economic policies; they could educate African leaders to their political ideology and they could prevent a revolution from taking place under "communists" thus allaying their Cold War fears. The British administration retained control over crucial sectors, including defense, external affairs, justice, and finance during the early years Nkrumah was in office.

One example should suffice to suggest the magnitude of the economic

[12] *Ibid.*, pp. 155–56.

motives behind Britain's maintaining this control over Ghanaian affairs. Britain faced severe monetary shortages following World War II, and in 1951, the same year semi-responsible internal government was granted in the Gold Coast, the United Kingdom suffered a serious balance of payments crisis. Not only were large sterling balances held in Britain and now demanded, threatening the pound, but during this period, Britain faced a severe dollar shortage. "For the United Kingdom, and for the whole sterling area, the year 1952 was dominated by the need to check this crisis." [13]

Britain held sterling balances for her colonies, and she could not afford to lose these at that point. The British government clearly recognized the role the colonies were to play in improving the balance of trade, as discussions at a meeting in 1954 of commonwealth finance ministers showed.[14] In effect these colonies were lending money to Britain—and at extremely low interest rates. Rather than providing development aid for the Gold Coast, the latter's foreign exchange earnings were transferred to Britain to bolster her assets. Thus, E. N. Omaboe has stated that:

> Capital outflow on government account from Britain into Ghana has been of minor importance in her economic advancement. It is rather that Ghana has made substantial investment in Britain through the holding there of almost all her foreign reserves.[15]

Ghana's reserves were extremely important in this period, accounting for 18.4 percent of Britain's total colonial sterling balances in 1951.[16] In 1951, the Gold Coast exported over $84 million, mostly in cocoa, to the dollar area of which the Gold Coast retained only 17 percent.[17] By 1954, the Gold Coast's Cocoa Marketing Board (CMB) held almost $92 million

[13] *Britain: An Official Handbook* (London: H.M.S.O., 1955), p. 272.

[14] Ibid., p. 277.

[15] E. N. Omaboe, "An Introductory Survey," *A Survey of Contemporary Ghana,* 1, p. 31.

[16] Calculated from total British balances of £908 million in 1951, of which Ghana's share was £137.2 million. See Bob Fitch and Mary Oppenheimer, *Ghana: End of An Illusion* (New York: Monthly Review Press, 1966), pp. 44–45, and Killick, "External Trade," p. 360. See also Emily Watts, "British Policy in the Federation of Rhodesia and Nyasaland," (Senior Honors thesis, Newcomb College, New Orleans, 1963) for an account of the similar position occupied by Britain's Central African territories.

[17] Gold Coast Legislative Assembly, *Debates,* August 9, 1955, cited in Fitch and Oppenheimer, *Ghana,* p. 46. Except where needed for emphasis or in quotations, all monetary figures have been converted to dollars to avoid confusion. For the period under consideration, the following equivalents are used: £ or G£, $2.80, until July 1965; Cedi (C), $1.17, until February 22, 1967; New Cedi (NC), $1.40, until July 1967; New Cedi devalued July, 1967, to $.98.

in United Kingdom Government Securities, about 79 percent of the Board's total reserves.[18]

> The British had a clear interest in the continuation of these policies following the CPP's rise to power in 1951. Had Nkrumah broken the CMB's marketing monopoly and adjusted the domestic cocoa price to the world level, or used CMB profits within the Gold Coast, the British economy would have been seriously affected.[19]

Nkrumah and the CPP permitted this policy to continue precisely because they were dependent upon the British for their own power.

This compromise supposedly served the interests of the nationalists, at least in their own eyes. However, as Fanon puts it, "The will to break colonialism is linked with another quite different will: that of coming to a friendly agreement with it." [20] The nationalists hoped economic aid would be gained through cooperation; the legitimacy of the authority of the CPP could be reinforced through association with the British; and party leaders gained time to consolidate their power vis-à-vis both the opposition parties and their opponents within the party.[21] Indeed, Nkrumah could not have come to power were it not for the backing of the colonial government. Neither the CPP nor its opposition were strong enough to mount any further political challenge after the initial electoral battle which the British administration was prepared, shrewdly, to accept.

The Opposition to the CPP

Once "complete" independence from the British was in sight, moving Ghana's economy from colonial relations to socialist development plans could not be accomplished until the CPP managed to quell its opposition, which promised to stand in the way of any sharply leftward moves. For the first nine years of CPP rule, roughly from 1951 until the republican election in 1960, the CPP used much, if not most, of its energy fighting opposition maneuvers designed to win power from the CPP. All combatants realized the importance of being the ones left in power when the British finally departed; therefore, in the period from 1951 until independence was gained in 1957, a variety of opposition groups attempted to delay independence or change its terms in their factional favor. Fanon seemed to be describing Ghana when he wrote,

[18] Calculated from figures in The Ghana Cocoa Marketing Board, *Seventeenth Annual Report and Accounts for the Year Ended 30 September 1964* (Accra, n.d.), pp. 22–23.

[19] Fitch and Oppenheimer, *Ghana,* p. 46.

[20] Fanon, *Wretched of the Earth,* p. 124.

[21] Cf. Austin, *Politics in Ghana,* p. 156. Also see Frantz Fanon, *Wretched of the Earth,* p. 74, and Wallerstein, *Road to Independence,* pp. 54–67.

> The occupying power has made its choice from among the two or three nationalist parties which led the struggle for liberation. The ways of choosing are well-known: When a party has achieved national unanimity and has imposed itself on the occupying power as the sole spokesman of the nation, the colonial power starts complicated maneuverings and delays the opening of negotiations as much as ever it can. Such a delay will be used to fritter away the demands of this party or get its leaders to put certain "extremist" elements into the background.[22]

The 1954 general election was meant to have been Ghana's final election before independence.

> The stage had been reached when the nationalists, the colonial officers, and the United Kingdom government were all in agreement, and when the forthcoming election was seen as the last act of an unexpected partnership which thereafter (it was assumed) would be dissolved.[23]

While the CPP had been legitimized through its three and one-half year rule, it had also been weakened by internal dissension over the pace at which self-government was being achieved. The 1954 election was a turning point. Behind were the years of rule since 1951; ahead the struggles of the pre-independence period. Neither the British nor the CPP foresaw the trouble to come. In April 1954, full, internal self-government was granted as a final stage before independence.[24] But, "while agitation may unite, elections tend to divide." [25] Or, as it has been seen by another writer, elections produce "cleavage mobilization." [26] Within months after the June, 1954, election an opposition movement centered in Kumasi was formed. The struggle grew so sharp and even violent that the United Kingdom withdrew from the prospect of surrendering control without a third general election,[27] which took place primarily at the instigation of Nkrumah's opposition, which demanded the Gold Coast be turned into a federal state at independence.

The formation of this new party, the National Liberation Movement (NLM), was precipitated by the government's announcement of its new Cocoa Ordinance in which cocoa prices would be set for a period of four years. In the context of rising world prices, this anouncement resulted in widespread discontent in the cocoa-growing areas, particularly

[22] Fanon, *Wretched of the Earth,* p. 119.
[23] Austin, *Politics in Ghana,* p. 194.
[24] Ibid., pp. 200–202.
[25] Ibid., p. 245.
[26] Nettl, *Political Mobilization,* p. 271.
[27] Austin, *Politics in Ghana,* p. 250.

Ashanti.[28] Ashanti farmers submitted grievances through the United Ghana Farmer's Council "which marked the beginnings of a definite revolt against the CPP within the farmers' associations" [29] (and provided, incidentally, another motive for eventual incorporation of a farmers' auxiliary within the party). The NLM wanted to halt negotiations between the CPP and the colonial offices; they demanded a fresh start to the process of constitution-making which would provide a chance to form a federation.[30] Although the CPP eventually won the 1956 election and went on to take office as the first government of independent Ghana, the level of attack was so great that the party, perhaps for the first time, realized that its ability to maneuver would be limited even though it had control of the legal powers available to the government.

Again, Fanon aptly describes the process in general terms:

> The nationalist parties which have not taken part in the negotiations engage in denunciations of the agreement reached between the other party and the occupying power. The party takes over the reins from the colonialists, conscious of the danger with which the extremely demagogical and confused attitude of the rival party threatens it, tries to disband its competitor and condemn it to illegality.[31]

Class Basis of Party Participation

In order to understand the position of the CPP relative to its opposition, it is necessary to return to the political and social context in which the struggle for independence occurred. The first demands for independence came from middle-class, educated professionals who viewed themselves as the logical heirs to colonial rule. Trained and socialized by the colonial regime, their vision of an independent Ghana was one in which they would play the same paternalistic role as had the colonial administrators before them, instituting a black "indirect rule" over their less-educated brothers. While the middle-class professionals would control national and international affairs with the continued close cooperation of the British, the traditional chiefs were to continue in the role of local authorities

[28] Lord Hailey, *An African Survey: Revised 1956* (London: Oxford University Press, 1957), p. 829. The agitation resulted in an increased price the following year, 1955. See also Austin, *Politics in Ghana*, pp. 254–57.

[29] Austin, *Politics in Ghana*, p. 257.

[30] Ibid., p. 276. The same groups which mounted this struggle in 1954–56 reappeared in the 1969 elections, suggesting the lack of fundamental social change over the period between these elections despite the organizational efforts of the CPP. See Emily Card, "Who Will Govern Ghana?" *Africa Report* 13 (April, 1968): 9–16; and Card and Barbara Callaway, "Ghanaian Politics: The Elections and After," *Africa Report* 15 (March, 1970): 10–15.

[31] Fanon, *Wretched of the Earth*, p. 1191.

whose traditional powers had been qualitatively transformed under the British.

Although the *legitimacy* of the traditional institution of chieftancy had been undermined by the imposition of the white man's authority over the chief, the actual *power* of individual chiefs had been strengthened by the presence of the colonial regime which protected them from traditional checks on their power so long as they supported the colonial administration.[32] The chiefs' interests, then, were linked to the preservation of the status quo, as were those of the professional and middle-class intellectuals. Hence, as Nkrumah's new nationalist CPP arose to challenge the professional classes for leadership of the nationalist struggle, a semi-permanent anti-CPP alliance was formed between the professionals and the traditional rulers.

Nkrumah, by contrast, directed his appeal to the emerging classes of the new urban environment and, very importantly, thought of the struggle for independence in mass terms. Not only did he appeal to the "young men,"[33] unemployed urban youths and school leavers, but he saw the struggle in terms of creating a nationwide base of supporters. The opposition professionals, on the other hand, thought primarily in terms of appealing to a limited class of educated and traditional elites.[34] The emergence of the CPP cast the nationalist struggle in a new light, and the effect was a fragmentation of the older nationalist opposition party, the United Gold Coast Convention (UGCC), and the subsequent development of essentially regionally based parties in opposition to the CPP.

While the CPP's opposition was regionally based, the CPP appealed to a geographically dispersed group of people. According to Genoud the party contained within it all the strata and, hence, all the contradictions of Ghanaian society; its mixed nature constituted both its strength and its weakness. The CPP "tried to appeal to as many people as possible, and, thus, was no more the party of the working class than the party of the lower middle class, or any other group or class."[35] Genoud also emphasizes the transitional nature of colonial society and the fluidity of the social structures of a colony.[36] While Fitch and Oppenheimer argue

[32] See K. A. Busia, *The Position of the Chief in the Modern Political System of Ashanti* (London: Oxford University Press, 1951); for a different but related pattern, see L. Fallers, "The Predicament of the Modern Chief," *American Anthropologist* 57, No. 2 (1955): 290–305.

[33] Traditionally, those in Ashanti society who held no royal office; used in modern politics to refer to often minimally educated commoners.

[34] Cf. Apter, *Ghana in Transition,* pp. 176–77.

[35] Genoud, *Nationalism and Economic Development,* p. 182.

[36] Ibid., p. 169, Cf. Roger Murray, "Second Thoughts on Ghana," *New Left Review* 42 (March-April, 1967): 31.

that the CPP should have joined forces with the urban proletariat and the rural peasantry,[37] it is only fair to point out that the classic alternatives to a nationalist coalition party such as the CPP—a working-class or peasant-based party—were not feasible at this moment in Ghana's history. The urban working class was too small to constitute a base for an electoral party, and a major struggle would have been necessary to overcome the deep tribal cleavages dividing the rural peasantry, by far the largest proportion of Ghanian society and the class necessary to any fundamental change.

It must be noted that Fitch and Oppenheimer have incorrectly seen the "landless agricultural laborers and sharecroppers" as "the Gold Coast's real oppressed class" and therefore the class from which a revolutionary movement would arise.[38] The problem with this analysis is that the migrant laborers, into which category these landless laborers and sharecroppers often fall, represent a mixed category of persons. Some are international migrants (17 percent of the male labor force, 7 percent of the female); some are "long distance migrants" (19 percent of male labor force, 11 percent female) and some "short distance migrants" (21 percent of male labor force, 29 percent of female). Those who were classified as "long distance" migrants, in 1960 numbering 403,770 male and female workers,[39] are the group Fitch and Oppenheimer might find potentially threatening to the colonial system. This group is relatively small—and not all migrants cited in these figures are agricultural workers. They make the point that "the other strata of the party bourgeoisie—teachers, clerks, independent artisans, et al.—had no direct economic conflicts with the chiefs."[40] Their point is interesting because they recognize, but interpret differently, one of the major problems with organizing a fundamental challenge to the colonial system, given the cooperation of the chiefs with that system. It is not only that migrants had *economic* conflicts with the chiefs, but that the migrants, like those in urban areas, move outside the tighter web of village-centered traditional relationships and hence, to some extent, beyond the influence of the chiefs. Often these persons joined ethnic associations, which have been recognized as politically important in the nationalist period. The point is that some 70 to 80 percent of the labor force in Ghana is engaged

[37] *Ghana: End of an Illusion,* pp. 20–25.

[38] *Ibid.,* p. 22.

[39] Killick, "Labor: A General Survey," *A Study of Contemporary Ghana: The Economy of Ghana,* eds., Walter Birmingham, I. Neustadt, and E. N. Omaboe (2 vols.; Evanston: Northwestern University Press, 1966): 1, 132.

[40] *Ibid.*

in the pre-industrial sector.[41] Those persons so engaged are likely to be living in a traditional setting where the influence of local chiefs is greatest. Yet the support of these persons would have been absolutely necessary to mount the alternative to a parliamentary electoral struggle, an insurrection in which force would be used. For guerrilla struggles must have the support of the peasantry, or some portion of it, to survive. Yet another complicating factor in Ghana is that such a large proportion of the farming population is engaged in cocoa growing. The 1960 Population Census recorded 533,350 persons engaged in cocoa growing, of which 312,350 were farm *owners*.[42] Other farmers engaged in field crop and foodstuff production numbered 910,460.[43] Thus, of a total farm labor population of 1,462,810, 21 percent were cocoa farm owners and 36 percent were in cocoa production—not exactly a mass of "starving peasants."[44]

The analysis by Fitch and Oppenheimer is extremely suggestive; yet, they appear not to understand fully the persuasiveness of traditional power at the historical point they are discussing (1948 to 1951), nor do they adequately perceive the land tenure system. Later Dien Bien Phu and the Cuban revolution might alter notions of potentials. Yet at this point, it was precisely because so few classes could, or would challenge the economic power of the chiefs that Nkrumah turned to the young men, a choice which Fitch and Oppenheimer criticize.

Parenthetically, and perhaps ironically, the example of "Gold Coastism" had tremendous impact on nationalist movement in other parts of Africa. Wallerstein sees the example of Ghana and the developments in North Africa and Indochina as the "two principal levers that forced a shift in the French pattern of constitutional development."[45] Ironically, although its later self-proclaimed goals were among the most "radical" to be found in Africa, the CPP's early ascension to power—almost a decade before many other African nationalist parties enjoyed the same fruits—almost certainly assured that even had its leadership wished to do so, the small territory would have had utmost difficulty in supporting a revolutionary armed struggle. The point in time at which crucial actions occur is extremely important in analyzing the political history of Ghana. The 1960's witnessed outbreaks of armed insurrection against the Portuguese in the territories under their control in Angola in 1961; Guinea, 1963; and Mozambique, 1964. Aside from questions of the relative interna-

[41] Killick, "Labor: A General Survey," p. 127.

[42] Killick, "Cocoa," *A Survey of Contemporary Ghana,* vol. 1, p. 239.

[43] Killick, "Agriculture and Forestry," *A Survey of Contemporary Ghana,* vol. 1, p. 221.

[44] Fanon, *Wretched of the Earth,* p. 61.

[45] *Politics of Independence,* p. 72.

tional power of Portugal as compared with Britain, the intervening years saw the growth of a much strengthened, if split, communist world, and the continuation of the struggle in North Vietnam.[46]

Genoud maintains that persons from all strata of Ghanaian society supported the party in the nationalist elections. In fact, in another study observing the 1969 elections, fifteen years after the first complete adult suffrage election in Ghana, this writer has suggested that voting patterns cut across socio-economic stratifications and reflected "tribal" or ethnic differences as much as any other socio-economic indicator such as education, urbanity, etc. This study suggests that the following of the parties which succeeded the CPP had as much to do with subliminally perceived "tribal" interests as it did with "class" interests,[47] and it may be suggested that the same held true for the nationalist votes. While it must be clearly recognized that ethnic, regional, and class interests often coincide, as for example, in the Ashanti area which is the center of cocoa farming, earlier ethnic animosities can still be perceived in voting patterns.

However, it is necessary to distinguish more clearly than has been done in past writing between the CPP leadership and the CPP followers in attempting to analyze the "class" basis of the party; often the failure to discuss the two separately is compounded by the tendency to see the CPP throughout its fifteen-year history as always representing the same interests.

When they began their careers, many of the leaders could rightly have been classified as independent radicals with little, or nothing to lose, in the Fanonist sense.[48] Over the years of CPP office, many of the early leaders gained access to the wealth and power of the state, and differ-

[46] See Gerard Chaliand, *Armed Struggle in Africa: With the Guerrillas in "Portuguese" Guinea* (New York: Monthly Review Press, 1969). On the impact of "Gold Coastism" on British colonial history, see Sir Andrew Cohen, *British Policy in Changing Africa* (Evanston: Northwestern University Press, 1959), esp. p. 44. On the usefulness of the distinction between "radical" or "revolutionary" and "moderate" regimes in Africa, see Immanuel Wallterstein, "Left and Right in Africa," *Journal of Modern African Studies* 9 (May, 1971): 1–10.

[47] See Emily Card, "When a Great Number of Mice Dig a Hole, It Does Not Become Deep," (Paper delivered at the annual meeting of the Western Political Science Association, Sacramento, California, April, 1970). Fitch and Oppenheimer are highly critical of those who would see tribes as a significant factor in politics in Africa, pointing out that " 'tribal' politicians like Professor K. A. Busia of Cambridge are still in exile" (*Ghana,* p. 4). Yet shortly after their book was published, Busia reappeared on the scene and began to draw upon the same tribally-related interests as he had in the 1954 and 1955 elections; he went on to become prime minister of Ghana in the 1969 elections.

[48] Fanon speaks of the peasants "alone who are revolutionary, for they have nothing to lose and everything to gain," *Wretched of the Earth,* p. 61.

ences in purely personal interests began to be reflected in differences over policy matters related to the extent and pace of Ghanaian socialism. By 1960, when inner party purges of the old leadership began in earnest, some of these formerly "radical" leaders had become wealthy men, whose prosperity was "linked to the State and to foreign capital." [49] These entrepreneurs—both men like Komla Gbedemah, who had entered politics from business, and men such as Krobo Edusei, who had been employed by the *Ashanti Pioneer*[50]—continued in positions of leadership in the party, and their presence contributed to the vacillation of the party in pursuing its socialist policies.

Regional Factors of Political Conflict

The opposition was formed from a shifting coalition of the same professional and traditional interests which had been split from the CPP during the early nationalist struggle. From the first national election in 1951 until the republican election of 1960, regional opposition along several dimensions developed. In the Trans-Volta-Togo area, the Ewe people demanded independence and then amalgamation with the Ewe in French Togoland. The CPP, on the other hand, wanted to annex both British and French Togoland into Ghana.[51] For the North, Nkrumah's emphasis on a unitary form of government and his radical ideology lost him the support of much of the tradition-bound and Muslim population of this region.

The main opposition, however, was centered in the cocoa-growing

[49] Amin quoted by Davidson in "West Africa's Blocked Economy," p. 477.

[50] Information about the backgrounds of party leaders and other elites is not always easily obtainable and a note on sources here will be generally helpful in indicating how such material has been obtained. The information here about Gbedemah is taken from a private interview (Accra, 1967) which was checked against other available sources. Krobo Edusei is described by Henry Bretton as the member of Nkrumah's "cabinet who was most loyal, least scrupulous about democratic principles, least informed and toughest-minded." *Rise and Fall of Kwame Nkrumah* (London: Pall Mall Press, 1967), p. 45; while David Apter notes that "Krobo Edusei was treated with great consideration by Nkrumah, who made him chief government whip, although his qualifications were by no means clear." *Ghana in Transition* (New York: Atheneum, 1968), p. 208. Austin, *Politics in Ghana,* p. 56, provides the information about Edusei's background as a newspaper employee but does not state his actual position. Some biographical information may be found in the *Ghana Yearbook* (Accra), published by the Graphic Corporation, but this source is not always accurate.

[51] Scott Thompson, *Ghana's Foreign Policy,* 1957-1966 (Princeton: Princeton University Press, 1969), pp. 81–87. See also Claude Welch, *Dream of Unity: Pan Africanism and Political Unity in West Africa* (Ithaca: Cornell University Press, 1966).

Ashanti areas. The Ashanti demanded a federal rather than a unitary form of government for Ghana. This opposition had its economic as well as geographic base in cocoa, Ghana's main export crop, 50.9 percent of which came from the Ashanti Region in 1954 to 1955.[52] Cocoa farmers and chiefs in the region could unite over a simple, shared common interest—the price paid to them for their cocoa. The cocoa growers opposed the policy of the Cocoa Marketing Board which purchased cocoa from them at a price set below prevailing world market prices. Cocoa growers resented the drain of resources from the cocoa growing regions to the government center where much of the capital obtained from their cocoa went into state or CPP projects. Under a federal system, farmers hoped to retain cocoa profits in the region and provide for themselves an economically prosperous, regional base of power.

Nkrumah's political opponents among the Ashanti professionals recognized the potential advantage of regionally based power. In 1954 they linked with the Ashanti cocoa interests to form the opposition NLM under the leadership of K. A. Busia. The NLM was also able to draw upon a network of economic relationships which the chiefs had built up under British superintendency in the prewar era. Many chiefs had utilized their new wealth to provide superior education for their children during the colonial era and, therefore, by the end of World War II, a sizeable segment of the most highly educated members of the "new elite" had kinship ties with the traditional elite.[53] Both Busia and the late J. B. Danquah, head of the UGCC, had ties to traditional elites. Given their common economic and political interests, it is not surprising that the professional classes were able to form an alliance with the chiefs in order to oppose Nkrumah and the CPP.

At this point, perhaps the British were not so sure about their choice of successors, for it was becoming apparent that the traditional and professional interests might, in the long run, cooperate more smoothly. While the control of cocoa by these interests might originally have prevented the continued accumulation of sterling reserves in Britain through the

[52] CMB, *Seventeenth Annual Report,* p. 26.

[53] For an elaboration of this theme, see La Ray Denzer, "The National Congress of British West Africa," (M. A. thesis, University of Ghana, 1965), and David Kimble, *A Political History of Ghana, 1850–1928* (London: Oxford University Press, 1963). Both studies show that a majority of the founding members of the Aborigines Rights Protection Society (an anti-colonial organization formed in 1898) and the National Congress of British West Africa, formed in 1920, were related to traditional rulers. It is maintained here that this interrelationship continues to the present day. See also Thomas Kerstiens, *The New Elite in Asia and Africa* (New York: Praeger, 1966), pp. 122–23.

Cocoa Marketing Board (which may help explain British acceptance of the CPP), the NLM group represented that strata of persons most likely to faciltate continued British investment after independence. Thus, British insistence on a fresh round of elections stemming from the federalism issue may be viewed as a rearguard action on the part of the British administration. Austin suggests that if the NLM had come to power it would have dropped the federal demand;[54] however, regional economic concerns might have dictated otherwise. In any case, the issue provided the British with a chance to take a second look at their successors, and, perhaps, from the British point of view, bring the CPP in line through forcing them to compromise to some extent with the more conservative opposition.[55]

In a distinctly unprincipled style (albeit true to the form of the political system they had adopted), the CPP, in combating the NLM opposition, played upon the same regionalism on which the opposition was based. In 1956, Nkrumah managed to split the NLM vote when he proposed the creation of a separate region for the Brong—who are not a "true Ashanti" group. In the 1956 election, the CPP used this issue of Brong separatism to divide the NLM vote in the Brong area of the Ashanti Region and thereby managed to deprive Busia's party of nearly two-thirds of the Brong vote.[56]

Having allowed itself the luxury of believing that once independence was obtained another path could be taken, the CPP found itself at independence a conglomerate of contradictory and often mutually exclusive interests. And it faced yet another opposition group, the United Party, which was formed in 1957 from some of the same interests which had earlier formed the NLM. Having postponed forming a solid-based mass movement among the people, the party began vainly trying to fill the gap from the top with the party auxiliaries. These centralized organizations, created by administrative fiat, were to have involved key sectors of the population in the development effort.

[54] *Politics in Ghana,* p. 356.

[55] Of course, the actual effect was quite different—the 1954-56 struggles helped defeat parliamentarianism in Ghana. Busia himself disavowed any automatic acceptance of the 1956 election results (Ibid., p. 329), foreshadowing the CPP's later disregard for elections.

[56] Austin, *Politics in Ghana,* p. 353. By creating this new region, Nkrumah was also able to split Ashanti economic power. Whereas in 1957-58, the Ashanti Region accounted for 50.7% of cocoa produced, and hence approximately 30% of Ghana's export earnings, in 1958-59, the Ashanti Region produced 33.3% of Ghana's cocoa output and the new Brong-Ahafo Region, 27.1% (Figures from CMB, *Seventeenth Annual Report,* p. 26).

Rise of the Single Party

Upon acheiving independence in 1957, Nkrumah embarked upon a program to consolidate the political gains of independence through strengthening the organizational and legal power of his Convention People's Party. From 1961 until 1964, which saw the legal institutionalization of the single-party state, the party attempted to make simultaneous major thrusts toward the development of the economy and mobilization of the population. This dual effort involved establishing a new institutional framework for political control while expanding government control of the economic sector. Although the CPP had gained control of the national government, it became clear to the CPP leadership that political mobilization for economic development could not occur in the context of a two-party system, particularly when the opposition, finding itself increasingly powerless, "hastened all the more anxiously to sponsor every outbreak of discontent with CPP rule."[57] While publicly keeping the parliamentary ideal as its model, inner party councils tentatively began to move toward the creation of a single-party state.

One of the first public signs of the CPP's new stance was a series of bills providing the regime with wide powers which could be exercised against the opposition. The CPP passed the Preventive Detention Act in July, 1958, which provided for imprisonment of persons for up to five years without trial, and soon members of the opposition were to be found occupying Accra jails under the provisions of this act and other legislative measures.[58]

Another set of steps to facilitate complete CPP legislative control involved centralizing the state apparatus. In 1958 a variety of legal procedures were initiated to remove restrictions governing constitutional

[57] Austin, *Politics in Ghana*, p. 271.

[58] Other acts included the Investigation of Crime Act which broadened the Attorney General's authority to compel any subject to supply information where crimes against the state were involved; an Offences Against the State Act which gave judges the authority to sentence persons up to fifteen years for making false statements about Ghana; a Sedition Bill which provided imprisonment for up to fifteen years of persons found guilty of intentionally exhorting the overthrow of the government by illegal means or inciting contempt of the government or judicial branch; a Criminal Procedures Act which provided for Special Courts to enact the death penalty for political crimes without trial by jury; and an Emergency Powers Act which gave the President the right to declare a state of emergency by legislative instrument with the approval of the cabinet. In 1962 the attempts on Nkrumah's life resulted in the issuance of emergency regulations which among other things provided for the suspension of habeas corpus. For details of the background to this legislation see Geoffrey Bing, *Reap the Whirlwind* (London: MacGibbon and Kee, 1968), pp. 377–82, and Austin, *Politics in Ghana*.

change, the main target at that point being the dismantling of the five regional assemblies which were the legacy of the compromises with the opposition following the 1956 election. In March, 1959, the regional assemblies were abolished and parliamentary power vested solely in the unicameral National Assembly.[59]

After its 1960 defeat in the republican plebiscite, the opposition became only a token force. It exhibited a "sense of defeat bred by the growth and assertion of CPP power." [60] Now the CPP began its move to consolidate the party's control over the country, and "a web of power was spun over the country, its threads reaching out from the central committee of the party into the constituencies through a number of satellite organizations." [61] These organizations were the auxiliaries.

The electoral opposition had no sooner been, in effect, removed, than the party had to combat a tendency toward internal deterioration. Some single-party regimes appear to have managed to combat this tendency toward increasing apathy by transforming themselves into mass mobilization organizations; for example, in Cuba observers indicate the party functions effectively through this device as a local link in the state apparatus and within other organizations such as labor unions, women's, youth, and neighborhood groups.[62] For a variety of reasons, however, the gap between the CPP's ideal as a mass party and the reality, a party of mass apathy, was not overcome. "Thus the belief that problems of the previous decade could be conjured out of existence by lumping them within a single party proved a dangerous illusion." [63]

In fact, it appeared that bringing together the segments that embodied these problems aggravated arriving at solutions. The party began to turn in on itself. In a series of internal party unheavals, the old leadership from nationalist days was forced into eclipse. Nkrumah replaced Kojo Botsio as Secretary of the Central Committee. In subsequent months, Gbedemah, Botsio, Krobo Edusei, A. E. Inkumsah, and other party stalwarts were asked to resign or were censured for their private wealth.[64] With the demise of the right, a left-wing group centered around Tawia Adamafio came to predominance:

> Tawia Adamafio had gathered around himself men in key positions in the country. . . . Under the guise of the indoctrination of a hard core of party cadre, he placed himself in a position of command with personal support

[59] Austin, *Politics in Ghana,* p. 380.
[60] Ibid., p. 384.
[61] Ibid., p. 382.
[62] See Lockwood, *Castro's Cuba, Cuba's Fidel.*
[63] Austin, *Politics in Ghana,* p. 402.
[64] Ibid., pp. 402–405.

> through these personalities from a wide section of the population and from very sensitive and important organs of Government.[65]

These "personalities" included Kwaku Boateng, Minister of the Interior; Dowuona-Hammond, Minister of Education; John Tettegah, Secretary-General of the Trades Union Congress (TUC); K. Amoako-Atta, Deputy Governor of the Bank of Ghana; T. O. Asara, Chairman and Managing Director of the Ghana Commercial Bank; Eric Heymann, Editor of the *Evening News;* T. D. Baffoe, Editor of the *Ghanaian Times*; Z. B. Shardow, head of the Ghana Young Pioneers; Cecil Forde, attached to the President's Publicity Secretariat; H. P. Nelson, Principal Secretary of the Ministry of Trade; Kweku Akwei, head of the Party's Education Wing at Party Headquarers; S. B. Ofori, of the Agricultural Development Corporation and later Chairman of the Ghana Fishing Corporation; E. N. Omaboe, Government Statistician; D. S. Quarcoopome, at that time in charge of security in the country; and A. C. Kuma, then State Professor at the University of Ghana.[66]

Genoud discounts the importance of Adamafio's group:

> Whether the rise and fall of Tawia Adamafio . . . actually represented an abortive attempt to radicalize the policies of the government and give the party a more important and direct responsibility in the running of the affairs of state . . . is not too clear nor too important.[67]

However, it would appear that Adamafio's efforts were crucial, for it was the group around Adamafio which was central to the establishment of the party auxiliaries with the concomitant far-reaching changes in the orientation of major sectors of the society in accordance with the party and the state. While Adamafio predominated, the concept of the auxiliaries seemed to have vitality; when his ascendency was halted by the Kulungugu bombing incident on August 1, 1962 (in which Adamafio was accused of involvement in the attempt on Nkrumah's life),[68] the barely established auxiliaries suffered a de-emphasis within the party-state, even though on the surface their strength appeared to grow.

By 1964, when the CPP became Ghana's only constitutional party, the internal factions had been reduced to peaceful coexistence within the party-state. The extreme left controlled the party and the state press and

[65] The Attorney General in his Opening Address at the Treason Trial on August 9, 1963, after Adamafio's fall from power. Cited in Austin, *Politics in Ghana,* p. 407.

[66] Ibid. See also Bretton, *Rise and Fall of Kwame Nkrumah,* p. 199.

[67] Genoud, *Nationalism and Economic Development in Ghana,* p. 185.

[68] Austin, *Politics in Ghana,* p. 410. Adamafio in a later private interview maintained that the bombing was the result of a plot by right wing CPP elements who wished to limit both his own power and that of the party auxiliaries.

the right found its place in the ministries,[69] hardly a combination conducive to a unified ideological theory and actual practice.

The "cult of personality" that centered around Nkrumah emerged fully. Fanon sees the growing importance of the leader in the African party as one of the "pitfalls of national consciousness." The cult of personality does provide an additional example of the CPP's tendency to resemble the Stalinist model and for the same reasons—that is, the centralization of power at the top at the expense of participation by the people. The distrust of and disregard for the people leads elitists, whether "communist" or "democratic," to an attempt to ignore the people, or, as one writer puts it, to "revolt from the masses."

> With the disenchantment with the common man, the classical view of the elite-mass relationship has become reversed: it is the common man, not the elite, who is chiefly suspected of endangering freedom, and it is the elite, not the common man, who is looked upon as the chief guardian of the system. The revolt from the masses has led to a second shift in theory: the emphasis is no longer extending or strengthening democracy, but upon stabilizing the established system. . . . Thus the political passivity of the great majority of of the people is not regarded as an element of democratic malfunctioning, but on the contrary, as a necessary condition for allowing the creative functioning of the elite.[70]

Fanon puts it this way:

> For if you think that you can manage a country without letting the people interfere, if you think that the people upset the game by their mere presence, whether they slow it down or whether by their natural ignorance they sabotage it, then you must have no hesitation: you must keep the people out.[71]

"At the heart of the elitist theory is a clear presumption of the average citizen's inadequacies,"[72] and rather than drawing its strength from the

[69] Austin, *Politics in Ghana,* p. 412. See also Legum, "Ghana," in *African Socialism,* pp. 149–154, and Fanon, who aptly notes that after the nationalists have won, "local party leaders are given administrative posts" (*Wretched of the Earth,* p. 171).

[70] Peter Bachrach, *The Theory of Democratic Elitism: A Critique* (Boston: Little, Brown, 1967), p. 32.

[71] Fanon, *Wretched of the Earth,* p. 189. While Fanon's analysis rests too heavily on the example of Algeria and his emphasis on the necessity of violence and the present potential role of the peasant in other areas is too great, some of his observations are strikingly reminiscent of Ghana, in all probability because of his visit there during this period.

[72] Jack L. Walker, "A Critique of the Elitist Theory of Democracy," *Apolitical Politics: A Critique of Behavioralism,* eds., Charles A. McCoy and John Playford (New York: Thomas Y. Crowell Company, 1967), p. 201.

people, the party relies on the leader.[73] But, in the process, the leader himself changes.

While the party's ideology continued to be directed toward mobilizing the people for the task of national development, through its attempts at rigid control it often served in Fanon's terms "to immobilize the people." [74] The dynamics of the party seemed to be directed toward internal competition for positions of influence, power, and wealth within the party heirachy and its auxiliaries. The party became "a means of private advancement." [75] Ultimately, the demeaning activities of some demoralized and corrupt party functionaries contributed to widespread popular alienation from the party.

In contrast to the CPP's own ideology of major social mobilization, meaningful popular participation was scant. It could not be characterized as an "empty shell"—for the party auxiliaries did continue to operate in a number of specifically defined areas. On the other hand, the CPP could only be called a mass party in the sense that it had, on paper, a large non-restricted membership and could mobilize large numbers of people for rallies and demonstrations.

The party appears to have failed to bring into the political arena a large number of politically conscious and dedicated participants. It lacked both the necessary internal dynamics to prevent stagnation and the organizational capacity to sustain its legal power. It did not correspond to Fanon's "living party, which ought to make possible the free exchange of ideas which have been elaborated according to the real needs of the mass of the people." [76] This failure was the logical consequence of a political superstructure erected upon an economic base with built-in contradictions.

The CPP also faced problems stemming from its expansion of the party machinery to provide positions for its younger lower echelons. For example, the United Ghana Farmers' Cooperative Council employed over 30,000 functionaries as regional, district, and local marketing officers, secretaries and receivers.[77] However, many of these functionaries were ill-equipped to handle their duties effectively, and corruption and inefficiency marked many undertakings of this kind.[78]

[73] Fanon, *Wretched of the Earth,* p. 165. See also Walker, "A Critique of the Elitist Theory of Democracy," p. 201.

[74] Fanon, *Wretched of the Earth,* p. 171.

[75] Ibid.

[76] Ibid., p. 170.

[77] Ghana, Ministry of Information, *Report of the Committee of Enquiry on the Local Purchasing of Cocoa,* J. C. de Graft-Johnson, Chairman (Accra: State Publishing Corporation, 1967), p. 137.

[78] See the several reports of commissions of inquiry appointed after the coup by the National Liberation Council (NLC) to investigate the affairs of the Nkrumah

After the 1960 elections, the local constituency organizations were no longer needed to turn out the vote since Ghana had become a *de facto* single-party state. Moreover, the local party branch never became an effective channel for grievances, and many participation needs were still being met at the local level by the traditional institutions.[79] The office of the district commissioner rather than the party secretary was often likely to be the center of local operations.

In order to revitalize the party as well as implement a new style of social and political life in Ghana, the party placed increasing emphasis on the functional auxiliaries within the party which, appealing to women, youth, farmers, etc., took precedence over constituency organizations. These new organizations, which were meant to link certain categories of individuals to the party-state, cut across other, more traditional forms of local, ethnic, and religious groupings. The most important of these auxiliary organizations were the Trades Union Congress (TUC), the United Ghana Farmers' Council Cooperatives (UGFCC), the National Council of Ghanaian Women (NCGW), the Ghana Young Pioneers (GYP), and the National Association of Socialist Students' Oraginzations (NASSO).

These organizations were heavily emphasized in Nkrumah's program for the transformation of Ghana into an African socialist society. However, these organizations met difficulties similar to those which the party itself faced. By remaining open to all and containing within itself all the factions in Ghanaian society, the party failed to develop the necessary cohesiveness. The continuance of the open party meant that as Nkrumah took steps to try to implement "socialist" goals, he met with resistance from within the party, where he did not have a sufficient group of tightly organized militants, as well as from the civil service, university, judiciary,

---

regime. These include reports such as the following: Ghana, Ministry of Information, *Report of the Commission Appointed under the Commission of Enquiry Act,* 1964 (Act 250) to *Enquire into the Properties of Kwame Nkrumah,* Fred Kwasi Apaloo, Chairman (Accra: State Publishing Corporation, [1967]); *Report of the Committee of Enquiry on the Local Purchasing of Cocoa;* Ghana, Ministry of Information, *Summary of the Report of the Commission of Enquiry into Irregularities and Malpractices in the Grant of Import Licences,* N. A. Ollennu, Chairman (Accra: State Publishing Corporation, 1967); Ghana, Ministry of Information, *Report of the Jiagge Commission of Enquiry into the Assets of Specified Persons,* Mrs. Justice Annie Jiagge, Chairman (Accra: State Publishing Corporation, 1969); Ghana, *Report of the Sowah Commission Appointed under the Commission of Inquiry Act, 1964 (Act 250) and NLC (Investigations and Forfeiture of Assets) Decree 1966, N.L.C.D. 72 to Enquire into the Assets of Specified Persons,* E. N. P. Sowah, Chairman (Accra: State Publishing Corporation, 1969).

[79] See Barbara Callaway, "Local Politics in Ho and Aba," *Canadian Journal of African Studies* (Winter 1970).

police, traditional leaders. Many key party officials were more interested in preserving their own positions than in achieving revolutionary goals.

The economic and social transformation of Ghanaian society required national actions that would create a new sense of national purpose. However, the lack of a real unifying struggle during the pre-independence period and the CPP's many compromises with the British prevented the party from developing into an instrument of revolutionary social change.[80] Its problems were many: lack of dedicated cadres to carry out the ambitious vision of Nkrumah, lack of committed leadership, and a decline of Nkrumah's own moral leadership. For instance, in the early days, Nkrumah had provided the model of asceticism for the nation, sleeping as he did in modest quarters in Accra. In the final days of his regime Ghana was noted for Nkrumah's palatial presidential residences and the ostentatiousness of its top politicians rather than the austerity of its leadership. Despite his "Dawn Broadcast" in April, 1961, in which Nkrumah denounced corruption, and the continued attacks on it in the press, it was evident that the party was a vast patronage machine, and talk of corruption in high places was common to Accra "rumor-mongers." Organizational inefficiency and weaknesses were exacerbated by the loss of moral force on the part of the party: the "cipipi" (CPP), once a source of national pride, became a national joke.

Economics in the "Political Kingdom"

Faced with the necessity for economic development, the Nkrumah government discovered that its failure to force a clear break with the colonial past severely limited economic alternatives. In the absence of complete, qualitative change, the government's strategy became that of decolonization or of post-independence, anti-colonial nationalism rather than socialist revolution.[81] Because an absolute break with the world capitalist "metropolis" did not occur Ghana has experienced a devastating "time lag" between formal political independence and the seizure of control over

[80] Fanon sees a violent struggle as necessary to party and national unity. "The mobilization of the masses, when it arises out of the war of liberation, introduces into each man's consciousness the ideas of a common cause, of a national destiny, and of a collective history" (*Wretched of the Earth,* p. 39). While it is probably true that the holders of power are not going to surrender *real* power, as opposed to the illusionary power of national independence, except through such struggles, Fanon tends to emphasize the psychoanalytic impact of violence more than other aspects of the struggle. It is the educational efforts which necessarily must accompany such a struggle which make the difference. See Eric R. Wolf, *Peasant Wars of the Twentieth Century* (New York: Harper and Row, 1969) for a comparative study of six peasant actions and accompanying reeducation.

[81] Genoud, *Nationalism and Economic Development in Ghana,* p. 73.

its own economic life. The occurrence of such a time lag is, according to Genoud, dependent on two main variables: the intensity of the power struggle before and after independence and the intensity of strain on the economy.[82] Genoud further states that:

> While the party leadership and government grow more concerned with economic problems and discover that independence also means underdevelopment, the conception of decolonization becomes less vague and tends more and more to be understood as a prerequisite for development. The instruments of economic control, in order to be applied to the reorientation of the economy, must be concentrated in the hands of the state.[83]

A model developed by Dudley Seers and used by Genoud in analyzing Ghana's economy provides general insights into the economic problems of the period under discussion. In Seers's model, the colonial (and immediate post-colonial) economy is an "open" economy in which the local currency is backed by and fully convertible into the currency of a major international power. Moreover, there are few quantitative restrictions on imports and tariffs are relatively low. In this model, "as the economy of the primary producer comes under stress, the net total of foreign exchange receipts available to finance imports . . . rises more slowly than exports." [84] Thus, the classic situation of a net loss in capital occurs.

A foreign exchange crisis is precipitated by the absorption of an increasing proportion of export earnings by foreign importers. Import substitution may alter this outflow of capital but the continued influence of the colonial power will be used to "keep the door open for the sale of its products, and will discourage or prevent the establishment of high tariffs or import quotas." [85] As the economy comes under stress due to the outflow of capital, the government tries to prolong the "open stage" so as to avoid making choices which will antagonize vested interests. Various

[82] Ibid., p. 107. Genoud points out an extremely suggestive relationship between these two variables—which he sees as independent but, "if the political power struggle involves economic or developmental issues, they may be thus related" (p. 107). Conversely, it is maintained here that if the struggle does not involve these issues, they will be falsely separated. A "political power struggle" which does not involve economic strain, or more precisely, a reorganization of economic relations producing economic strain, has nothing to do with real power.

[83] Genoud, *Nationalism and Economic Development in Ghana,* p. 108.

[84] Dudley Seers, "The Stages of Economic Development of a Primary Producer in the Middle of the Twentieth Century," *Economic Bulletin of Ghana* 7 (1963), cited in Genoud, *Nationalism and Economic Development,* p. 101.

[85] Seers, "Stages of Economic Development," cited in Genoud, *Nationalism and Economic Development in Ghana,* p. 102. *The Ghana Report* confirms the influence of the British on trading patterns in Ghana immediately after independence (p. 21).

devices may be employed to delay making the politically difficult choice: the government can deplete its foreign reserves, raise rates of taxation on foreign companies, or make mild increases in tariffs. Using these devices, "income can grow for some years more quickly than exports without an economy essentially ceasing to be open." [86] This period in Ghana may be equated to the "Lewis era," in which the economy was guided by W. Arthur Lewis and other advisors along these lines.

However, these devices to prolong the "open" stage are, at best, short-lived.

> Despite the temporary reliefs which have just been described, the period of stress cannot be endured indefinitely. Whereas the pressure for economic development persistently mounts, the markets for primary products show a chronic tendency to sag, while countries supplying financial assistance do not provide it at a fast enough rate. Moreover, in the current political climate of the world, it is becoming increasingly difficult to suppress by violence political demands for economic development. After a while, the forces acting to close the economy become cumulative. Governments may concede general wage increases to reduce political tensions. But such rises in cost may hamper exports (by making production in marginal farms or mines too expensive) and at the same time they are bound to stimulate imports. Official measures to encourage local industries involve an increase in outlays for imported equipment. Furthermore, as the foreign exchange crisis deepens, it is found that loans are harder to float in overseas markets; foreign capital may become more reluctant to enter; and domestic private capital tends to seek safety overseas. . . . At a certain point the open economy loses its capacity to cope with the socio-economic demands on it, and a crisis develops, triggered off perhaps by some quite small event (such as a dip in the price of a leading export or a change of government). The symptom is a fast decline in reserves of foreign exchange.[87]

As this last stage in the "open economy" was reached in Ghana, industrialization, according to Genoud, was perceived in much clearer and more realistic terms than the vague and happy notions of earlier days when a CPP election manifesto promised "to make the Gold Coast a paradise so that when the gates of heaven are opened by Peter, we shall sit in heaven and see our children driving their aeroplanes, commanding their own armies." [88]

At this stage, there were only two possibilities: the government either had to reduce its expenditures (public consumption) or reduce private

[86] Seers, "Stages of Economic Development," cited in Genoud, *Nationalism and Economic Development in Ghana,* p. 103.

[87] Ibid., pp. 103–104. Bracketed insertions in Genoud.

[88] Cited in Genoud, *Nationalism and Economic Development in Ghana,* p. 116, from *The Evening News,* July 13, 1956, quoted in Austin, *Politics in Ghana,* p. 334.

consumption. In either case, it had to impose general controls on foreign trade and the movement of capital and other transfers so that it could push ahead with its industrialization and other development projects. According to Seers, Ghana confronted these problems in 1961 and moved toward closing its economy.[89]

The government did not make a clear-cut choice between reducing public or private consumption. It had to continue to allow private consumption to rise in order to keep its political support. Consequently, capital continued to flow out of Ghana at an even faster rate after 1961. In fact, the government failed to make this choice for precisely the reason that Seers suggests as contributing to the earlier continuation of the "open" economy, i.e., the inability to "mobilize sufficient support" for more stringent policies.[90] In fact, not even the government's own economists were aware of the magnitude of the decline in reserves of foreign exchange or the level of debts incurred—such was the dizzying rapidity with which the Ghana government plunged ahead after 1961, trying vainly to find the formula which would allow the contradictions of its open economy to persist. Despite the development of machinery for central planning (which took place rather late, since the Seven Year Development Plan was not even introduced formally until 1964), the planners overestimated the government's ability to attract foreign private investment and underestimated the rate at which recurrent expenditures from previous projects would consume reserves.[91]

Following independence, the government made an effort to speed up economic growth, but during those first few years of its independence, Ghana followed the economic growth plans constructed by W. Arthur Lewis. This advisor stressed a "pragmatic" approach based upon continued reliance on foreign capital and trade with Western Europe and North America. Ghana's economic policies therefore reinforced the country's status as a neo-colonial society.

For the first five years after independence, 1957–1961, the policy was

[89] Seers, "Stages of Economic Development," cited in Genoud, *Nationalism and Economic Development in Ghana,* p. 104.

[90] Ibid., p. 102.

[91] I happened to be at the University of Ghana when the plan was introduced, and I was engaged in research in the regions as the government publicized its plan. Both in the University and in the regions, the plan prompted great discussion, for it appeared that the government had finally stated clearly its long-term plan for socialism, even if it were to be achieved gradually. However, the plan had only begun to be implemented when it was abandoned following the coup of February, 1966. See Office of the Planning Commission, *Seven-Year Plan for National Reconstruction and Development, Financial Years 1963/64–1969/70* (Accra: Government Printing Department, 1964).

one of gradualism, coexistence and restraint. No direct efforts were made to eliminate foreign influence. During this period of "competitive coexistence," [92] only the Ghana Commercial Bank, founded in 1953, provided any serious competition to foreign business enterprises. During this time, CPP-affiliated and state ventures were launched in insurance, shipping, lumber, construction, and cocoa-purchasing, but there was no government restriction of foreign competition with these enterprises. Part of the rationale for this pattern of coexistence was Nkrumah's recognition of the difficulties in trying to impose socialism on this new nation, as he pointed out in 1961:

> At this juncture, Ghana is not a socialist state. Not only do the people as yet not own all the major means of production and distribution, but we have still to lay the actual foundations upon which socialism can be built, namely, the complete industrialization of our country. All talk of socialism, of economic and social reconstruction, is just empty words if we do not seriously address ourselves to the question of basic industrialization and agricultural revolution in our country, just as much as we must concentrate on socialist education.[93]

In order for meaningful development to occur, Nkrumah and other top party leaders believed that it was necessary to break the pattern of colonial economic relations. In the period beginning 1960 to 1961, "socialism after industrialization" emerged in government circles as a distinct, immediate goal, replacing an earlier emphasis on decolonization through "open" expansion of the economy. In a similar manner, during the same period, increasing emphasis was placed upon the party as the agent through which socialism would be achieved.[94]

The ultimate goal of the Nkrumah regime was a socialist economy free of foreign control. This result was to be achieved through a transitional period of rapid industrialization within a "mixed" economy. Nkrumah expected, naively as it turned out, that "the growth rate of the public and cooperative sector of our economy will exceed the growth rate of the private sector, particularly in industry and agriculture," [95] and that through effective competition with foreign firms, the Ghanaian govern-

[92] John D. Esseks, "Economic Decolonization in a New African State, Ghana 1956–66" (Paper presented at the Annual Meeting of the African Studies Association, 1967), p. 3.

[93] Nkrumah, "Address to CPP Study Group in Flagstaff House," *Accra,* April, 1961, reprinted in *The Spark* (June 12, 1964).

[94] These plans were spelled out first in the *Program of the Convention People's Party for Work and Happiness* (Accra: Government Printing Department, 1962) and later translated into technical terms in the *Seven-Year Development Plan.*

[95] Kwame Nkrumah, *Blueprint of Our Goal: Osagyefo Launches the Seven-Year Plan* (Accra: Government Printing Department, 1964).

ment would eventually gain control over the entire economy. Parenthetically, it may be noted that the Nkrumah government's belief that it could successfully compete with foreign firms and eventually squeeze them out was paralleled in the political realm by its relations with the opposition.

It was asserted that, with indigenous private enterprise mainly restricted to small-scale activity, direct government action would be necessary in almost every field. The central emphasis was upon state investment as the major source of capital in the absence of large accumulations in Ghanaian hands. Foreign capital was also considered important temporarily, but local capital from Ghanaian entrepreneurs was excluded on the grounds that it was unequal to the magnitude of the development task.[96]

Over the eight years from 1957 to 1965, the changing pattern of government expenditures reflected the shift in official development policy.[97] The pattern of government development expenditures after 1959 changed from a predominance of expenditures for social and economic infrastructure to an increasing emphasis on direct investment in productive facilities. In the late 1950's, investment in development of Ghana's infrastructure accounted for the greatest part of development expenditures. Transportation and communication represented approximately 40 percent of all development expenditures in 1957 to 1958 and 1958 to 1959. After 1958 to 1959, expenditures for transportation and communications remained constant and consequently fell sharply in relation to total development expenditures. Spending in these areas dropped to an average of 16 percent of development expenditures in the three years from 1962 to 1965. Starting in 1961, the government began to invest heavily in the means of production in agriculture, fisheries, and industry. These expenditures increased from 10 percent of development expenditures in 1957 to 1958 to one-third of the total in 1965.[98] Investment in agriculture and industrial production accounted for the bulk of these funds.

[96] *Program for Work and Happiness.*

[97] The fiscal years were changed as follows: financial year 1955–56 should have ended March 31, 1956, extended to June 30, 1956; 1961–62, should have ended June 30, 1962, extended to September 30, 1962; the year commencing October 1, 1963, was extended from September 30, 1964 to December 31, 1964. "These frequent changes in accounting periods, far from facilitating comparisons, introduced a great deal of confusion and were nothing but desperate attempts by the Government at postponing the day of reckoning since it was becoming increasingly difficult to balance the budget, the Government having resorted to deficit financing for a number of years." Ghana, Ministry of Information, *Report and Financial Statements by the Accountant General and Report Thereon by the Auditor General for the Year Ended 31st December 1964* (Accra: State Publishing Corporation, 1967), p. 1.

This shift was combined with a growing government share in the rapidly expanding total investment by all sectors. In the eight years from independence to the military coup, capital expenditures by the government rose by an annual average increase of approximately 23 percent. The public sector accounted for more than 67 percent of gross fixed capital formation in 1965, the peak year of centralized economic activity (compared to 20 percent in 1958).[99] The seriousness of the government's intention to obtain greater national control of the economy and encourage rapid economic growth is apparent from this level of investment.

However, in spite of these programs, the internal structure of the economy did not change sufficiently to offset continuing losses in export earnings and generate sufficient development capital. Changes in the internal economy as well as revised external trade are equally vital to freeing a dependent economy. Since Ghana's external trade continued to follow the colonial pattern, not surprisingly, the country's internal economy did not change its composition significantly either. In 1955, total agricultural output accounted for 50.4 percent of the Gold Coast's Gross Domestic Product; in 1964, despite the push for industrialization, 51.4 percent of Ghana's GDP originated from agricultural activities.[100]

The development effort necessitated a changing pattern of imports. Beginning in 1961, strict import licensing controls were instituted so that the government could assure that the country's limited foreign exchange earnings would be used largely to finance the purchase of essential capital goods. Although total imports rose by 47 percent from 1957 to 1961, from 1961 onwards, when cocoa prices began to drop *and* when the government gained control of key economic pressure groups through the party's auxiliaries, it was able to hold the level of imports at a steady 20 percent of GNP. As a consequence of its policies (and the control it could now exercise over key groups), consumer goods were cut from 57 percent of imports in 1957 to 34 percent in 1965; importation of essential capital goods and industrial materials rose correspondingly. In 1957,

[98] Cf. the projections based on the Seven Year Plan in E. N. Omaboe, "The Process of Planning," pp. 455–57. The projected level of government investments in agriculture and industry was 37.3% of the total. See also Central Bureau of Statistics, *Economic Survey, 1965* (Accra: State Publishing Corporation, 1966), and Central Bureau of Statistics, *Economic Survey, 1966* (Accra: State Publishing Corporation, 1967).

[99] These figures do not include autonomous agencies such as those in charge of the railways, ports, the Housing Corporation or the Cocoa Marketing Board, which themselves had independent capital expenditures of over $15.4 million in 1965. They do include suppliers' and contractors' credits.

[100] Robert Szereszewski, "The Performance of the Economy, 1955–62," *A Study of Contemporary Ghana,* vol. 1, p. 57.

capital goods accounted for 13 percent of total imports; by 1965, they amounted to 30 percent.[101]

On the one hand, the government became increasingly dependent on certain imports for its program of industrial development, while on the other hand, diversification of the economy did not advance to a point where local production of goods could substitute for imported consumer items.

Consequently, in spite of its apparent (for Africa) prosperity at independence (i.e., foreign exchange reserves of $800 million in 1957), its impressive civil service, its relatively well-developed infrastructure, and despite the governmental efforts described above, by 1966 Ghana found itself confronted with a major economic and financial crisis. By 1966, its reserves had dwindled to less than a half million dollars, and Ghana had more than two hundred separate debts totalling some $710 million. Total debt service alone amounted to 25 percent of Ghana's earnings in 1966.

External Economic Relations

Paradoxically, the Nkrumah regime tried to reorganize the internal economic and social order of Ghana while still maintaining the country's major colonial trading patterns. Although on the surface it appeared that greater control of the internal economy by the government was being achieved, internal economic policies continued to be dominated by external influences. The economic choices made during the dyarchy and Ghana's continuing position as an exporter of raw materials combined to circumscribe severely Ghana's ability to free herself from continuing economic dependency through building an integrated economy.

The economic bind in which Ghana found herself in 1966 began with the decision, made during the dyarchy, that development had to proceed from an industrial rather than a peasant agricultural base. In contrast to development efforts in Tanzania (after 1967), North Vietnam, and Cuba (after 1962), Nkrumah saw industrialization as the immediate means to modern economic development. For example, in the Arusha Declaration, Julius Nyerere outlined a policy for Tanzania in which further development would be based upon building a peasant agricultural base rather than utilizing foreign capital.[102]

"A program of industrialization, and the urbanization that would go

[101] Figures compiled from the *Economic Survey, 1965* and *Economic Survey, 1966.*

[102] T.A.N.U., *The Arusha Declaration: Socialism and Self-Reliance* (1967), reprinted in Julius K. Nyerere, *Uhuru Na Ujamaa: Freedom and Socialism* (London: Oxford University Press, 1968), pp. 231–250.

with it, would be an electricity-intensive pattern of growth, while a process of development deriving more from increases in agricultural productivity would require relatively small amounts of power."[103] Once having committed the nation to the very ambitious and costly Volta River Project (VRP) from which the necessary electric power would be obtained for industrialization, Ghana had no choice but to invest in other industrial undertakings. The hydroelectric plant raised "the country's potential for industrialization by making available in the southern half of the country power in sufficient quantities to serve a substantial industrial sector."[104] But, to make the project pay, this "substantial industrial sector" had to be created. In the meantime, the country would continue her dependency upon exports of raw materials in order to finance imports of necessary industrial components. Since the financial arrangements for the Volta River Project were completed at considerable disadvantage to the Ghana government, it had to locate industrial consumers to utilize the power and pay off the large, long-term expenses for the construction of the project. In order to understand how Ghana got herself into this position, it is necessary to review briefly the history of the Volta River Project.

When the possibilities for the Volta River Project were being investigated after World War II, the Gold Coast's sizeable bauxite deposits located near the Volta River attracted the interest of the British.[105] Aluminum was scarce and available supplies came from the dollar areas. By 1956, when the investigating commission reported, world aluminum production had increased, the British dollar shortage had eased, and there was growing uncertainty on the part of the British about the political future of the country. By this point, however, Nkrumah had become committed to the VRP. In fact, in order to assure its financing, Nkrumah was willing to compromise with foreign investors on other projects to preserve a favorable climate for the VRP, and his commitment to this project appears to have constrained the government from taking radical actions in other areas of the economy.[106]

In 1957, Nkrumah approached the United States Government regarding financial assistance for the Volta River Project and through U.S. governmental encouragement, subsequently made contact with the Kaiser

[103] Tony Killick, "The Volta River Project," *A Study of Contemporary Ghana*, vol. 1, p. 400.

[104] Ibid., p. 409.

[105] The following discussion of the VRP is drawn primarily from Killick, Ibid., pp. 391–410.

[106] See Thompson, *Ghana's Foreign Policy*, pp. 26–27, 31, 94. See also John D. Esseks, "Economic Independence in a New African State, Ghana: 1956–65" (Ph.D. dissertation, Harvard University, 1967), pp. 449–50.

Aluminum and Chemical Corporation. After a series of negotiations, an agreement was signed in November, 1960, with the Volta Aluminum Company (VALCO), a partnership between Kaiser (90 percent) and Reynolds Aluminum (10 percent). At this point, "Ghana needed Valco more than Valco needed Ghana. Valco struck an accordingly hard bargain." [107]

First, the cost to Valco was lowered by separating the industrial costs, which Valco was to cover, from the public utilities project, for which the Ghana government had to locate financing. Ghana took loans from British, United States, and international agencies totaling $98 million, 72.6 percent of which were at near-commercial rates of 5¾ percent and 6 percent interest. Second, significant tax concessions were granted which allowed Valco to operate virtually tax-free. Third, power sales to the aluminum smelter were to be virtually at cost. Combined with the cheap labor available in Ghana, these rates made it economical for Valco to operate a smelter using *imported* partially processed bauxite in the form of alumina. Since very little profit would be obtained by the government from sales to the smelter for thirty years, the government had to find other users of the power in order to meet the then estimated $8.4 million yearly loan payments beginning in 1967. Thus, Ghana was committed to industrialization in order to make the VRP viable.

Finally, although the original plan had included the subsequent installation by Valco of a plant which would have converted Ghanaian bauxite into alumina and thus have provided Ghana with an integrated aluminum industry, the final agreement contained no such commitment. With the low power rates and tax concessions, Valco could more profitably continue to import alumina, mainly from Haiti, on ships owned by a Kaiser subsidiary. The installation of the alumina plant was clearly dependent on its potential profitability to the foreign concerns, on one hand, and to the "climate of the investment" on the other.[108]

"The investments in Ghana by the two aluminum companies are seen by them as merely a part of a far larger set of integrated investments throughout the world," [109] so Ghana's needs were largely irrelevant to Kaiser and Reynolds in determining whether or not the alumina plant and related new bauxite mines were to be forthcoming. This pattern of "extractive development" [110] is a common mechanism whereby the "devel-

[107] Killick, "The Volta River Project," p. 393.

[108] Ibid., p. 406.

[109] Ibid., p. 403.

[110] Or, *croissance extravertie,* as used by Amin, *L'Afrique De L'Ouest Bloquee.* The translation is Basil Davidson's in his review, "West Africa's Blocked Economy," *op. cit.,* p. 477.

opment of underdevelopment"[111] continues in former colonial territories like Ghana. The international capitalist system to which these small economies are tied is not geared to their own development. The Volta River Project provides a perfect example of this pattern, in which "these economies may grow but they do not develop: they do not change in structure. What does develop is the rate of transfer of real wealth. More is put in, but more is taken out."[112]

Given the lack of capital accumulation by an indigenous class during the colonial period and the government's wish to prevent the growth of a capitalist class, much of the new investment capital for industrialization had to come from abroad, either in the form of exchange from export earnings or from foreign governmental or private sources. Thus, Nkrumah's economic development program continued Ghana's excessive dependency upon the same external forces which governed its economy during the colonial period.

Of the total development investment under The Seven-Year Plan of $2.85 billion, about one third or $952 million was expected to be new foreign capital. This figure included the $148 million proposed investment by Valco, $112 million from private foreign companies, and $672 million in foreign loans and grants to be raised by the government. In addition, another $280 million was to be financed by the government through cocoa surpluses.[113] Nkrumah thought that, although their ultimate goals were different, both foreign firms and the Ghanaian government would find a common interest in industrializing the Ghanaian economy in order to increase the market for manufactured products and to open up new areas of investment.[114] In a 1963 speech to businessmen Nkrumah made his position clear:

> Our ideas of socialism can exist with private enterprises. I also believe that private capital, and private investment capital in particular, has a recognized and legitimate part to play in Ghana's economic development. . . . Ghana's

[111] Andre Gunder Frank, "The Development of Underdevelopment," *Monthly Review* (September, 1966). Parenthetically it might be noted that the *absence* of an integrated industry represented some assurance that the Ghana government would not threaten the investment through nationalization. This pattern of investment is not uncommon: by scattering their fixed capital investments in a variety of countries, investors provide themselves with insurance against nationalization since most of these small nations would have difficulty in completing the missing parts to form an integrated industry.

[112] Davidson, "West Africa's Blocked Economy," p. 477.

[113] Figures from the *Seven-Year Development Plan,* cited in E. N. Omaboe, "The Process of Planning," pp. 455–457.

[114] See *The Ghana Report,* pp. 9–13, 166.

> socialism is not incompatible with the existence and growth of a vigorous private sector in the economy.[115]

It was thought, naively, that the influence of foreign capital on the direction of development could be curtailed by simultaneous Government involvement in investment enterprises.

Backing into the corner

Nkrumah's version of socialism contained initial contradictions which circumstances only further exacerbated. While continued reliance on foreign sources of capital would have, in itself, inhibited the government's attempt to free Ghana from external control, the inability to attract such investment placed Ghana in an even more precarious position. The militant political stance of the Nkrumah government did not attract investment, and it may have caused some investors to shy away from Ghana. Even the control of Ghana's import-export sector by foreign firms provided a problem which militancy only amplified.

The composition of trade determined broadly its direction, which was almost overwhelmingly with the industrial countries of Europe and North America. Particularly, trade with the United Kingdom continued to be high; in 1960, 37 percent of Ghana's imports came from the United Kingdom, while 31 percent of her exports went to the former colonizer.[116] Eleven British-owned firms dominated this trading sector.[117] During the dyarchy and the first years of independence, the government was cooperating with these entrenched trading firms and "discouraging other foreign distributive enterprises."[118] Predictably these firms which wielded considerable influence over both the Ghanaian government and their home governments were not inclined to encourage local manufacturing that would undercut their own importing and distributing interests.

Ghana was plagued by other constraints on her ability to maneuver. With the failure to attract the expected capital, Ghana had to rely increasingly on her export earnings, and she was unable to diversify these earnings sufficiently to offset the continuous decline in the world price of cocoa.

At the same time cocoa prices were falling, Nkrumah's government

[115] "Ghana Socialism Creates 'Happy Atmosphere' for Private Capital," from a speech by President Kwame Nkrumah at a dinner for businessmen at Flagstaff House, Accra, February 22, 1963. Quoted in *African Socialism,* eds., William H. Friedland and Carl G. Rosberg (Palo Alto: Stanford University Press, 1964), Appendix VII, p. 275.

[116] E. N. Omaboe, "An Introductory Survey," p. 31.

[117] *The Ghana Report,* p. 21.

[118] Ibid., p. 21.

found itself committed to an economic plan which required a continued expansion of imports to keep the ambitious state projects operating. Complementary supplies of materials for mechanized agriculture and industry were not available when needed; and the inefficiency of the import licensing system[119] added to the financial problems caused by the deteriorating balance of payments. For example, Ghana had thousands of tractor-plowed acres with no improved seeds for high value crops.

By 1963, the growing balance of payments crisis had caused the government to concentrate on a maximization of export revenues at the expense of programs for Africanizing the economy. However, major exporters took their profits in sterling in 1964 and 1965, even though foreign exchange at this time was at a premium. The government was fearful that, if it took steps to limit these outflows, the companies' export earnings, which were economically important given the thin margin of the balance of payments, would be lost completely.[120]

In addition, the particular nature of Ghana's main export crop, cocoa, made it imperative not to alienate Western investors. Even had Nkrumah been so inclined to nationalize foreign firms operating in Ghana, as was Nyerere in Tanzania, the essential earnings from cocoa could have been jeopardized. Ghana depended almost entirely on sales to the West for her cocoa earnings. While Ghana consistently produced about a third of world cocoa output, in 1956 to 1958 the entire Soviet and Eastern European consumption of cocoa was only 6 percent of the world supply; in contrast, in the same period, Western Europe and North America consumed 80 percent of all cocoa produced.[121] Because of the luxury nature of cocoa, and since most of it is consumed by the capitalist nations, cocoa is particularly vulnerable to purchaser boycott and/or world commodity market price manipulation. In fact, this possibility was explicitly recognized by potential investors in Ghana as a guarantee against nationalization. One report prepared by a New York investment consulting firm noted specifically in relation to the spectre of nationalization that "Ghana's dependence on her cocoa exports make her vulnerable to a cocoa boycott."[122]

The final calamity for Nkrumah's economic strategy came with the sharpest decline in the world price of cocoa in 1965. Between 1958 and 1964, world consumption of cocoa increased at an average annual rate

[119] *Report of the Commission to Enquire into Import Licensing.*

[120] Esseks, "Economic Independence in a New African State," p. 451.

[121] *Review of the World Cocoa Economy,* FAO, Rome, 1963, Table 5, cited in Tony Killick, "Economics of Cocoa," *A Study of Contemporary Ghana,* vol. 1, p. 372.

[122] *The Ghana Report,* p. 167.

of 5.7 percent while world production rose by 7.8 percent. As a result, the world price dropped steadily from thirty-nine cents to twenty-two cents a pound. Over the same period, cocoa production in Ghana increased by 12.6 percent annually, thus raising its share of world production (and dependency on the world market) from 26 percent to 35 percent. The final breakdown in prices occurred in 1964 to 1965 when world production increased by more than 25 percent. Ghana accounted for half of the increase. By July, 1965, just six months before Nkrumah fell, the world price of cocoa was twelve cents a pound, almost half the average of the preceding year. Clearly cocoa, which accounted for an average of 64 percent of Ghana's foreign exchange earnings, and thus was crucial for its economic development, offered little or no basis for financing Ghana's economic development. Production increases could barely keep up with world price declines. In 1965 the price drop was so drastic that Ghana's foreign exchange reserves were nearly exhausted.[123]

After Nkrumah

Almost exactly six years later, the world price of cocoa had dropped to a five-year low. The drop was not so drastic as in 1965—from twenty-nine cents a pound a year earlier to twenty-three cents a pound in December, 1971—but combined with other economic factors the decline had the same effect on a shaky civilian government. In February, 1966, Nkrumah's government had been overthrown by the military, the Convention People's Party disbanded, and the constitution dissolved. The undemocratic excesses of Nkrumah's regime were denounced and a "new era" was hailed by the military leadership, the National Liberation Council. In January, 1972, after a two-year interlude of civilian rule under K. A. Busia's Progress Party, the military again interceded. The new National Redemption Council took power from the civilians, dismissed the Prime Minister, dissolved all political parties, and abolished the constitution of Ghana's "Second Republic" which had been instituted in September, 1969.

In 1966, the military had cited Ghana's critical economic position, widespread corruption, and political restrictions as the precipitating factors in the coup. In 1972, again the deteriorating economy, continued corruption, and Busia's sometimes arbitrary actions against political opponents finally caused the military to take power.

In both coups, specific military grievances had played their role. In

[123] See Killick, "The Economics of Cocoa," pp. 345–57; Douglas Rimmer, "The Crisis in the Ghana Economy," *Journal of Modern African Studies* 4 (May, 1966); and Alan Rake, "Is Ghana Going Bankrupt?," *Transition* 24 (1965).

1966, the possibility of Ghanaian intercession in Rhodesia and the confusion resulting from both Western and Soviet training had been added to the military's list of complaints. Since the transfer of power back to the Busia government, the military had not fared well. General economic conditions had contributed to cuts in the defense budget. Other stringency measures which affected the army particularly were the National Development Levy introduced in the July, 1971 budget and the abolition of a vehicle maintenance allowance shortly afterwards. The National Development Levy required a one percent salary contribution from all workers earning more than one thousand new cedis a year. Combined with the end of vehicle maintenance allowances, the real income of officers was considerably lowered.[124] Yet in both coups, it was the general economic situation which was the real contributor to political instability. Officers "grievances" alone were insufficient to generate coups. At both points, the deteriorating economy spelled doom for civilian regimes.

Despite the resemblances between the two coups, the 1972 military leadership initially began to take measures which should have been taken by the first military regime or the Busia government. One of the first actions following the 1972 coup was a repudiation of some of the foreign debts incurred by Nkrumah at the height of his economic crisis. These debts had been necessitated as much by the unfavorable position of cocoa on the world market as by the excessive expenditures of the Nkrumah government, and the attempt to honor them by the two successive governments had caused all Ghanaians to suffer. The policy with regard to the debts was one indication of another difference between the leaders of the first coup and the second. The first military council had appeared particularly eager to legitimize itself on the world stage, a posture continued by Busia's civilian government. In repudiating the debts, the 1972 military leaders showed somewhat less regard for Western opinion which had previously hampered independent political or economic action.

The 1972 regime also contained a new set of officers. Following the upheavals of the 1966 coup and the changes occurring with the return to civilian rule in 1969, the top military leadership had virtually been replaced due to retirement, reassignment, or death. The officers of the first period were products of the colonial system, and these middle-class gentlemen emphasized the virtues of Christian ethics rather than Ghanaian needs. The new officers are generally somewhat younger and more inexperienced than the leaders of the first coup, although the commander

[124] Valerie Plave Bennett, "The Military Under the Busia Government," *West Africa* (February 25, 1972): 222–223.

of the coup, Colonel Ignatius Kutu Acheampong had training in both Britain and the United States.

For both military governments as well as Ghana's two civilian regimes, the problems to be dealt with were essentially the same: Ghana's external debts, foreign earnings, especially the world price of cocoa, continued reliance upon imports for essential food stuffs, and internal problems of corruption and lack of commitment to the development effort. The population, which would necessarily have been involved in a successful development effort, had historically been left outside development efforts. Nkrumah had made an attempt at mass involvement, but his efforts ended with the apparent necessity to control the population in order to retain power. Busia's liberal democracy cast participation in electoral terms, again hardly sufficient participation to ensure support for stringent measures such as a 44 percent currency devaluation or the National Development Levy.

If the 1972 coup looked like a rerun of the 1966 coup, the 1969 elections resembled a rerun of the 1954 to 1956 elections. The leading characters and their roles had changed very little in the intervening years. K. A. Busia again led the opposition against the ghost of the CPP. Although Nkrumah was gone, the man credited with creating the grass roots organization of the old CPP, Komla Gbedemah, took his place in organizing essentially similar bases of support. Busia waged as bitter a personal campaign against Gbedemah in 1969 as he had against Gbedemah as Nkrumah's field organizer thirteen years earlier. And, just as Busia had showed his disdain for parliamentary procedures by declaring in advance of the 1956 elections that his party would not necessarily honor the results, before Busia had even taken office as prime minister he was maneuvering to prevent Gbedemah taking his place as leader of the opposition. By the time the new parliament had convened in November, 1969, Gbedemah had been declared ineligible for office due to his role during the Nkrumah period.

The Progress Party in the 1969 elections directed its appeal to the same regional groups upon which the former opposition to Nkrumah had relied. It had been in the Akan-speaking areas, especially Ashanti, that the opposition demand for federation had crystallized against Nkrumahist centralism during the 1956 elections. The alignment between the Akans and the traditional leaders in the north formed the basis for the old opposition, just as it formed the basis of support for the Busia government.[125] Thus, since his support was centered in the cocoa producing areas, Busia's gov-

[125] Card and Calloway, "Ghanaian Politics: The Elections and After," p. 11.

ernment was perhaps rendered even more susceptible than Nkrumah to the pressures resulting from a decline in cocoa prices.

The similarities between the 1956 elections held before independence and the 1969 elections held following both Nkrumah's period and military rule indicate the lack of fundamental social change in Ghana. Despite Nkrumah's attempt at consolidating the country under the single party espousing African socialism, the military's attempt to purge the country of corruption and place it more nearly back in the Western camp, and Busia's attempt to institute parliamentary multi-party democracy, Ghana in 1972 still faced the same problems she had at independence in 1957. The reason should be clear from the analysis of the Nkrumah period. The structure of economic relations had remained essentially unchanged from the colonial period. Despite Nkrumah's development efforts, no clear break from the colonial past occurred in order to reconstruct the national economy, and the succeeding regimes reinforced, rather than weakened, the colonial economic legacy.

Conclusion

Nkrumah had been unable to lead Ghana out of the trap of dependency and underdevelopment which was bequeathed the country by its colonial rulers. Even though he was ideologically committed to socialism, he did not have a sufficient political base to take either the initial steps, such as applying rigid import controls, or more radical ones, such as nationalizing the foreign-owned sectors of the economy or turning decisively to the Communist bloc for new trade relations. At this time, Ghana had no choice but to continue within the neocolonial pattern, hopefully biding her time while consolidating a political base capable in the future of mobilizing the population in support of the economic hardships necessary to achieve economic independence.

The agents for building this support were to have been the party and its auxiliaries, but the neocolonial economic *cul de sac* in which Ghana found herself and the political legacy of Ghana's colonial past undermined both Nkrumah and his efforts to build Ghanaian "socialism." In view of the neocolonial structure of Ghana's economy, Nkrumah's reliance upon a purely political instrument—the party and its auxiliaries—to achieve the goal of economic independence was doomed to failure since the party could not affect the basic structure of Ghana's economy.

The problem of changing the internal structure of the economy, i.e., gaining control of the major sectors of the economy, while still remaining at the mercy of fluctuations in the world price of cocoa, placed Ghana in an impossible situation which none of the succeeding regimes altered. Any success in eliminating foreign domination of the major sectors of the economy could have only been achieved under Nkrumah's strategy if sufficient foreign exchange had been available to obtain essential imports needed for the operation of the state enterprises. With increasing state involvement in every sector came dependence of the state upon success in these areas, and as the government became overextended in its efforts to cover operating losses of some state enterprises, the concomitant drain on foreign exchange from cocoa earnings spelled disaster.

Similar factors prevailed for succeeding regimes, although the structural inadequacies were temporarily masked with a brief rise in world cocoa prices and a postponement of some debt payments. In actuality, the first military regime and the Busia government aggravated rather than alleviated the structural faults of the economy. If the military had repudiated foreign debts upon assuming power in 1966, this act would have been ample justification for the coup. Instead, the military relied upon negotiation with international financial powers, hoping for generous debt terms but receiving instead the "right" to postpone payment (and thereby pay developed nations higher interest). The Busia government continued this policy despite its high social costs to the regime. Trade patterns continued as before, with trade with the United States and other Western countries growing as a proportion of total trade. There was almost no new foreign industrial development in Ghana during the post-Nkrumah period, but there were few new Ghanaian industries either. The foreign exchange crisis necessitated strict import controls, but these could not offset the high rate of smuggling. Finally, Busia was forced to devalue Ghana's currency for the second time in four years.

The second Ghanaian military government has recently attempted to follow an international economic policy which diverges from previous governments. It has adopted stances declaring its non-acceptance of previously incurred financial obligations resulting from the vagaries of the international economy. Whether the government will be able to achieve a real measure of economic independence in current international economic circumstances is not clear.

Ghana's problems are the result of her external dependence rather than domestic incompetence. In these circumstances it is unlikely that the new military leaders can effectively alter Ghana's position unless they are willing to strike out in radically different directions. As long as this alternative appears unlikely, Ghana's position will continue to remain a dependent one. Changes in the form of her government will matter little until the structure of the economy is significantly altered.

Nigeria

THE POLITICAL ECONOMY OF NIGERIA

by

Barbara Callaway

Introduction

Nigeria, containing within its boundaries some eighty million of West Africa's one-hundred million people, may yet offer an alternative to the usual Third World stereotype of underdevelopment, dependency, and political instability due to external forces beyond its control. In Nigeria the structure of underdevelopment is the result of both external forces and internal conditions. Inherent traditional divisions within the country were underscored and reinforced by the former colonial power, Great Britain.

In this Introduction a brief overview of Nigeria's historical development will be used to analyze the present political configuration in light of the process of decolonization. This historical analysis of Nigeria's political and economic history will then be followed by more detailed description of the economy and post-independence political developments. The implications of this discussion for future economic and political developments will then be analyzed in a concluding section.

The structure of the economy is related to pre-colonial cleavage, colonial exploitation and post-independence political maneuvering. Divisions in Nigerian society are both horizontal and vertical. Emerging class distinctions were deeply cut by ethnic cleavages while a colonially inherited federal structure reinforced social inequalities and economic imbalances. These imbalances exacerbated perceptions of political domination and unequal modernization. The result was full-scale civil war.

This essay is a revised version of a paper written with C. S. Whitaker, Jr., "Competition and Enmity: Social Conflict in Nigeria" presented at the annual meeting of The American Political Science Association in Chicago, September, 1971.

In Nigeria, as economic forces set in motion forces of social change, financial wealth became the means by which members of a political class tried to render the actions of others predictable. Foreign economic interests found this process to be quite compatible with their own concerns and therefore an informal symbiosis of interests developed. Shortly after independence the integrity of the entire political class became suspect and popular disillusionment was reinforced by increasing economic frustrations brought on by rising inflation, rising unemployment and disappearing opportunities inherent in the structure of a neo-colonial economy. In Nigeria these tensions were briefly channelled into a bloody civil war. The intervention of the military had served only to postpone the working out of a more permanent solution, however. A military elite now rules in place of the old politicians, but whether the dynamics of the system have been altered is the crucial question. Social confrontation remains a factor in Nigeria's future.

Historical Background

Nigeria is a British imperial creation and as such its history reflects British imperialistic concerns. The roots of serious divisions between peoples and cultures which bedevil any quest for Nigerian unity existed before the British arrived on the scene, but British colonial policies greatly exacerbated these tensions.

The grasslands of Northern Nigeria were, by 1831, under the control of the Fulani peoples who conquered the pre-existing Hausa states in a Jihad, or Islamic holy war, which began in 1802. The Fulani-established empire in the upper North had many of the characteristics of medieval feudalism where clients owed nearly total obedience and allegiance to patrons who were members of a heirarchical, deeply entrenched ruling class. After fighting a series of wars, the British conquered the area in 1902 and established the Protectorate of Northern Nigeria. In 1914 northern and southern Nigeria were amalgamated into the Colony and Protectorate of Nigeria.

Between 1902 and 1914 in Northern Nigeria, the British developed what was to become a philosophy of colonial administration—Indirect Rule. Briefly, the central tenet of Indirect Rule is the idea that traditional authorities in the colonies should be recognized wherever possible and that the metropolitan power should seek to coopt them into the colonial administration by calling them Native Authorities and ruling through them at the local level.

In Northern Nigeria both the Hausa and Fulani who conquered them understood the meaning of conquest and the workings of a hierarchial system of authority. The addition of one more tier of authority over a many-tiered structure which was based on the allegiance of the masses to traditional patrons, while dramatic, was not revolutionary. Indeed, it has been argued that the superimposition of colonial power actually was supportive of the traditional hierarchial nature of authority in Northern Nigeria.[1] The Emirs, or traditional leaders of the North, soon recognized that "identity of interests" which was at the theoretical heart of Indirect Rule and quickly learned to appreciate the advantages of British "protection" which insured order and enlarged trade while not threatening their over-lordship in the area.

Indirect Rule was developed in response to the particular circumstances found in Northern Nigeria. Southern Nigeria was characterized by totally different structural systems of authority and the transfer of the Native Authority system to this area had vastly difficult results.

The southwestern portion of Nigeria is the home of the Yoruba people. The British did not understand the system of chiefly rule among the Yoruba. Here, traditional rulers, call *Obas,* ruled over large towns whose populations worked on farms in the surrounding countryside. While the Yoruba share a common cultural heritage and each large Yoruba town is governed by an *Oba* and his council, the people as a whole lacked any overall central authority. The British assumed the *Obas* had autocratic powers similar to that of the Emirs. In fact, theirs was a limited constitutional monarchy built upon overlapping family, lineage and clan units. The British, failing to perceive the true nature of the system, gave the chiefs powers they would never have had in the traditional society and removed the traditional checks on their power, thus corrupting traditional authority. This bastardized chieftancy in Western Nigeria was thus coopted first into the colonial bureaucracy and later they formed an alliance with the new politicians in an emerging political class.

In southeastern Nigeria the British were totally frustrated in their efforts to implement Indirect Rule. Here, traditional rule was essentially para-democratic or consensual and there was no formal administration. Further, Eastern Nigeria's population density of 550 per square mile is the densest in Africa and one of the densest in the world. In spite of this great density of population, the predominant tribal group here, the Igbo,[2]

[1] For two definitive statements on this subject see: M. G. Smith, *Government in Zauzau* (London: 1964) and C. S. Whitaker, Jr., *Politics of Tradition: Continuity and Change in Northern Nigeria* (Princeton: 1970).

[2] Igbo is the more correct spelling of the word which has been spelled 'Ibo' in much of the literature. Colonial officials did not hear the 'gb' sound and therefore spelled the word incorrectly. Recent publications which have acknowledged this phonetic error include the revised edition of M. M. Green's *Igbo Village Affairs*

live in small village groups rather than in "traditional urban centers" as do the Yoruba.[3] Each Igbo village is a unit unto itself and owes allegiance to no higher authority. In these acephalous villages, elders elected on the basis of age and achievement ruled by concensus. Central political authority was completely lacking. The density of population and the high degree of social fragmentation made the administration of this area particularly troublesome for the British. A central concept of Indirect Rule was that all communities possessed indigenous leaders who wielded authority, who could demand a certain degree of obedience and respect, and who could be coopted into the Native Authority system. Northern Nigeria corresponded to this preconception clearly, but the situation in the East was far more complex and hence the conditions of control much more elusive. In their frustration at not being able to "find" the traditional authorities, the British created chiefs by warrant and armed them with powers which from a traditional perspective were arbitrary and in direct conflict with accepted custom.[4]

The concentration of Nigeria's three main cultural groups in three distinct areas of the country made the British division of the country into three regions appear logical. Yet, each of the resulting three regions, North, West and East, was characterized by a cultural makeup which made the three-part division less than fully logical. Although Nigeria indeed has three major cultural groups, some 250 different peoples live within its boundaries. Thus, in each region a preponderant majority dominated a heterogeneous group of cultural and linguistic minorities.

Indirect Rule had a profound impact on subsequent developments within the country. Rather than act as a force for national integration,

---

in 1965; Victor Uchendu's *The Igbo of Southeastern Nigeria* (New York: 1965) and Beatrice and William E. Welmer's *Igbo* (Los Angeles: 1968).

[3] For more detail concerning Igbo social and political organization see: Victor Uchendu, *Ibid.*, Daryll Forde, *The Igbo and Ibibio-speaking People of Southeastern Nigeria* (London: 1950); and Simon Ottenberg, "Ibo Receptivity to Change," in William R. Bascom and Melville Herskovits, eds., *Continuity and Change in African Cultures* (Chicago: 1969). For more information on the Yoruba political system see Peter C. Lloyd, *Yoruba Land Law* (London: 1962); "The Changing Role of Yoruba Traditional Rulers," West African Institute of Social and Economic Research (WAISER) (Ibadan: 1956); "Kings, Chiefs and Local Government," *West Africa* (January 31, 1953); "The Traditional Political System of the Yoruba," *Southwestern Journal of Anthropology* (Winter, 1954); and "Some Change in the Government of Yoruba Towns," WAISER, (Ibadan: 1953).

[4] Recent Igbo writers have viewed the extreme vitriolic expressions of anti-British feelings evidenced in Biafra during the war as a release of long-standing resentments toward the British dating back to the inept attempts to impose Indirect Rule there. See Arthur A. Nwankwo and Samuel U. Ifejika, *The Making of a Nation: Biafra* (London: 1969), pp. 10–34.

the object of Indirect Rule was to preserve traditional divisions and keep the country divided into small, distinct units. The most conservative elements within the traditional power structure gained most by Indirect Rule and hence developed an interest in preserving the status quo.

British policy in the realm of religion further accentuated regional differences. By agreeing not to interfere with Islam in the North and giving the Emirs the option of accepting or rejecting the Christian missions (and thus also mission schools), the colonial power in effect fostered religious cleavages between the north and south. The numerically superior Islamic and largely illiterate North lagged behind the more urbanized, Christianized and literate south. After the amalgamation of the two sections in 1914, the Igbo, in particular, began moving to other sections of the country where they filled positions both in the civil service and increasingly in small-scale businesses. The overcrowding in the East and the exposure to Western education meant that the Igbo, more than any other group, had incentives to migrate out from their home area. The system of Indirect Rule, however, helped to keep them apart from the societies into which they moved.

During the years between the two World Wars, a small middle class of businessmen, civil servants and professionals developed in the new cities, primarily in the South. It was from this group that the leadership of the Nigerian nationalist movement came. The system of Indirect Rule through Native Authorities excluded them from the colonial decision-making process and their resentment found expression in the growing nationalist movement which developed after the Second World War. The expanding war-stimulated economy added a small but significant class of wage earners to the nationalist cause. The early years of nationalist agitation culminated in the formation of the National Council of Nigeria and the Cameroons (NCNC),[5] under the leadership of Dr. Nnamdi Azikiwe, an American educated Igbo born in Northern Nigeria.

With increasing commercial activity and the greater involvement of a growing Nigerian bourgeoise class, Igbo-Yoruba competition and tension in the cities divided the nationalist movement. In 1951, Obafemi Awolowo, a Yoruba businessman and lawyer, founded the Action Group (AG), a Western-based predominantly Yoruba party created primarily to counteract the NCNC.

The northern section of the country entered politics formally in 1951 with the creation of the Northern People's Congress (NPC). This party

[5] The party was founded as the National Council of Nigeria and the Cameroons, but became the National Council of Nigerian Citizens in 1961 when the people of the Cameroons Trust Territory voted to terminate their association with Nigeria.

was created partly in response to the threat of southern domination and the growth of northern radicalism among small segments of northern intellectuals. From the time of its inception until its final overthrow in the military coup d'etat of 1966, the NPC represented conservative, regional interests epitomized by the Emirs (traditional leaders of the North), their kin and clients, both traditional and nouveau.

Immediately after the War, the NCNC was in outlook a truly national political party attempting to propogate the nationalist cause throughout the country. Within a few years, however, as new parties were born with tribal or regional-religious bases, the NCNC itself became increasingly an inward-looking Eastern and Igbo-dominated party.

The British supported this increasing regionalization of Nigerian politics in a series of constitutional conferences held in London and Lagos in 1953 and 1954.[6] It was firmly decided at this time that Nigeria would be a federation with three strong regions. One consequence of this decision was that each of the regions would come to be dominated by one of the three main cultural groups and one of the three political parties. Thus, fissaparous tendencies, rather than unitary tendencies, were reinforced.

Internal self-government was formally granted to the Eastern and Western Regions in 1957 and to the Northern Region in 1959. On October 1, 1960, Nigeria became an independent state within the British Commonwealth of Nations. The first Prime Minister, Sir Abubakar Tafawa Balewa, headed an uneasy coalition government representing the major parties of the Northern and Eastern Regions—the NPC and the NCNC. Azikiwe, the first Governor-General, became President when Nigeria adopted a republican form of government on October 1, 1963.

Nigeria's economic history is the result of its colonial past. One result of the British insistence that each colony pay for itself and produce profits for British companies was the promotion of the export trade. In Nigeria this export economy centered on cocoa in the West, palm oil in the East, and peanuts in the North. British colonialism was designed to protect, improve, promote and direct the export trade of Nigeria.

Following World War II the British effort to better organize the export trade centered upon the establishment of the first marketing boards. Monopolistic boards were created for Nigeria's main export crops in 1947. The primary object of these boards was to buy the local crop through local purchasing agents who were usually employees of commercial firms which had dominated the trade prior to the establishment of the boards. The boards monopolized the sale of these products on the world market and attempted to stabilize the price paid to indigenous farmers when

[6] See Eme Awa, *Federal Government in Nigeria* (Berkeley: 1964).

the world price of commodity products was high. The difference between the world price and the price paid to the farmer was banked by the boards in London banks where it was held as sterling balances credited to Nigeria's account.

The question of "who gets the board" became a critical constitutional issue. The Yoruba, in particular, were interested in the regionalization of the marketing boards since the richest board, the Cocoa Marketing Board, and 90 percent of Nigeria's cocoa, came from the Yoruba dominated Western Region. In 1954 three regional marketing boards were established, each responsible for marketing all the produce from that region and inheriting the assets. The marketing boards provide a key to the power system of Nigeria's first Republic.[7]

The Regional Marketing Boards rapidly became major conduits of commercial patronage and thereby instruments of political control. Marketing board funds deposited in regionally created Nigerian banks could then extend credit to Nigerian businessmen. The businessmen were then expected to support the party in power, both politically and financially. The regional marketing boards funded loan and development corporations which undertook various projects in cooperation with private business interests. These corporations and their related loan associations were invariably managed by politically reliable administrators. Naturally, those who received loans from the board or banks were powerfully induced to support the regional government. In each region the mechanism of the marketing boards thus served to forge a tight and mutually supportive alliance of politicians and nascent businessmen committed to maintaining the status quo.

All during the period of the first republic the three dominant political parties, each electorally based on the allegiance of one of the three predominant nationality groups, grew fat in the house of patronage and financial control. Those who held political power in the regions were able to create economic opportunity for their own kin and clients and thus to determine the pattern of social stratification. As a group they formed the most fundamental power group in the federation. Indeed, they became, in Richard L. Sklar's trenchant designation, a "political class," controlling access to the important positions in all major institutions in Nigeria.[8] Clearly, for anyone seeking any significant change in

[7] For more detailed analysis of the connection between the marketing boards and politics in Nigeria see Richard L. Sklar and C. S. Whitaker, Jr. "Nigeria," in Gwendolyn Carter, ed., *National Unity and Regionalism in Eight African States* (Ithaca: 1966), pp. 128–206.

[8] Richard L. Sklar, "Contradictions in the Nigerian Political System," *Journal of Modern African Studies* (1965): 201–213.

the Nigerian economic and political power structure, the grip of this class would have to be broken.

The role of the marketing boards is also the key to another fundamental feature of the Nigerian political economy—namely, its foreign domination. Foreign firms dominated both the import and export trade and through them limited industrial growth was promoted, but always primarily with an eye to attracting foreign investment into Nigeria. International trade and capital formation alike depended upon expatriate profit as the prime mover.

Economic History

The principal motive of the British in creating Nigeria was not to advance the interests of the various peoples of the area, but to serve Britain's own economic interests.[9] Once her authority was firmly established in Nigeria, Britain had the orthodox colonial preoccupations of maintaining law and order while extracting raw materials for the home market and creating Nigerian demands for British manufactured goods. Under British colonial rule export crops such as groundnuts (peanuts), cocoa, palm oil and cotton were introduced and Nigeria's timber, tin, and coal were exploited—products which today (along with the more recently developed oil industry) are the mainstays of the Nigerian economy.

Following the colonial trade wars and the consequent consolidation of the 1920's, the Nigerian market was dominated by a small number of large and highly integrated foreign trading companies—the United Africa Company (Unilever affiliate), John Holt, Paterson, Zachonis, Compagnie Francaise de l'Afrique Occidentale (CFAO), Societé Commerciale de l'Ouest African (SCOA), and the Swiss-owned Union Trading Company (UTC). UAC and John Holt operated both ocean and shipping companies and inland water transport services for evacuating the country's export produce which they purchased and to bring in imports which they sold. These large merchant wholesalers provided credit to small scale Nigerian businessmen and market women who were committed to buying their products for their trade. In this way the foreign firms in effect controlled even small-scale retail trade.

As outlined above, immediately after World War II, the British created monopolistic marketing boards to control Nigeria's export trade. In spite of Nigerian control of the marketing boards after independence in 1960, expatriate firms continued to monopolize both import and export trade. Measures were taken to promote Nigerian industrialization, but these

[9] This argument is developed at length by Nwankwo and Ifejika, *The Making of a Nation,* pp. 10–34.

measures in fact were designed to attract foreign investment into Nigeria. The result of these policies was continued foreign domination of the Nigerian economy through a network of structural relationships now termed neo-colonial.

Neo-colonialism is the process by which colonial patterns of dependency are sustained after the granting of formal political independence. The primary objective of neo-colonialism is to maintain the former colony as a controlled source of raw materials as well as a market for investment and the sale of goods manufactured overseas by local subsidiaries of foreign firms. The realization of a mass market and the promotion of certain types of consumption habits are crucial to the foreign investors. Thus, the major private foundations and commercial firms of the Western, developed countries invested heavily after Nigerian independence in national market and feasibility studies.[10]

Nigeria is a neo-colonial state in that political independence did not significantly affect the country's economic dependency before the post-1970 development of the oil industry. During the first ten years of its existence as a nation, Nigeria followed a conservative monetary policy, avoiding foreign exchange restrictions and remaining open to foreign investment and foreign companies. Thus, at the beginning of the 1970's, foreign interests still controlled savings, investments, the money supply and the prices of most consumer items. All large trading and manufacturing firms were foreign controlled or owned. Nigerian firms were small and there was little Nigerian investment.

The high capital requirements of merchandise trading discouraged the development of indigenous commercial activity until after the Second World War. The large foreign firms pursued a policy of pre-empting the market by handling all ranges of merchandise. The large investment needed in storage and handling facilities and the long capital turnover period discouraged investment by medium- or small-scale enterprises.[11]

Given their control of Nigeria's market, the merchant firms were understandably not enthusiastic supporters of Nigerian industrialization. They did not wish to cut their own throats and those of the manufacturers and

[10] Since 1954 the Ford Foundation has given over $20m. to various projects, including the expertise for developing the first six-year development plan. The Carnegie Foundation has given $700,000 to the Ashby Commission which studied the Nigerian educational system. The Rockefeller Fund established a Lagos office in 1957 to prepare feasibility studies for American investors. Arthur D. Little, Inc., assumed this function after 1962. See Africa Research Group, *The Nigerian Civil War* (Cambridge: 1970), pp. 6–9.

[11] On the actual use of market power see P. T. Bauer, *West African Trade* (Cambridge: 1954), chps. 10–11.

processers with whom they had contractual relationships, nor did they want to lose the import trade in manufactured commodities. The import trade reduced the overhead costs on the purchase of goods for export and helped to keep profits up in spite of falling prices of the major export crops (e.g. cocoa) on the world market.[12]

Although historically the merchant firms were not enthusiastic about local industrialization, their position began to change in the late 1950's.[13] The post-war growth in imports affected the structure of competition. Imports increased from £20m. in 1946 to £66m. in 1958. Many new sellers were attracted and Nigerian businessmen began to enter the import market on their own. Indian importers and distributors contributed to the competition as did Greek produce-buyers and Levantine retailers. The near monopoly held by the merchant firms began to give way. In 1949 the three largest importers (UAC, John Holt and Paterson Zochonis) accounted for 49 percent of all traded commodities, in 1963 they controlled only 16 percent of this trade.[14] Since 1934 the British manufacturers have lost one-third of their share of the Nigerian market to non-Commonwealth suppliers and more than 50 percent of this shift has occurred sinced 1959. Nigerian traders imported 5 percent of total goods imported in 1949 and 20 percent of the 1963 imports.[15]

As the competition increased the overseas manufacturers began financing Nigerian importers on the basis of ninety-day credit and the services of local confirming and warehouse agents employed by the expatriate firms. Thus, the local Nigerian importers developed a symbiotic relationship with overseas manufacturers extending them credit. For this reason they later supported the government in its conservative economic policies.

After independence in 1960 a new form of financing was available to Nigerian politicians cum businessmen which enabled them to enter both the commodity and nascent manufacturing sectors. This took the form of supplier credits to contractor-financed projects. In such projects the contractor sets the terms of the loans, which are notoriously disadvantageous to the contractee—usually the government. The usual governmental controls and guarantees which normally accompany foreign aid or investment are absent in this type of financing.[16] Thus, through this form of financ-

[12] See J. Mars, "Extra-territorial Enterprises" in Margery Perham, ed., *Mining, Commerce and Finance in Nigeria* (London: 1948), p. 68.

[13] Peter Kilby, *Industrialization in an Open Economy: Nigeria 1945–1966* (Cambridge, Mass.: 1969), pp. 53–137.

[14] *Ibid.*, p. 63.

[15] Bauer, chap. 5 for 1949 and Federal Office of Statistics, *Nigerian Trade Summary* (Lagos: 1963) for 1960's.

[16] See Douglass A. Scott, "External Debt-Management in a Developing Country,"

ing Nigeria's politicians made costly and unviable commitments to private foreign creditors. By 1965 Nigerian government initiated contractor-financed projects were the most important form of new investment in the country. In 1966 they accounted for 80 percent of the value of new plants under construction.[17]

Many of the private entrepreneurs who entered the country on contractor-finance projects were "on the make." A Britisher, Ernest Shinwell, attempted to promote a clothing factory and supermarket in Eastern Nigeria in 1963 using £50 million of forged securities as collateral for government-sponsored loans.[18] Contractor-finance or suppliers' credits were also characteristic of long established manufacturing companies seeking outlets for their redundant equipment. Indian Head Mills, a U. S. firm, was given a contract for a £2.4 million textile plant at Aba after contributing £72,000 cash and forty-year-old machinery valued at £699,000 in return for 70 percent equity.[19] This was not an exception. Old and redundant equipment was frequently brought into the country under contractor-financing and supplier credits. Often various pieces of plant equipment were not made by the same manufacturer and therefore part replacement was most difficult if not impossible. Whether managed by Nigerian or expatriate supervisors, these enterprises were generally over-staffed, had unresolved technical problems and did not earn profits. In spite of their unprofitability and questionable contribution to the Nigerian economy, these arrangements were popular because they directly benefited the politicians. A system was institutionalized in which the contractor paid a 10 percent "kick-back" fee into the treasury of the ruling party and a similar fee to the politician responsible for the contract award.[20]

In marked contrast to the profitless operation of these enterprises were the joint ventures between Nigerian and foreign firms. Firms with a prior interest in the market turned to supporting import-replacing industrialization in order to meet the rising competition. Most of the manufacturing enterprises in this form of industrialization consisted of the old merchant firms lowering the cost of imported commodities through processing, assembling, or packaging them in Nigeria. The government granted tariffs to protect such finished products ("made in Nigeria") from "out-

in Tom J. Farer, ed., *Financing African Development* (Cambridge: 1965), pp. 50–57.

[17] Africa Research Group, *The Nigerian Civil War,* p. 12.

[18] *West Africa,* February 6, 1965, February 13, 1965.

[19] *Idem.*

[20] Richard L. Sklar, *Nigerian Political Parties: Power in an Emergent African Nation* (Princeton: 1963), Chp. X.

side" competition, while leaving imported materials as well as capital and equipment for construction of the plant duty free, and provided "tax holidays" and permitted repatriations of profit. UAC, for instance, built sewing machine assembly plants, cigarette and beer factories and bicycle assembly lines in order to maintain its dominant share of the consumer market. It is thus very profitable for foreign firms to engage in this type of import substitution and the scope for it is great. Consequently, imports of consumer goods have been declining while imports of chemicals, machinery and transport equipment have been increasing.[21] Local industry replaced imports of flour, beer, household utensils, cement, corrugated iron sheets, tires and tubes by 1963.[22] However real substitution can be achieved only when foreign personnel and capital are replaced by trained Nigerian personnel and capital. There is some indication that these facts of economic life are now recognized by Nigerian leadership. The weekly journal, *West Africa,* in its February, 1972 editions, outlined the major components of a new decree which would establish Nigerian control over the business sector. These provisions will be discussed in the concluding section of this essay.

The four largest import replacing industries—cigarettes, beer, cement and textiles—account for 40 percent of industrial output and 21 percent of industrial employment in the sector employing ten or more.[23] They receive preferential tax treatment and a 100 percent import duty has been placed upon the importation of competing products. The rate of return on investments in such industries is 20 percent, and thus they furnish high profit-yielding investments for foreign capital. The need for high capital investment in such enterprises so far has prevented effective Nigerianization of these projects. The Nigerian government now speculates, however, that as indigenous technical skill grows and financing becomes available (apparently from oil profits) the foreign interests can theoretically be bought out.[24] At the present time the foreign firms involved are required to reinvest a certain percentage of their profits over specified periods of time. This reinvestment of profits, however, is used primarily to pay back loans originally granted for the purchase of capital equipment for such enterprises. Both the Nigerian government and the foreign investors find this a convenient arrangement. Should the Nigerian government implement foreign exchange restrictions, debt servicing is unlikely

[21] See Bank of Nigeria, *Nigerian Trade Journal* (Lagos: 1946–1964).

[22] Kilby, *Industrialization,* p. 28.

[23] See Federal Office of Statistics, *Industrial Survey of Nigeria, 1963* (Lagos: 1963).

[24] *West Africa,* February 4, 1972.

to be curtailed since Nigeria needs to maintain its credit standing. Profits, however, might not be so protected. By providing capital in the form of loans, the foreign investors limit their loss in the event of a business failure. Credit losses are tax deductible and equity investments are not.

In addition to supporting import substitution the large merchant firms responded to intensified competition by transforming themselves from general trading companies handling the full range of merchandise into a series of smaller specialized marketing and manufacturing units. They have attempted to concentrate in the least competitive markets, i.e. those requiring considerable capital and technical servicing skills. They have specialized in department store merchandise, earth-moving and civil engineering equipment, air-conditioning and other electrical goods, office equipment, pharmaceuticals, and motor vehicles. Machinery trade was particularly popular because investment was small—3 to 4 percent of the combined equity-debenture capital commitment. In effect this means that the investor is required to put down in cash only 3 to 4 percent of the total investment, but will be paid back, at high rates of interest, in proportion to the total amount committed. This approach has the distinct disadvantage that in practice the government assumes most or all of the risk of failure while the private promoter and his associates secure both a gain on promotion and construction and the bulk of the profits if the venture succeeds.

The promotional activities of German, Italian, and Israeli machinery merchants obtained over £30 million in public investment from 1962–1966 in support of largely uneconomic privately operated projects. For example, Coutinho Caro of Hamburg accounted for £18 million invested in glass factories at Port Harcourt and Ughelli, a textile factory at Asaba, a cement factory at Ukpilla, clinker grinding factories at Lagos and Koko, a cocoa processing factory at Ikeja and a palm kernel processing plant at Port Harcourt.[25] None of these firms produced a profit for the Nigerian investors, but the repayment of the loans plus interest guaranteed profits to the creditors. In this way foreign firms were able to use local capital to finance their operations because very little cash outlay was required from the foreign investors, whose loans were generally guaranteed by their governments. The results of these projects was the *decapitalization* or a net capital loss for Nigeria. Since these investments are obviously not particularly economically beneficial to Nigeria, the explanation for their existence is largely political. These prestigious capital-intensive projects can be achieved quickly, they provided well-paid directorships for politicians and were an important source of party finance via "kick-

[25] Kilby, *Industrialization,* pp. 77–78.

backs."[26] Moreover, the selection and location of these projects were also based on political rather than economic considerations. Little consideration was given to promoting an integrated national economy in financing these projects largely because the arrangements were negotiated with politicians in the regions. Even politicians active on the national scene sought to direct projects to their own regions because they depended on support from a regional basis of power.

In the highly competitive markets for soap and beer and the non-differentiated commodities such as flour and cement, the very short capital turnover period and the minimum handling, storage, and invoicing enabled low-overhead Nigerian distributors who operated on bank overdrafts to capture a large share of this trade. The desirability of using Nigerian distributors does not disrupt but rather reinforces market patterns as individual Nigerian businessmen benefit from their association with the foreign producers of the products they distribute and, in turn, are encouraged to establish their own local monopolies.

In trying to promote industrialization prior to 1966, the government provided foreign investors with essential infrastructure (i.e. roads, communications, electric power, etc.), guaranteed private investors against uncompensated nationalization, and gave them freedom regarding the sale of their assets and repatriation of profits. These incentives encouraged foreign capitalists to make direct investments in public projects through loans to the government. By 1966 £35m. had gone into public investment projects which were yielding no profits but the loans for which had to be repaid with interest. The explanations for this was also political since these were the pet projects of certain politicians. These non-profit yielding enterprises included a fruit cannery, four cement mills, two sack factories, a paper mill, two breweries, an integrated textile mill, two soft drink bottling plants, a ceramic factory, a mint, a glass factory, and four oilseed crushing plants. Also, there were the big prestige projects such as the five-ship merchant marine, an international airline, three olympic-sized sports stadia, four television stations and five luxury hotels.

Contractor-financing and the marketing boards gave the regional political class reason to be satisfied with status quo politics. These people did not fully comprehend the consequences of economic breakup. Both the Northern and Eastern politicians seriously considered secession before the events of 1966. National politicians were basically regional in their outlook and also benefited from the financial arrangements that characterized regional politics. National politicians were concerned with

[26] A list of firms reported to have paid bribes in order to obtain government favors was printed in the *Daily Graphic,* January 27, 1967.

directing funds and projects to their own districts and did not have a particularly national outlook. The foreign firms played the political game in that they acceded to the wishes of the politicians. The corruptness and uneconomic ventures of the system were of no particular concern to them so long as their profits were guaranteed. For an agreed upon kickback these guarantees were forthcoming. The foreign investors, however, were depending upon the existence of a mass market. Even the investors in the oil industry had an interest in the existence of a large market for their affiliate enterprises. Therefore, although they were not so interested in whether Nigeria had a unitary or regional-federal form of government, they were concerned that there be "one Nigeria." One Nigeria, however, was seriously in trouble by mid-1966.

Post Independence Politics

The threatened disintegration of Nigeria which culminated in the civil war of 1967–1970 had its origins in the breakup of the regionally based political class and the political status quo in Western Nigeria. The crisis in the Western Region resulted from a basic split within the Action Group, the dominant party of that region, during 1962–1963. The Action Group crisis represented a basic conflict in ideology and in the prevailing view of the "rules of the game" in Nigerian politics. It provides the key to much of subsequent Nigerian history. The conflict brought into the open a fundamental conflict between the business oriented political class committed to the status quo and the younger, more progressive elements increasingly committed to programs promoting social change.

The crisis began building almost immediately after the first federal elections held just before independence in 1959. In these federal elections no party had won a constitutional majority, although the NPC (Northern People's Congress) had a clear plurality. It was thus necessary to form a coalition government at the federal level. Partly because the NCNC (National Council of Nigeria Citizens) was a strong opposition party within the Western Region, the NCNC and the Action Group were not able to agree upon the conditions for a coalition government even though they had much in common in ideological and socio-economic terms. Instead, an alliance was formed between the two most unlikely bedpartners—the conservative, regionalistic NPC and the progressive, nationalistic NCNC—forcing the Action Group into the role of the opposition party at the federal level. Chief Awolowo, the leader of the Action Group, almost immediately began forging the AG into an effective national opposition party. Since the NPC dominated coalition at the federal level represented a victory for the proponents of regional power, the logical position of the opposition to that stance was one of anti-regionalism. Thus, the Action Group continued to support the creation of new states in the country and appealed to minorities in both the East and the North to support that program. Such a platform posed a serious threat to the entrenched regional parties. Parodoxically, the Action Group itself depended upon a regional power base for its own existence. In addition to attempting to expand the arena of the Action Group's appeal through seeking minority support for the creation of new states, the AG under Awolowo's leadership began to take an increasingly radical position on matters of national policy. Domestically, the Action Group dedicated itself to the "reconstruction of a democratic socialist society in Nigeria." In the federal parliament the AG delegates spoke out against Nigeria's close ties with Great Britain and appealed for a more "positively neutral" foreign policy. Specifically, the AG successfully opposed the signing of a Defense Agreement with the British and pushed for establishing more ties with Eastern bloc countries. Awolowo and his followers at the national level espoused a preference for moving Nigeria more to the left in Pan African affairs and giving more serious attention and support to the southern African liberation struggles.

As the Action Group began to replace the NCNC as the party of the intellectual and radical elements in Nigeria and as it increased its following outside the Western Region, the NCNC and the NPC began to perceive it more and more as a serious threat to their interests. In 1961 the NCNC initiated a press campaign exposing some of the more glaring irregularities in the relationship between the Western regional government, the banking and investment and loan agencies in that region, and party personnel. Indeed, a commission of inquiry appointed in 1962 revealed that the Western Regional Marketing Board had made loans in excess of six million dollars to a private company owned entirely by four leading members of the Action Group.[27] While the relationship existing between the marketing board, the regional government, its banking institutions and members of the government and party was a characteristic feature of the political scene in all the regions, the public exposure of such relationships did much to discredit Awolowo and the role of the Action Group as a radical opposition party. Meanwhile, the regional wing of the AG, under the leadership of the Regional Premier, Chief Samuel Akintola, became quite concerned with the new image of the party being projected at the national level. The Action Group politicians at the regional level had the same interests at stake as their counterparts in the other two

[27] See the Report of the *Coker Commission of Inquiry into the Affairs of Certain Statutory Corporations in Western Nigeria,* 4 vols., (Lagos: 1962).

regions, and they had no desire to alter the status quo. Thus, the businessmen-cum-politicians (or vice-versa) in all three regions had much in common with each other and were equally concerned with the stance of the national wing of the Action Group.

In May, 1962, the inevitable clash between the regional and national wings of the Action Group occurred. The Federal Executive Council of the party, under the leadership of Awolowo, asked for the resignation of Akintola, who was accused of indiscipline and anti-party activities. Akintola sought support for his position from the national government. Such support was forthcoming when the federal government declared a state of emergency in the Western Region after a riot, perpetrated by the followers of Akintola, erupted in the Western House of Assembly. During this federally imposed state of emergency, the civilian government of the West was suspended and martial law declared.

Once the national government interfered with the internal problems of the Action Group, the political status quo was undermined. During the state of emergency in the West, Awolowo was placed under house arrest. By the end of the year Akintola was reinstated as the regional premier, Awolowo was charged with felonous treason on grounds that he had plotted a coup d'etat and was active in sending young men to Ghana for training in illegal and subversive activities. He was found guilty as charged after a dramatic trial in 1963. It was evident that Awolowo had become irresponsible from the point of view of the ruling political class and thus had to be eliminated as a force in national politics.[28]

1963 saw the imprisonment of Awolowo, the country's first organized nation-wide strike, the creation of a new region out of the minority areas of the Western Region,[29] and a series of crises centered around the politically sensitive issue of acquiring new census data upon which constituency realignments would be based for the upcoming 1964 general elections.[30]

[28] See Richard L. Sklar, "The Ordeal of Chief Awolowo" in Gwendolyn M. Carter, ed., *Politics in Africa: Seven Cases* (New York: 1965), pp. 119–167. and Anthony Enahoro, *Fugitive Offender* (London: 1963).

[29] In mid-1963 the Federal Parliament acted to create a new state, the Mid-West State, from the minority areas of the Western Region. The Action Group had favored the creation of at least three new states, one carved from each of the existing regions. It was at first opposed to the creation of only one new state, and that at its expense, but eventually the party did support the resolution. The NCNC, however, had sponsored the bill and there was a sizeable Igbo minority in the Midwest. Therefore, the NCNC won the new regional elections in the Mid-west and cut deeply into AG strength in the area.

[30] Nigeria's 1962 census was rejected and revised in 1963. In the revised version, which was never published officially, the North was given 30m. of Nigeria's 55m. people. This meant that the Northern party could win enough seats to form a

The division of power in the West, the elimination of an effective organized national opposition, and the dismemberment of the Western Region greatly unbalanced the political system. The Action Group's attempt to nationalize its appeal succeeded in disrupting the party's cohesion and pushing the conservative, ethnically-oriented wing of the party toward a common accord with the NPC.

Ironically, in order to discredit the opposition-minded section of the Action Group under the leadership of Awolowo, the allies of the Western Nigerian political class loyal to the status quo commissioned spectacular inquiries into the depths of the Action Group's corruption, which, in the end, seriously undermined their own position by exposing the whole corporate nature of the political class.[31] This revealing of massive misuse of funds had the effect of discrediting the legitimacy of the political class in all the regions and providing a rallying symbol for reform-minded elements throughout the country. Once the security of one section of the political class had been broken, the security of all was threatened.

Regionalism was the fundamental characteristic of the first four years of Nigeria's independence. Each region was controlled by members of the dominant ethnic group in that region. Each region had its own government, its own university, divergent religious, political, economic and cultural interests, and largely separate economies centered around regional marketing boards, public corporations for major services, and development and loan associations. Regional issues were consistently given prominance over national ones and the ethnically oriented, regionally-based politicians dominated the political system. Nepotism and patronage were rife. Although the politicians and middle class became prosperous under the first regime, the subsistence farmers and marginal wage earners who constitute 70 percent of Nigeria's work force were no better off than before independence. The progressive forces represented by the national wing of the Action Group appeared to be crushed.

However, following the splintering of the Action Group, a gradual realignment of forces began to take place. The NCNC remained in the coalition government, but increasingly took an independent line. The census crises effectively broke up the coalition government for all practical purposes, and the NPC began to strengthen its ties with Akintola's splinter party in the West. The division in the West thus gave the NPC its first genuine southern ally. While the conservative elements in the North and West were drawing closer together, the census crisis had the effect of

---

government without going into a coalition with a southern-based party. The NCNC and the Eastern Regional Government expressed 'no confidence' in the census.

[31] Coker Commission, 4 vols., (Lagos: 1962).

driving the easterners into consolidation along communal lines—all easterners (Igbo and the minorities) felt threatened and thus began to turn inward. The eastern elite, under the leadership of the regional premier, Michael Okpara, began to fear northern domination and to seek common cause with the opponents of regional power wherever they were. The Eastern-based party, the NCNC, had historically been the party of "one Nigeria" and expressed the Pan-Nigerian outlook of the Igbo. Having migrated from the overcrowded East to cities in other regions, the Igbo became active in cultural and political affairs. Outside their own region they became the "radicals" of Nigerian politics and reflected the unitary emphasis on constitutional issues which became characteristic of all Nigerian radicals as the hold of the political class became more entrenched.

For the first time since independence the more natural partners, the progressive forces of the East and West, and the conservative forces of the North and West, formed alliances on political lines which took on increasingly serious tribal connotations as the crisis progressed. As the federal elections of December, 1964, approached, after the first nationwide strike and bitter electoral campaigning, the country drifted toward violent confrontation. Because of the inability of many of its candidates to campaign in the North due to false arrests, denial of meeting permits, lawlessness and other irregularities, the United Progressive Grand Alliance, primarily the NCNC and the Action Group, together with several minor parties, decided to boycott the elections. Consequently, no elections were held in the Eastern Region. The Nigerian National Alliance, primarily the NPC and Akintola's Nigerian National Democratic Party, won the occasionally contested elections in the West and in the North where the Alliance was largely unopposed.[32] When President Azikiwe at first refused to appoint a prime minister and claimed the election was invalid, the country seemed close to disintegration. However, a compromise was reached in which Balewa, the prime minister, formed a "broad-based national government" with eighty cabinet ministers. Further compromises resulted in new elections being held in the East and some 51 UPGA candidates being elected to the federal parliament from that region.

A final crisis occurred following the Western Region elections in October, 1965, when the regional government announced, amidst rising violence and rioting, that Akintola's NNDP had won a huge majority in the hopelessly rigged elections. The federal government again stood behind the Akintola group, thus lending its support to an illegitimate splinter regime. It became clear that the northern politicians, together

[32] For details of the election developments and crises, see *West Africa,* October-December, 1964 and January, 1965.

with their southern allies, would not permit political change through constitutional channels.

The political crisis intensified as actors increasingly saw their ends as mutually exclusive. The deepening political crisis was reinforced by deepening ethnic awareness in the south. The degree of animosity and tension was clearly evident in the Lagos University crisis of 1965.[33]

This five-month crisis centered around the controversy regarding the appointment of a vice-chancellor for the university. At this time Nigeria's three most prestigious universities (at Ibadan, Lagos and Nsukka) were all headed by Igbo academicians. The University of Lagos Act, placed before parliament in 1964, renamed Professor Eni Njoku as the vice-chancellor at Lagos. Parliament adjourned for the 1964 elections before this item was acted upon, however. The new NNDP/NPC dominated government decided to make the appointment of the vice-chancellor a political issue. In February, 1965, the University's Academic Senate recommended that Njoku be reappointed. A ten-member provisional council, however, had the formal authority to overrule the senate. The council was a politically appointed body which, in 1965, was composed of six Yoruba, one Hausa, one minority and one expatriate member. No Igbo was appointed to this council after 1965. The Council, against the advise of the academic senate, recommended that a Yoruba Professor, Saburi Biobaku, be named the vice-chancellor. A Lagos newspaper expressed the feeling that went into this appointment: "Lagos was a Yoruba city and its University ought to be headed by a son of the soil." [34] After the announcement, all the university deans and academic staff protested, and after demonstrations and a student strike, the university was closed. The crisis was not resolved until six of seven faculty deans had been dismissed or fired and fifty members of the academic staff had resigned. Lagos, once a cosmopolitan university drawing students from throughout the federation, became a Yoruba University. This crisis at Lagos was followed, in December, 1966, by the resignation of Dr. Kenneth Dike, the Igbo vice-chancellor at Ibadan. Rather than coalesce around class interests, competition in national institutions, education and the civil service increasingly reflected ethnic interests. At the center, conflict grew out of the attempt of the NPC dominated federal government to balance the regional composition of the civil service in which southerners were greatly over-represented because of their greater access to education. As less qualified northerners were advanced over their southern counterparts in order to give some regional balance to the civil service, the frustration

[33] Ifejika and Nwankwo, *The Making of a Nation,* pp. 55–71.
[34] *Daily Sketch,* p. 8, quoted *ibid.,* p. 56.

of the southerners increased. The consolidation of interests along ethnic lines took place as a result of this situation. The political class began dividing into its ethnic components as entry into privileged positions in the system became more difficult.

Immediately before and after independence there was rapid advancement in the civil service. The rapid advancement of young men early in their careers to the top had the effect of freezing the opportunities for advancement to the high echelons of the civil service. As more university graduates appeared on the scene, a confrontation began to shape up along ethnic lines due to the intense competition for the remaining civil service posts. With a growing number of equally qualified candidates available for the few positions, ethnic ties became the important determinants. The clear emergence of ethnic considerations in career advancement within the public service was detrimental to national unity, for it caused animosity and distrust between members of the political elite at the national level. This growth of ethnic awareness in the civil service reinforced the regional and communal orientations of Nigeria's politicians.[35]

Nigeria's politicians during this period naturally tended to favor the areas from which they derived their political support in allocating scarce national resources. Without much consideration for economic planning and paying little attention to myriad reports and studies by international agencies and corporations (who were interested in promoting the economic viability of projects supported by their sponsors), the politicians invested in many projects which were unviable and too costly. The politicians of the First Republic tended to formulate their fundamental political identity in terms of their region of origin and ethnic community rather than along cross-ethnic or national class lines. They fostered communalism or tribalism which militated against a national outlook and deepened feelings of ethnic differences and antagonism. The political class sought to guarantee their continued power and privileges through maintaining their regional power bases and securing popular support by ethnic appeals—i.e., they began to foster "tribalism" for their own political purposes. However, the ethnic animosity which they unleashed ultimately set them against themselves in their scramble to get as much of the "national political pie" as possible. In sum, the political class attempted to consolidate their class power privileges through fostering "tribalism" and to eliminate all further competition for access to these positions. This

[35] For an extended theoretical exposition of the concept of communalism see Robert Melson and Howard Wolpe "Modernization and the Politics of Communalism: A Theoretical Perspective," in *American Political Science Review* 64 (December, 1970): 1112–30.

dynamic led to the breakdown of the political regime and the downfall of the First Republic.

As opportunities for advancement and entrance into the political system narrowed, there was a breakdown in trust and cooperation. The ruling politicians sought to control events and consolidate their continued privileged position through the power of money and the judicious use of patronage. Those men who sought to challenge the system on ideological grounds found that they lacked a viable constituency. The national politicians had a stake in preserving the communal basis of their constituencies and the regional politicians found the status quo to their political and economic interests. No program which promoted genuine change toward social equality could be tolerated by the Nigerian political class, either at the national or at the regional level.

Nationalism and Economics

Nationalism in Nigeria was limited to the elimination of outright foreign political domination. The fundamental economic relationships established during the colonial era were not judged detrimental to the interests of the political class. The foreign firms paid well for "protection" from radical elements and offered a certain amount of patronage to the members of the ruling groups by allowing them to serve on boards of directors, and advisory councils, and allowing them to influence staff appointments. At the same time, many Nigerian politicians were businessmen themselves and the government and indigenous business community were mutually supportive of each other. Thus, the politicians found that cooperation, both with the foreign firms and with the local businessmen, was consistent with their own interests.[36]

Because Nigeria inherited substantial reserves from the colonial marketing boards, public capital was available for the "wheeling and dealing" of the Nigerian politicians. Insulated from the more urgent problems of sheer economic survival faced by many African countries at independence, the political class inherited British colonial attitudes in regard to living conditions, salaries, and privileged treatment, and were able to indulge

[36] A review of banking, development corporations, loan boards, and schools run by politicians and their friends makes clear how the new political and economic elite shared government resources. See C. V. Brown, *Government and Banking in Western Nigeria* (Ibadan: 1964); M. S. Baratz, "Public Investment in Private enterprize: A Western Nigerian Case Study," in *Nigerian Journal of Economic and Social Studies* 6 (March, 1964); G. K. Helleiner, *Peasant Agriculture, Government and Economic Growth in Nigeria* (Homewood, Ill.: 1966), chap. 10; *Report of the Inquiry into Fees Charged by Public Secondary Grammar Schools and Teacher Training Colleges in Western Nigeria* (Ibadan: 1963).

themselves in the free pursuit of these things. Increasingly, politicians who depended on communal or ethnic support defended themselves from the growing opposition of intellectuals and students demanding social change. They ignored national considerations for the sake of consolidating their own narrow political power bases. Thus, the Nigerian political system became more fragmented while it became more corrupt.

The vested interests of those entrenched in the public sector (the main source of employment) led to a closing of the job market, especially to southerners. Meanwhile, the country's educational system was overproducing, even at the university level. The growth in unemployment, the staggering underemployment, the slower than hoped for economic growth, the reduced share of southern political control, the erosion of constitutionalism through two rigged censuses, and the fraudulent elections in 1964 and 1965, contributed steadily rising frustrations.

Balewa's precariously balanced "broad-based national government" came to an abrupt end on January 15, 1966 when a group of junior army officers, based primarily in Kaduna, initiated a coup d'etat which resulted in the assassination of three of Nigeria's most important political leaders —Prime Minister Balewa, the Northern Premier Sir Ahmadu Bello, and the Western Premier Chief Samuel Akintola. In this coup attempt many Northern army officers were also assassinated.[37] The available members of the national government, meeting in extraordinary session in Lagos, decided to hand power over to the Army Chief of Staff, Major General Aguiyi Ironsi.

The coup was not successful in that its originators never came to power, but the attempt was successful in ridding the country of a regime now unpopular in almost every segment of the Nigerian society. General Ironsi, however, was not able to take advantage of the initial popularity enjoyed by his regime. Ironsi was not involved in the coup, but he came to power as a result of its attempt and he hesitated to punish its perpetrators. A career officer with no experience in politics, Ironsi made several critical mistakes. Perhaps the most serious miscalculation occurred on May 24,

[37] Literature on Nigeria prior to 1963 is rich and relatively complete as public records are available. However, from the census, general strike and Federal elections of 1964 onwards, the political story has yet to be fully recorded and analyzed. An extremely valuable collection of official and unofficial documents, Nigerian newspaper accounts, radio broadcasts and verbatim statements made by the leading actors of the Nigerian tragedy of 1966–1970 has been collected by A. M. H. Kirk-Greene. See A. M. H. Kirk-Greene, *Crisis and Conflict in Nigeria: A Documentary Sourcebook, 1966–1970, vols. I and II,* (London: 1971). On the first military coup see "Special Branch Report of the Events of 15 January, 1966" in Vol. I, pp. 115–124.

1966, when Ironsi declared by decree that Nigeria was now a unitary state with a unified civil service.[38]

Increasingly the coup and the Ironsi regime were viewed as anti-northern by northerners: Ironsi himself was Igbo, his regime appeared to be Igbo dominated, mostly northern army officers were killed during the coup, and the unification decree meant that more than ever the North would be dominated by southerners. Slowly but quietly, the ousted northern politicians, with the aid of British civil servants still employed in the northern Nigerian civil service, were able to capitalize on the growing fears of southern domination posed by the unification decrees.[39] In reality, the "unity" decree affected very few civil servants in the North and the very nature of military rule had already established a de facto unitary state in the country. It appeared to northerners, however, that they were to be subordinate to southerners in the army (where most of the officers were Igbo) and in the civil service.[40]

Partly as a result of this discontent and anxiety, riots were initiated in the North against easterners, most of whom were Igbo. Some 3,000 people were killed and many thousands more fled to the Eastern Region. At the urging of both Ironsi and the Eastern Military Governor, Lt. Còl. Chukwuemeka Odumegwu Ojukwu, the panic subsided and most of those who fled returned to their homes in the North.[41]

Then, on July 29, 1966, when he was touring the country for the cause of national unity in the wake of the northern riots and distrust generated by the unification decree, Ironsi was kidnapped and subsequently murdered by mutinous northern army officers.[42] Negotiations began on the

[38] See "The Unification Decree: No. 34 of 1966" *ibid.*, pp. 169–173.

[39] Prior to 1966 the North, in pursuing its policy of 'one North' had refused to give positions in its civil service to non-Northern Nigerians. Instead, a number of retired or redundant British civil servants, whose skills were no longer needed after independence by the Federal Government, found employment in the North where they were considered less offensive than southerners. As pointed out earlier, the North lagged behind the south in education and skilled manpower and therefore could not staff its bureaucracy from its own resources. For a rebuttal of the contention that Britishers were involved in developments in Northern Nigeria in 1966 see "British High Commission Denies Complicity in Northern Disturbances, June, 1966" *ibid.*, pp. 180–181.

[40] For a discussion of the development of these feelings see: Walter Schwarz, "The Fall of the Fulani Empire," in the *South Atlantic Quarterly* 67: 591–607, (Autumn, 1968): 597–8; and Murray Last "Aspects of Administration and Dissent in Hausaland, 1800–1968," *Africa,* 40 (October, 1970).

[41] See "Broadcast by Military Governor of the North, 29 May, 1966," in Kirk-Greene, *Crisis and Conflict,* pp. 177–179 and "Ojukwu Appeals for Calm among Easterners in the North," pp. 179–180.

[42] This coup is outlined in great detail by Robin Luckham, *The Nigerian Mili-*

evening of July 29 and continued through the morning of August 1, 1966, when Lt. Col. Yakubu Gowon, the highest ranking northern officer and Army Chief of Staff under Ironsi assumed control. Initially, it appears clear that a majority of the northern officers favored a de-facto secession of the North from Nigeria. A number of prominent civilian figures, including a northern judge of the supreme court, several federal permanent secretaries, the British high commissioner and the American ambassador, urged against secession. Gowon responded to these urgings and was able to persuade his fellow officers that some framework of common authority should be maintained. The only condition under which the Northern officers would accept any alternative to secession was that Gowon, as the most senior Northerner in the army, take up the cloak of power. Because several non-Northern officers outranked Gowon in terms of seniority, Ojukwu consistently refused to recognize the legitimacy of the regime. Over a period of four days the senior officers of the North were unable to control their other ranks and virtually all Igbo army officers stationed outside their own region were systematically murdered. On August 1, Ojukwu stated in a radio broadcast that:

> The brutal and planned annihilation of officers of Eastern Nigerian origin in the past few days has cast serious doubt as to whether the people of Nigeria, after these cruel and bloody atrocities, can ever sincerely live together as members of the same nation.[43]

Prior to this time, separatist sentiment had been much stronger in the North than in the East. The Igbo, in particular, had been more mobile and more nationally oriented than other Nigerian groups. The paradox of what was to become briefly the Republic of Biafra was that the dominant Biafran people, the Igbo, with what appeared to be a nationalist orientation, adopted a tribal outlook. This was partly because there was scarcely a village in Igboland which did not have members of its community working as traders, laborers and civil servants in the North. Virtually every Igbo family lost someone in the riots and pogroms directed against them in 1966. Thus, in their trauma they turned inward.

As mentioned above, the Igbo were more dispersed within the Federation than other peoples because of the density of population in their own area and because of their possession of education and skills needed elsewhere. Ethnic identity assumed new dimensions as an explicit referent through which members of the Igbo community outside the Eastern

---

tary: A Sociological Analysis of Authority and Revolt 1960–1967 (Cambridge: 1971), pp. 51–83.

[43] Kirk-Green, "Statement by Ojukwu, 1 August, 1968," in *Crisis and Conflict,* p. 198.

Region could distinguish themselves from those amongst whom they lived. Wherever they went the Igbo established town and clan improvement associations which channelled resources back to home villages in the East and emphasized the apartness of the Igbo. Their domination of the professions, their widely acknowledged acquisitive spirit and their increasing ethnic solidarity earned the Igbo the ill will of the peoples among whom they settled.

After the second coup, Gowan convened a constitutional conference which broke up after the outbreak of more killings in the North. This time, in late September and early October, 1966, many thousands of easterners and many millions of dollars worth of their property were destroyed in a full-scale pogrom carried out simultaneously in all northern cities.[44] After this outbreak of animosity against them, the Igbo returned en masse to the East. Between two and three million people flooded into the overcrowded Eastern Region as refugees, causing a crisis which could not be solved. From this point a major crisis seemed inevitable as pressure for secession began to mount in the East and the Igbo began to develop a more definite concept of their separate destiny.

After the events of mid-1966, the easterners (particularly the Igbo) felt they would be better off with a state of their own. By 1965 the East had the most extensive hospital facilities in Nigeria. The region was producing the most electricity by 1954 and had most of the registered motor vehicles on the roads by 1964. The Igbo formed more credit associations than any other group in the country—in 1964 the East had 68,220 individual memberships in credit associations, the West had 5776 and the North 2408.[45] The region led the nation in the percentage of children in schools, the percentage of villages with electricity, and in trade and industry. It had tremendous oil reserves which could be the mainstay of the economy and the skilled manpower necessary to ensure its growth. The region had resources, ports and the natural energy of a skilled and frightened people.[46]

As mentioned, after the July 29 counter-coup, it appeared that the North rather than the East favored secession.[47] On assuming office as

[44] Estimates of the number of people killed range from 30,000 (the Official figure) to 300,000.

[45] Ministry of Finance, *Abstract of Statistics* (Lagos: 1965), pp. 139–140.

[46] According to an estimate of Carl Liedholm, Eastern Nigeria in the early 1960's possessed the fastest growing industrial sector in the World. See "Preliminary Estimates of an Index of Industrial Production for Eastern Nigeria from 1961–1966," (Enugu: Economic Development Institute), March, 1967.

[47] For discussion of the specific position of the Northern officers and the position of Gowon vis-a-vis the Northern officers, see Luckham, *The Nigerian Military,* pp. 67–68.

the supreme military commander on August 1, 1966, Lt. Col. Gowon gave evidence of this ambiguity when he stated:

> I have now come to the most difficult part, or the most important part, of the statement. I am doing it, conscious of the great disappointment and heartbreak it will cause all true and sincere lovers of Nigeria . . .
>
> As a result of the recent events and the other previous ones, I have come strongly to believe that we cannot honestly and sincerely continue in this wise, as the basis of trust and confidence in our unitary system of government has not been able to stand the test—political, economic, as well as social—the base of unity is not there . . .[48]

By the time of the eastern secession, however, the North, with the aid of external advisers, particularly British and American, had come to recognize its dependence on eastern oil revenues, eastern skills and eastern access to the sea.[49]

In January, 1967, Ojukwu and Gowon met with the other three military commanders in Aburi, Ghana to try and reconcile the deteriorating relationship between the East and the national government. Aburi resulted in a potential resolution of the major issues of discord and distrust that had brought Nigeria to the threshold of disintegration. The Aburi accords were reached by mutual agreement of the five military leaders. The agreements reached, however, were never implemented and in the absence of other evidence so far not available, it is reasonable to accept Ojukwu's assertion that the civil service advisers to the federal government found the agreement so out of touch with their interests that it was impossible to implement them.[50] On March 27, 1967, the concessions made at Aburi were formally abrogated by Gowon (Decree No. 8).[51] Citing the non-implementation of the Aburi agreements as cause, Ojukwu unilaterally declared that all federal revenues collected in the East would

[48] "No Trust or Confidence in a Unitary System of Government: Lt. Col. Gowon's Broadcast on the Assumption of Office, 1 August, 1966," in Kirk-Greene, *Crisis and Conflict,* pp. 196–197.

[49] "Crisis 1966: The View of Nigerian Intellectuals," *ibid.,* p. 311.

[50] See Ojukwu, Preface to *Aburi: The Verbatim Report* (Enugu: 1966). Ojukwu also specifically accused Gowon of bad faith at Aburi. See also Kirk-Greene, *Crisis and Conflict,* pp. 312–359.

[51] At Aburi it was decided that force be renounced as a means of settling the country's differences, the army was to be reorganized, funds were to be provided for displaced persons, 'displaced' civil servants were to continue on full salary until March 31, 1967, and the *Ad Hoc* Constitutional Conference, adjourned after the September-October pogrom, should reconvene. The federal and Eastern governments had different interpretations concerning what these agreements actually meant and how they were to be implemented. For statements regarding the various interpretations, see Kirk-Greene, *ibid.,* pp. 312–359.

be paid to the Eastern Government after March 30, thus precipitating the crisis which led to Gowon's announcement of Decree Number 8 and the initiation of a complete blockade of the Easterrn Region.

On May 29, 1967 a three hundred-member consultative assembly in the East mandated Ojukwu to declare "at the earliest practicable date Eastern Nigeria a sovereign and independent state." On May 30 Ojukwu announced that the union with Nigeria was "totally dissolved" and declared the independence of the Republic of Biafra.[52] On July 5, 1967, federal troops invaded from the North and the three year civil war was under way.

In the Federation the Yoruba quickly filled the vacuum created by the departure of Igbo in the administration, in business and in the universities.[53] After some hesitation, Awolowo, who had been released from prison by Gowon, rallied to the federal military government and accepted the top civilian post in the federal executive council as vice-chairman and commissioner for finance.

When Biafra invaded and won and then lost the Midwest early in the war, the buffer area which had offered some protection to the East was gone. When the war was going reasonably well for Biafra, Ojukwu proposed a loose association of states in place of the Federation. This was a position Biafra was to continue to propose but which the federal government categorically refused to discuss.[54] On May 27 Nigeria had been divided into twelve states by decree and the federal government insisted that this twelve state division must stand. Six of the twelve states were in the North, but none of the large traditional units of the upper North had been broken up.[55] The West and Midwest were to remain as they were. The real change was to be in the East where three new states were

[52] *Ibid.*, "The Republic of Biafra: Resolution by the Eastern Region Consultative Assembly," pp. 449–450; and "Ojukwu Secedes and Declares the 'Republic of Biafra,' " pp. 451–453.

[53] "In the meantime what best could the West do but expect to pick up the mantle of leadership and use the stalemate (between North and East) to benefit themselves." "Nigerian Crisis: The View of the Intellectuals," *Nigerian Opinion* (November, 1966): 123, cited in Kirk-Greene, *ibid.*, p. 312.

[54] See "Ojukwu's Press Conference before leaving for Niamey," July, 1968, and "Biafra Puts Forward Counter-proposals, Addis Ababa, 9 August 1968" in Kirk-Greene, Vol. II, *ibid.*, pp. 242–243 and 279–280.

[55] Luckham, *The Nigerian Military*, pp. 326–328 for discussion of changes in the North in order to satisfy both the demands of the minorities for new states and the concerns of the traditional leaders of the far North. In the end the Emirs supported the creation of new states as the "only way to preserve traditional institutions in the 'dry' North from changes originating further south in the diaspora and Middle belt." *Ibid.*, p. 328.

created, isolating the Igbo in their "heartland" without a seaport and without oil. The loss of Port Harcourt, an Igbo city and the eastern port and industrial center, was particularly unacceptable to Igbo leaders.[56]

The war itself was excruciatingly long and tragic. Civilian deaths were higher in this war than in any other war in modern history. The International Red Cross reported that this was "the gravest emergency it had handled since WW II." [57] Egyptian pilots flying Russian planes bombed civilian centers such as markets, hospitals, and schools. Because Biafra produced no protein and was not a food producing area, the blockade was particularly disastrous and contributed to the exceedingly high rate of starvation. By August of 1968 the Red Cross estimated that ten thousand Biafrans were dying each day from starvation.[58] It was this aspect of the war, rather than the rightness of the cause, that caused Tanzania to become the first state to recognize Biafra on April 13, 1968.[59]

The war was not ideological, although the Biafrans spoke of the "Biafran Revolution" and hoped for support from the "progressive"

[56] Port Harcourt was an Igbo speaking city in a disputed area of the former Eastern Region. The local people here, the Ikwerre, who formed only 15% of Port Harcourt's population, speak a dialect of Igbo but claim to be non-Igbo people. For a discussion of the Ikwerre and their relationship with Port Harcourt's 85% Igbo population see Howard Wolpe, "Port Hartcourt: Ibo Politics in Microcosm," (Paper delivered at the Annual Meeting of the African Studies Association, Los Angeles, California, October 16–19, 1968). A series of articles written by former British civil servants with service in Northern Nigeria evaluating the significance of the breakup of the North are in *West Africa* in the 1969–1970 editions.

[57] *Africa Report* (October 28, 1968): 53.

[58] In a confidential report to U. Thant, Dr. Herman Middlekoop estimated the rates of starvation at 6,000 per day in July and 10,000 per day in August, 1968. See *New York Times* (October 20, 1968): 4.

Reports on the tragedy varied widely, however. For example: "Reporting to Parliament on Lord Hunt's mission, Commonwealth Secretary George Thomson stated that the Biafran starvation death rate was 2–3000 per day. On the same day (July 22) the *Washington Post* reported that official Biafran sources set the number of deaths by starvation at approximately 3% of its population per week. The announcement was unclear as whether the figure 3% was to be applied to the whole population of 12 million or only to the refugee population of 4.6 million. In any case, according to the *Washington Post* article, this estimate "exceeds" the estimates of private relief agencies. It was estimated that if the war continued, in a year more than five million Eastern Nigerians would be dead. Later, the International Committee of the Red Cross representative in Geneva set the death rate for July alone as 100,000." Carolyn K. Colwell, "Biafra: A Chronology of Developments Attending the Secession of the Eastern Region of Nigeria" in four parts, Washington, D.C.: Library of Congress Legislative Service, November 22, 1968, February 26, 1969, July 31, 1969 and January 28, 1970, Part I., p. 26.

[59] For Nyerere's statement see "Tanzania Recognizes Biafra," in Kirk-Greene, Vol. II, *Crisis and Conflict*, pp. 206–211.

African states.[60] African states, however, feared secession far more than they favored revolution. The unexpected major role played by the Soviet Union in supplying arms to federal Nigeria further confused the situation by escalating the arms supply. Oil was of crucial importance and accounts for much of the outside intervention in the war on the side of Nigeria. Nigerian oil represented some 10 percent of all British crude oil imports in 1967. Therefore, the British had important economic interests to protect which motivated them to support the federal government. The Biafrans attempted to buy French support by bargaining with its potential oil reserves, but, although DeGaulle made statements of support, French recognition of the regime was not forthcoming. Two states in former French Africa, however, did recognize the Ojukwu regime (Ivory Coast and Gabon). Recognition in each instance was based on humanitarian grounds and came too late in the war for any material gains to be a relevant consideration. Hopelessly out-gunned and out-manned, the Biafrans could hope to hold on but certainly not to out-fight the Nigerians. The Biafran surrender came on January 17, 1970.[61]

Nigeria faces serious problems of reconstruction and reconciliation. As a result of the war Nigeria's ten thousand-man army has been expanded into a 250,000-man leviathan composed "mainly of young, unemployable school leavers from the towns and underemployed peasants."[62] The existence of this large army poses great problems for the future. A large proportion of the budget must be allocated for its maintenance and with the war concluded there is little to keep it occupied. Already it has been alleged that corruption in the army is more rampant than during the last days of the First Republic.[63] Gowon has pledged to eradicate corruption in public life and has announced that the military will remain in power until such a task has been accomplished. No program has yet been announced for the attainment of this goal. The government has announced that the army will stay in power indefinitely.[64]

[60] The principles of the 'Biafran Revolution' were outlined in the Ahiara Declaration broadcast on Radio Biafra on June 1, 1969. For the text of this Declaration see "Ojukwu: the Ahiara Declaration," in Kirk-Greene, *ibid.*, pp. 376–393.

[61] "Lt. Effiong Announces Surrender of Biafra," *ibid.*, pp. 451–452.

[62] William Gutteridge, "Military Elites in Ghana and Nigeria," *Africa Forum* (Spring-Summer, 1967): 31.

[63] Pauline Baker, "The Politics of Nigerian Military Rule," *Africa Report* (February, 1971): 19.

[64] Gowon has announced nine conditions for a return to civilian rule:

1. Reorganization of the armed forces.
2. Implementation of the Second Year Development Plan (1970–1974).
3. Eradication of corruption in political life.
4. Settlement of the question of the creation of more states.
5. The preparation and adoption of a new constitution.

One of the problems with a military regime, in Nigeria as elsewhere, is that the army has no popular base of support, but bases its legitimacy on a monopoly of force. The army is steadily losing its popularity and is becoming itself unacceptable.

An irony of the military regime in Nigeria is that it undermines the very stability it professes to seek as it attempts to repress the re-emergence of post-war political parties or of any opposition to its policies. None of the issues which led to the breakdown of the first republic have really been solved. There has as yet been no effort to create a framework and a milieu within which competing political forces can function. Thus, political issues and groups forming around them have been forced underground where rumors of intrigue and repression flourish. The creation of twelve states and the resultant breakup of the three large regions is a significant beginning for a realignment of political forces. Leaving the Western Region virtually intact, however, and not breaking up the large emirates in the North, while creating new states for them to dominate, means that it is only in the Eastern region that drastic changes have taken place.[65] The deep effect of the war on the East Central State cannot yet be evaluated.

The predominance of minority elements in the military, however, is a potentially significant feature of the current situation and could result in a dramatic reordering of the Nigerian political scene in which majority group domination comes to an end. The repression of political activity on the other hand could result in increasing instability. The army, with its disproportionate size and seemingly eradicable corruption, seems incapable of carrying out the tasks set for it by General Gowon.

Conclusion: (Prospects for Genuine Political and Economic Independence)

This paper has focused upon the internal dynamics of Nigeria's political system and their inter-relationship with the country's economy domi-

---

6. Introduction of new revenue allocation formula between the federal and state governments.
7. Conduct a national population census.
8. Organization of genuinely national political parties.
9. Organization of elections and installation of popularly elected governments in the states and at the center.

Baker, *Africa Report* (February, 1971): 18.

[65] Lagos state was created out of the Western Region, but this state basically is only the Federal Capital and its absence from the Region does not basically change the nature of future Western area politics. For details of the state division see "Gowon's Broadcast to the Nation, dividing Nigeria into Twelve States," in Kirk-Greene, *Crisis and Conflict*, vol. 1, pp. 444–449.

nated by foreign interests. Normal political processes were temporarily interrupted as the country diverted its energies into a three-year civil war. The efforts at reconstruction following the Biafran surrender in 1970 do indicate major changes of direction in Nigeria's political economy, but it is too early to determine whether or not these changes will result in major restructuring of the political system or of the economy.

During the first four years of Nigerian political independence the three one-party regions within a superficially competitive system became increasingly self-contained as legal procedures were ignored, rules abandoned and elections rigged. The legitimacy of the national government collapsed as the imbalances between the regions and within the system became more conspicuous. The absence of clearly ideological parties and the open economy encouraged the self-seeking communally oriented politicians in their pursuit of personal fortunes and in their disregard for the people they supposedly served.

Social, cultural and economic dynamics reinforced the constitutional framework of regionalism created by the British. The export economy was completely dominated by foreign capital while regional power provided fertile grounds for a merging of entrenched political and economic interests. A political class developed in each region with a vested interest in the maintenance of the status quo and a distaste for fundamental restructuring of the society. No party in Nigeria became a significant national force without a regional ethnic base. Each of the three dominant parties had a virtual monopoly of power in its home region which alone allowed it to be competitive on a national basis. This monopoly of the regions was crucial and each party strove to remain impregnable in its own area. So long as all parties could hope to remain secure in their own regions the polity could function. Each major party felt secure enough not to want "to upset the applecart." Some politicians did talk about "socialism" but their basic insensitivity to social problems was indicated (as documented by the Coker Commission) by their improper and excessive accumulation of property while in office, their lavish style of dress and entertainment, the large number of their personal retainers and other forms of conspicuous largesse. Their position was regarded as sufficiently irresponsible to make their overthrow initially seem a fortunate development in the eyes of most Nigerians.

During a series of crises between 1962 and 1965 the country gradually degenerated into near anarchy—a process which was interrupted by the first military coup d'etat in January, 1966. The effort to bind the country together after the first coup was a failure and after the second coup, in July, 1966, the country rapidly slid into civil war. The war ended in January, 1970, and since that time the military regime has been slowly trying to restructure the Nigerian political system, primarily through the emphasis given to the creation of twelve new states and the consequent extension of the sources of political patronage. Even so, however, the regional-ethnic basis of power in the past appears to be in a process of reproduction. Undoubtedly the majority tribes will still control their own state governments—the Igbo will control the East Central State, the Ibibio the Rivers State, the Yoruba the West, the Tiv the Plateau State, etc. And, despite the fact that the three regions dominated by three ethnic groups institutionalized during the colonial period and polarized in the conflict of the late 1960's appears to be at an end, the military attempt to restructure Nigerian politics and promote rapid economic development holds promise only if more basic problems are faced.

In summarizing the past, before projecting our analysis into the future, it is interesting to note a major ironic theme in Nigerian politics. The Igbo, who had once been Nigeria's most energetic nationalists and who had advanced most rapidly on the indices of "modernization," became more tribalistic in orientation as they slid into secession in 1967. "Modernity" here brought a self-consciousness on a regional level which was previously lacking. Not only the regional political class, but the masses of the people in the former Eastern Region and easterners wherever they might be in the Federation, became immersed in the forces of ethnic nationalism as opportunities for their advancement began to close and the political dominance of the Northern Region offset the superior education and economic advantages of the southern regions. The final turning point was the violence against easterners in the North. Thus, the disintegration which began with the playing out of ideological and class differences in the Western Region assumed devisive and fatal connotations in the northern massacres, solidifying both the regional political classes and the masses over the issue of separation.

In the past, the Nigerian economy provided the political class with many opportunities to entrench itself both at the national and regional levels. It was not necessary for foreign capital to seek to manipulate internal politics, since the politicians themselves took every advantage offered them to feather their own nests. The only stance for those opposed to this class to take was to challenge the entire structure of Nigerian politics. The politicians, however, closed off the avenues of opposition, and distrust between the various ethnic components of the political class become predominant.

The military regime and its civilian advisers have shown no inclination to investigate the underlying causes of the Nigerian civil war. The Commission appointed by Ironsi to investigate the May, 1966 riots was discontinued by Gowon. There has been no in-depth study by the Nigerian

Federal Government of the structure of the First Republic and the implications of that structure, both political and economic, in the disintegration of Nigeria. In addition, civilian advisers tend to be former "out" politicians. With the exception of Tony Asika and Sam Ikoku in the East Central state, ironically, none of these former politicians have offered analyses of or alternatives to the old Nigerian political system. In this regard it is perhaps significant that Ikoku has now been removed from the important post of minister of finance.

In terms of specific actions since the war, as opposed to retrospective analyses, however, the military has at least introduced the possibility of both political and economic restructuring. The creation of twelve states to replace the three regions means more complicated coalitions will be necessary before any one political group can establish dominance. On the economic front the military government has taken the first steps toward real economic independence by introducing a new development plan which calls for government ownership of at least 55 percent in all strategic ventures. A new Business Decree has divided all "medium sized industry" into two categories—those concerned with fixed capital under $450,000 and those with fixed capital over $450,00. Foreigners are to be totally excluded from the first group while enterprises in the second must have indigenous equity participation of at least 40 percent by 1976.[66]

It is Nigeria's oil, however, which offers the potential resource base for the country's economic development and perhaps genuine independence. Oil dominates the present Nigerian economy and in 1970 foreign investment in the oil industry was $1.4 billion. Shell-British Petroleum accounts for two-thirds of this investment, for three-quarters of total production and owns two-thirds of existing productive capacity.[67] Oil has increased from 7 percent of government revenues in 1964 to 14 percent in 1969.[68] Nearly all this money is in the form of tax revenues for the government, which means that large new sums of money will be available for Nigeria's development. In 1965 Nigerian export earnings made the greatest jump in their history, jumping some $148 million over 1964, thanks largely to oil. Nigeria is already the world's ninth largest producer of oil and the industry will continue to expand for the next five to ten years, making it the most dynamic sector of the economy. Yet, the oil industry provides direct employment for only 17,178 at the

[66] For details of these arrangements see *West Africa,* July 2, 1971 and December 17, 1971.

[67] Scott and Sandra Pearson, "Oil Boom Reshapes Nigeria's Future," *Africa Report* (February, 1971): p. 14.

[68] *Ibid.,* p. 15.

present time and has a projected employment of only 220,000 over the next twelve years.[69] On the other hand, in 1965 the industry generated $44 million tax revenues for the federal government, paid $5 million in harbor dues and earned $84 million in foreign exchange.[70] In 1970, resumption of full scale operations in the industry after the war resulted in a 40 percent rise in export earnings over the previous year and accounted for 55 percent of Nigeria's foreign exchange.[71] Most importantly, the prospect is that the oil industry will contribute significant growth linkages to other sectors of the economy and unbind it from the distorting restraints that other developing countries face.

A look at Nigeria's balance of payments indicates the salutary effect of oil on the economy. Since the beginning of the first five-year plan in 1955, merchandise imports surpassed exports every year until 1966, reaching a cumulative balance of payments deficit that year on current account of $173.8 million.[72] The deficit, common to Third World countries, was met by utilizing foreign reserves, foreign aid, external borrowing, the progressvie raising of tariffs to discourage imports, and the support given to import-substitution. However, typically, demands for a wider variety of imported goods increased and raising tariffs resulted in rising prices for the consumer rather than in reduced imports. Thus, the debt and the drain on foreign reserves continued to grow before 1966. In 1971 the 40 percent increase in oil production allowed for a 50 percent increase in imports which helped to keep prices down and resulted in greatly increased government receipts from tariffs and excise taxes. It is now obvious that oil will be able to free the economy from deficit foreign exchange problems and inadequate domestic savings. With ample domestic saving and foreign exchange insured, important industrial linkages can be accomplished within the economy.

The Petroleum Decree of December, 1969, represents a major step in Nigeria's effort at attaining economic independence.[73] This decree requires that 60 percent of all senior staff in the oil industry be Nigerian within ten years. In addition, 75 percent of the total managerial, professional and supervisory grades in the petroleum industry must be "Nigerianized" by the end of the decade. Plans for meeting these standards must be submitted by the major companies now in Nigeria within twelve months after receiving their licenses under the decree. In February, 1970, two months after the Petroleum Decree was promulgated, it

[69] "Nigerian Rehabilitation and Development," *Africa Digest* (August 1970) : 82.
[70] Kilby, *Industrialization,* p. 15.
[71] *West Africa,* September 17, 1971.
[72] International Monetary Fund, *Balance of Payments Yearbook,* Vols. 10 and 19.
[73] *Africa Confidential,* June 25, 1971 and *West Africa.*

was announced that the government would participate in the oil industry on the basis of a previously agreed upon percentage in each license granted to oil companies. The government reserved the right to purchase up to 12½ percent of total crude production of any company or its total requirements for internal consumption and announced that it would fix the prices of all petroleum products sold in Nigeria. The decree established restrictions for prospecting in the five thousand square miles of offshore reserves and required licenses for the construction of refineries and for engaging in marketing petroleum products in Nigeria. The oil negotiations of 1971 included a new taxation agreement with Shell-BP (the largest exporter of Nigerian oil) which will bring Nigeria's earnings from oil more closely in line with those of other members of the Organization of Petroleum Exporting Countries (OPEC). Nigeria joined this association during the summer of 1971. Even though assurances have been given to the various petroleum companies that nationalization is not contemplated, recent policies may indicate a trend in that direction. The Nigerian National Oil Corporation (NOC), which began operations in April, 1971, is already exploiting crude petroleum, and the intention is to develop it into a fully integrated oil company engaged in exploration, production, transportation, refining, marketing and other "spin-off" and ancillary industries. This corporation is 100 percent owned by the government and will be a totally Nigerian-run industry as soon as skilled manpower is available. It has been given extremely wide powers to "buy, or otherwise acquire or take over" assets of other companies.[74] The federal government's asquisition of a 35 percent share of SAFRAP, an affiliate of the French state-owned ELF, was announced a few days before the establishment of NOC. Apparently SAFRAP was not allowed back into Nigeria until agreeing to this arrangement because of French aid to Biafra during the war. The arrangement is particularly advantageous for NOC because it will save the new company exploration costs and other initial expenses. The concession includes the Obagi field in the East Central State which was producing 40,000 barrels per day prior to the war. This concession also comprises an immense natural gas reserve and thus the "and allied products" has special significance. NOC's share is to rise to 50 percent when the company produces 400,000 barrels per day, but the 35 percent will increase with the attainment of 250,000 barrels per day until the 400,000 figure.[75] If SAFRAP today, why not Shell-BP, Mobil, Texaco, Gulf or Agip/Phillips tomorrow?

The recent efforts of Nigeria to set the course for future developments

[74] *Ibid.*
[75] *Ibid.*

in the oil industry offers encouragement for the ending of economic dependency. There are other indications that Nigerians can run their own economy and bring about their own development. A 1965 rural economic survey of 199 rural villages in Eastern Nigeria found nine hundred thousand households engaged in manufacturing enterprises such as food processing, textiles, palm oil extraction, clothing, mats and metal products.[76] During the war the Biafrans established oil refineries in village compounds and kept their entire fleet of moving vehicles on the road. This activity in Biafra and in rural sectors where the large foreign firms were absent indicates that Nigerians can operate and develop large portions of their own economy without foreign capital or management. Given the opportunity, Nigerians could utilize their own human and material resources to develop their country in a manner which would free them of their present neo-colonial dependency on foreign capital and foreign companies. The Business Decree of June, 1971[77] and the Petroleum Decree of 1969 indicate that Nigerians now understand this and are taking steps which will bring the economy under Nigerian control.

In spite of the apparent determination to establish control, however, true restructuring of the economy remains a political issue which will only be settled when the ban on "politics" is lifted. In spite of announced intentions the fact at present is that the economy is still characterized by a modern export enclave geared to producing raw materials in exchange for a limited range of imported manufactured goods for those with incomes high enough to buy them—the classic neo-colonial structure. It is not as yet clear whether or not the government intends to redirect investment surpluses in the export sector to programs designed to raise productivity and incomes throughout an increasingly integrated national economy. Breaking the neo-colonial pattern means developing a basic orientation towards meeting internal demands and developing the capacity to satisfy those demands. Continual riots and threats of strikes in the most "developed" areas of Nigeria suggest that these demands are not being met. Political activity has been forbidden for the immediate present. This means that no radical proposals for restructuring Nigerian society can be promoted. The middle-class army officers and their civilian advisers, most of whom come from the ranks of former opposition politicians, do not appear inclined to develop a radical ideology which is essential if neo-colonial interests are to be overcome.[78]

[76] *Productive Activities of Households,* Federal Office of Statistics, (Lagos: 1966), p. 4.

[77] *West Africa,* February 4, 1972.

[78] For detailed accounts of Who's Who in Nigeria under the military regime see

The current emphasis on import substitution means that for the foreseeable future the economy will continue to be heavily biased toward producing luxuries, such as beer and cigarettes, rather than necessities, such as food and clothing, for mass consumption. The essential institutional changes needed if economic reconstruction is to take place do not appear to be feasible under the present regime.

In spite of real progress toward reclaiming at least the export sector of the economy, recent developments in Nigeria illustrate that the political distribution of economic benefits continues to be in the interest of a limited class of ex-politicians, civil servants, businessmen and expatriates even though national economic policy is development oriented and a genuine concern with mass economic welfare is expressed. The recommendations of the recent Adebo Commission appointed to study the wage and price structure will result in continued differentiation between the privileged and deprived sectors of the society.[79]

> The recommendations (of the Adebo Wages and Salary Review Commission) must be looked upon by any well-meaning Nigerian as an overt act to fleece the poor majority of the little they have to consolidate the financial stand of the wealthy minority.[80]

A statement regarding Ghana by G. Mennen Williams when he was undersecretary of state for African affairs appears appropriate for describing Nigeria:

> This is an area where the British developed a very soundly based civil service, a well trained military . . . The middle class is a sizeable one, and the amount of free enterprise is considerable.[81]

An economic system which continues to be based on the consumption habits of a privileged elite can easily lead to misallocation and corruption. Nigeria's politics of scarcity leaves room for increased corruption in the future. Indeed, it has already been alleged that corruption in the army is more rampant than during the last days of the reign of the politicians.[82]

"Nigeria: Anatomy of the West," in *Africa Confidential* (November 7, 1969) and "Who's Who in Nigeria," *West Africa* (October 22, 1971) "Who's Who in the West," *West Africa* (November 19, 1971).

[79] Basically, the Commission recommended that present wage levels and thus differentiations be maintained in order to stabilize prices. See *West Africa* (November 12, November 26, December 3 and December 10, 1971).

[80] *West Africa* (December 17, 1971).

[81] Hearings before the Committee on Foreign Affairs, House of Representatives, Eighty-eighth Congress, Second Session on H.R. 10502, To amend further the Foreign Assistance Act of 1961 as Amended and for Other Purposes, Washington, D.C., 1964, p. 160.

[82] Baker, *Nigerian Military Rule,* p. 19.

Under the present plan adequate foreign exchange must be generated to cover the needs of an expanding investment program and a rapidly growing manufacturing and transport sector which requires imported inputs and replacements. Foreign influence is likely to continue for some time because there is unlikely to be a reduction in consumer import requirements without the development of a revolutionary ideology. Given the proclivities of the present power-holders, such a development is unlikely. In addition to consumer import requirements there is a continuing need for foreign exchange for imports of capital and intermediate goods.

Structural change of the economy, while still a possibility, is not expected to be rapid. What appears at first to be an inconsistent pattern of economic management may yet develop into a more cogent process. The path has not yet been set. At a minimum, however, structural change requires direct intervention in productive sectors. It is precisely at such a time as the present, when the traditional export-oriented economy is working well that long-range plans to replace it should be developed. The folly of launching such plans during a period of decline in the export economy is well documented in the Ghanaian case.[83] If the creation of an independent political economy aimed at national development is the goal, then the ability to achieve that development depends on a clear understanding of the implications of that goal.

The Ghanaian experience further indicates that the pace of change cannot be accelerated without limit and that attempts which outrun available human, institutional and financial resources are likely to result in levels of waste, misallocation, demands for sacrifice and structural dislocation which raise doubts as to the feasibility and desirability, let alone the necessity, of making economic independence a primary political and economic goal. Ghana illustrates the failure that can result when such an attempt outruns both ideological dedication and human and material resources. The 1961 to 1965 effort in Ghana, while impressive, nevertheless failed to produce adequate positive results to justify the costs or, ultimately, to allow the government to survive.[84]

The present Nigerian stance offers some hope that public sector productive units can engage in partnership with foreign interests under conditions which give real voice to Nigerian interests and decision-making.

[83] Roger Genoud, *Nationalism and Economic Development in Ghana* (New York: 1969).

[84] Barbara Callaway and Emily Card, "Political Constraints on Economic Development in Ghana," in *State of the Nations,* ed., Michael Lofchie (Los Angeles: 1971), pp. 53–92.

Such partnerships apparently need not rule out phased movement toward African dominance.

However, substantial sacrifices will be necessary to carry out energetic development strategies. Such sacrifices require a level of national mobilization and mass support not likely to be available if Nigeria is to continue within the framework of its present neo-capitalist system. The Adebo report suggests that the current system in which there is a prospering foreign enclave, a moderately well-off and increasingly closed African elite, a relatively well-off labor "aristocracy" and a stagnant mass of rural farmers and unskilled urban laborers will be perpetuated.

While change and restructuring within the present model are possible, it is perhaps more likely that the more complex and interrelated with foreign interests the Nigerian economy becomes, the harder it will be to reverse the trend toward greater dependence. This is particularly true as substantial indigenous elites with vested interests in the status quo re-emerge and as horizons of national aspirations are re-cast in a neo-colonial economic framework. The first requirement for breaking this cycle is a belief in national self-reliance and all that this implies. The basic support for this belief is ideological, thus there is a need to construct a national socio-political ideology. The re-emergence of old political alliances, however, makes it doubtful ideology will play much of a role in future Nigerian politics. Without an embracing ideological framework, intervention in the economy is likely to be on an *ad hoc* basis. *Ad hoc* intervention opens avenues for individuals and interest groups to distort allocations to their particular benefit, and for the inculcation of widespread corruption to such a degree that there will be massive resource misallocation with costs to the economy far exceeding the direct cost increases themselves.[85] If this be the case, then it is likely that the description of the economy given by a prominent Nigerian economist will continue to be apt:

> . . . the simple truth that Nigeria was not really sovereign and independent . . . but particularly dependent both on its foreign trade sector and, at the growing points of its domestic economy, on foreign private initiative and leadership; not to mention the high degree of influence exercised by foreign powers in the formulation and execution of public policy . . . On the ideological plane, everyone was fashionably one kind of socialist or another; but in practice everybody accepted the ethical basis of capitalism.[86]

[85] For a conservative criticism of *ad hoc* intervention see W. F. Stolper, *Planning Without Facts,* (Cambridge, Mass.: 1966) especially chps. VII, VIII.

[86] O. Aboyade, quoted by Reginald Herbold Green, "Political Independence and the National Economy: An Essay on the Political Economy of Decolonization" in *African Perspectives,* eds., Christopher Allen and R. W. Johnson (Cambridge: 1971), p. 307.

It is often stated that prerequisites for economic independence are investment finance and high level manpower with managerial and technical expertise. Nigeria appears well on the road to meeting these requirements. Nigeria intends to be virtually independent of foreign high-level manpower within the decade; and the oil economy will generate the essential foreign exchange. What is missing in Nigeria is the development of an ideology which requires commitment to a conscious policy of economic independence. Here the relevant question to ask is whether a mixed economy with a large and basically capitalist productive sector provides a viable institutional setting for such a strategy or whether a transformation to a basically socialist mode of production is also essential. This question is open to debate and is dependent upon value judgements—judgements which the Nigerians themselves will have to make.

Kenya/Tanzania

UNDERDEVELOPMENT OR SOCIALISM? A COMPARATIVE ANALYSIS OF KENYA AND TANZANIA*

by

Lionel Cliffe

Introduction

This contribution focuses on two neighboring East African states. Their proximity, their common colonial past under British rule, and their continuing close links with each other and with their common neighbor Uganda in the East African community provide some basis for treating them together. More important for the purposes of this essay are the opportunities thus provided for comparison. These two cases offer a good prospect for realizing those familiar advantages associated with the comparative method—of drawing attention to variables which may explain differences in development patterns, as well as indicating those similarities which may be of some general significance. In their post-independence policies, they offer contrasting examples in their approach to the problems of neo-colonialism and underdevelopment. Kenya has been content to Africanize, and thus end racial barriers to elite privileges, but has otherwise left unaltered the basic inherited economic and social structure. Tanzania is attempting to implement a development policy of "Socialism

* Tanzania—a republic in East Africa, comprising the former country of Tanganyika, the islands of Zanzibar and Pemba and adjacent small islands. Formed in 1964.

Tanganyika—a former country in East Africa, became independent in 1961, now the mainland part of Tanzania.

Acknowledgement are due to John S. Saul whose comments on an early draft and whose intellectual stimulus over the years have improved my understanding; the Sociology Department of the University of Wisconsin, Madison through its Sociology of Economic Change Program provided hospitality during part of its writing.

and Self-Reliance"[1] aimed at breaking its reliance on export crops and on foreign investment for future development, and has instead provided for more social control of the economy and thus more effective use of the country's surplus.

Our analysis must therefore point out the contrast between these two strategies and seek to explain their adaptation by exploring the different sets of social forces at play in each. This latter task is not straightforward. A cursory glance at the major historical differences between the two countries might suggest that Kenya's colonial situation—with its settler economy, the racialism and the violent form of nationalist rebellion to which it gave rise—meet Frantz Fanon's prescription for avoiding what he called "false decolonisation:"

> Violence alone, violence committed by the people, violence organised and educated by its leaders, makes it possible for the masses to understand social truths and gives the key to them. Without that struggle, without that knowledge of the practice of action, there's nothing but a fancy-dress parade and the blare of the trumpets. There's nothing save a minimum of readaptation, a few reforms at the top, a flagwaving; and down there at the bottom an undivided mass still living in the Middle Ages, endlessly marking time.[2]

Tanzania, on the other hand, at first glance appears to correspond much more closely to the general pattern of independent Africa, of "decolonialisation in areas which have not been sufficiently shaken by the struggle for liberation."[3] Yet it is in that country that the leaders have realized the danger of settling for what they refer to as mere "flag independence."[4] Some effort will be made to resolve this apparent paradox and also to offer some speculation about the likely course of these alternative paths. Explanations of phenomenon in two countries offered within the context of a short essay cannot hope to be exhaustive, but however tentative, they must be sought beyond the official ideological statements and the form of the political institutions—different as these are in the two countries. Similarly it is pointless to treat the contrasting development policies as givens and merely compare the "effectiveness" and per-

[1] Tanganyika African National Union: 'The Arusha Declaration and TANU's Policy of Socialism and Self Reliance' (Dar es Salaam, 1967). The text is reprinted in J. K. Nyereré: *Uhuru na Ujamaa-Freedom and Socialism,* (Oxford University Press, Dar es Salaam, 1969).

[2] Frantz Fanon: *The Wretched of the Earth,* (English edition, Penguin Books, Harmondsworth, 1967), p. 118.

[3] ibid., p. 37.

[4] For instance, in Tanganyika African National Union: *T.A.N.U. Guidelines 1971,* (Government Printer, Dar es Salaam, 1971), p. 1, a major policy statement which has followed further some of the logic of the Arusha Declaration.

sistence of the regimes, as many modern theorists would have us do, for the ideologies, in so far as they do not remain rhetoric, represent the total agenda of the political authorities, and in Tanzania at least the total transformation of the society is on that agenda! A search for the roots of such initiatives and an analysis of the scope for alternative political options must include in its focus an investigation of the social forces that are at work within the society.

But here we run into another theoretical problem, for much of the political sociology of Africa has discussed systems in terms of "ethnicity." The "political elites," a favorite subject, are analyzed in the same terms, and if the content of their ideologies are at all discussed it is in terms of whether they represent "modern" as opposed to "traditional" values. Thus if we are not to ignore the actual ideas of the Tanzanian leaders themselves when they speak of their concern for the interests of "workers" and "peasants," our analysis of social structure must probe its horizontal dimensions as well as the vertical divisions.

Indeed, the two sets of cleavages, the "class" and the ethnic, must be viewed in their inseparable relationships one with another in order to grasp the precise nature of the social formation, which is both the source of any impetus for structural change and the target of it. But this approach inevitably involves an explanation of the emerging economic structures of these East African states. For the colonial patterns of producing "strategic" crops to be exported to the metropolis and in turn absorbing an increased volume of imported manufactures (some of them even in time produced on the spot) created new kinds of social groups: of peasants, artisans and laborers, teachers and clerks, trader and businessman. Even the ethnic character of contemporary politics owes as much if not more to the uneven impact of these processes as to "traditional" animosities and primordial identities.

Yet once attention is directed towards these underlying socio-economic realities, the significance of the differences in policy and in some of the historical conditions pale to insignificance beside the basic similarity of the environment of neo-colonial underdevelopment [5] in which political life in

[5] There is a growing literature which sees the problem of underdevelopment as stemming not from some 'natural' state of backwardness but from the deprivations of imperialism. See, principally Paul A. Baran: *The Political Economy of Growth,* (Monthly Review Press, New York, 1957); A. Gunder Frank: 'The Development of Under-Development', *Monthly Review,* (New York), Vol. 18, No. 4, September, 1966, which is also reproduced in a useful collection of readings, Robert I. Rhodes: *Imperialism and Underdevelopment,* (Monthly Review Press, New York, 1970); in the African context see Giovanni Arrighi and John S. Saul: 'Socialism and Economic Development in Tropical Africa', *Journal of Modern African Studies,* (Cambridge), VI, 2, July 1968.

both countries is set. This familiar state of affairs—of the preponderance of a range of agricultural products whose world price is deteriorating, the dearth of any significant industry, and the future direction of growth depending on whims of overseas investors—takes similar patterns in the two countries. The major crops—coffee, cotton, tea and sisal—are virtually the same, and the prices of each of them were less in 1969 than 1960, thus skimming off much of the benefit from increased volumes of production. About 90 percent of the population live in the rural areas, yet almost all of the benefit of post-independence growth has been felt in the towns. In both countries breweries, tobacco and textiles and a few similar consumer goods industries are the only major ones, except increasingly for the organizing of what Fanon described as "centres of rest and relaxation and pleasure resorts to meet the wishes of the Western bourgeoisie—tourists avid for the exotic, for big-game hunting and for casinos." [6] The overall indices of national impoverishment are equally of the same order—the Kenya annual per capita income in 1970 being only slightly higher than Tanzania's ninety dollars per head.

This economic pattern of underdevelopment was fostered and is maintained by a state which was created by colonialism. It is underpinned politically by the political institutions of independence and the new incumbents. These political forms have two basic characteristics now common to most African politics: 1) the domination of government and other institutions by a tiny, western-educated, highly privileged elite, largely unhampered by any popular political influence; 2) in so far as there is any connection with the mass of the population, a manipulative system of local patronage politics which gives some apparent legitimacy but serves to promote a fragmented, ethnic political culture which serves to mystify the exploited peasant farmers, landless and manual workers.

Thus the main variables in this analysis will be the class forces and the ethnic character of the two countries, viewed in terms of their historical development, stemming from the incorporation of the area into the world economy. This will provide the basis for an examination of the political institutions, and their expressions of prevailing interests—in particular, what development strategies are likely to spring from these socio-economic and political circumstances and finally, what scope there may be for defining an alternative to the neo-colonial pattern.

Development of Kenya's Economic Structure

In applying this mode of analysis first to Kenya, it is hard to escape the conclusion that "the impact of colonial settlement on the economy and

[6] Fanon, *op. cit.,* p. 123.

society set up a highly visible framework for a neo-colonial pattern of development (or "development of underdevelopment") which has been followed with singular consistency since 1963."[7] This assessment suggests that the country provides a classical example of the familiar African pattern, but it also reminds us that the particular form of Kenya's colonial exploitation was the medium of a settler economy which established particular socio-political structures and development policies.

Thus, as compared with her neighbors, Kenya has a more diversified and modern economy, characterized by a more significant manufacturing industrial sector, a large-scale and technically advanced capitalist element in agriculture, and consequently a much larger employed labor force. The involvement of foreign capital is also more pronounced and occurs in three distinct forms: 1) much of Kenya's industrial and commercial development has been associated with the larger multi-national corporations, although there is a degree of local enterprise mainly by Asian and some European residents; 2) overseas companies are also found in the agricultural sector, owning large tea, sisal and occasionally coffee estates; 3) a significant part of agricultural production was and still remains in the hands of a resident class of European settlers who were the dominant stratum in Kenya politics throughout almost all of the colonial period.

During that period, the historical role of the African population was seen chiefly as a labor supply to the town-based industries, estates and settler farms. Beyond that, it was restricted—physically by being confined in tribal "reserves," and economically by being denied opportunity for cash crop production. Only relatively recently, therefore, have Kenya peasants turned to the cultivation of export crops on any significant scale. A post-independence process of Africanization has blurred the former three-layered racial structure—with the Europeans occupying the large farmer, manager and administrative roles; largely immigrant Asian petty bourgeoisie in minor executive posts and dominant in trade; and an African labor force emerging from a subsistence peasantry. The same basic class structure persists, however. It may be summarized in the chart below:

Although the Kenya figures show some differences from the Tanzania statistics, the comparison shows that Kenya is still a predominantly peasant society producing chiefly primary products for export; there is only limited development of a local bourgeoisie and a local proletariat. A closer scrutiny of the economic structure is thus indicated in order to see whether the more emphatic presence of international capital, the marginally greater opportunities for a local property-owning class to entrench

[7] Colin Leys: 'Politics in Kenya—the Development of Peasant Society', *British Journal of Political Science,* Vol. I, 1971, p. 307–37.

LABOR FORCE IN KENYA AND TANZANIA

		KENYA (1968)			TANZANIA (1970)	
1. *Wage employment*						
—urban		500,000			270,000	
—agriculture						
—estates	190,000			110,000		
—peasant	360,000			40,000		
	———	550,000		———	150,000	
Total		1,050,000	(25%)		420,000	(8.5%)
2. *Self-employed in agriculture*		3,100,000	(72)		5,050,000	(80)
3. *Other self-employed*						
—employers	20,000			10,000		
—traders, etc.	100,000			70,000		
Total	———	120,000	(3%)	———	80,000	(1.5%)
Labour Force Grand Total		4,270,000			5,550,000	
TOTAL POPULATION		9,900,000			12,900,000	

(These figures can only be roughly correlated with the categories of "worker," "peasant," "bourgeois" and "petty bourgeois," as they are extrapolated from sources which present data in terms of source of income.)

itself, and the existence of a somewhat larger working class, do in fact tend to promote contradictions in the political life of the country which are significantly different than those in Tanzania.

The particular features of Kenya's colonial economy owe much to the fundamental physical characteristics of the country. First there is a rather remarkable concentration of population into two clusters. Much of the country is in fact arid semi-desert and it is estimated that only 15 percent of the land area has sufficient rainfall for permanent agriculture. Yet on the slopes of the central highlands and around Lake Victoria there is medium to high density of the peasant population. In fact over 60 percent of the population is concentrated in some 8 percent of the total land area in these two foci. It is these areas that are responsible for almost all of the peasant cash-crop production; their somewhat overcrowded populations have provided almost all of the labor force both in the urban centers and on the settler estates.

The second geographical feature which is of some historical significance is the existence of well-watered highlands in the area bordering on, and

[8] These figures are derived from Leys, *ibid* and Tanzania Government: *Economic Survey, 1970,* (Government Printer, Dar es Salaam, 1970).

located within, the Great Rift Valley. Many of these areas were either too high or perhaps slightly too dry for normal African subsistence crops and tended to be the preserve of people who are predominantly pastoral. They were thus only sparsely occupied; their small population and great beauty attracted the first European visitors, who saw a vast temperate, potential farming area opened up by the Uganda railway. It was this area between the two main clusters, covering the Rift Valley, the area down to Nairobi and towards Lake Victoria, which came to be known as the "White Highlands." European settlement began about the turn of the century and even before the first World War the main outlines had in fact been set. Essentially three types of settler agriculture grew up:

1. *Large plantations and estates,* growing crops like coffee, sisal and later tea, often in fact owned and run by large companies.
2. *Ranching areas,* some of these being the basis of huge personal estates, like that of the Lords Delamare who have been settler leaders over two generations.
3. *Mixed farms,* producing smaller amounts of either export crops or often food crops like wheat, maize, and dairy products in the temperate highland areas.

Certain structural characteristics of this inherited settler economy can be noted. First, there is the continued existence of what is now officially called "the large farm sector," even though over a million acres of the former European-owned mixed farming areas have been divided up into smaller peasant settlement plots and many large farms have been bought by members of the emerging African elite. Thus, much of the most productive farming land in Kenya (a total of some six million acres) is still made up of large farms, plantations and ranches. In fact the large-farm sector consists of holdings which average 1,900 acres, and account for almost 50 percent of agricultural exports from the country. Patterns of productive relations in this sector of agriculture continue to be characterized by large capitalist farmers employing a sizeable work force of agricultural laborers (somewhat less now than in the late fifties but still almost two hundred thousand people). Other sectors have also been shaped in a way that was appropriate to settler interests. For instance, the development of road and rail, marketing, extension and other services in fact served the Highlands and not the peasant areas. The sizeable holdings also necessitated the availability of credit, which was provided by government.

Along with their virtual monopoly of an array of parastatal marketing and servicing agencies and their paramount influence on government economic policy,[9] the settlers' fundamental need to guarantee a cheap supply of labor meant that they also sought control over the so-called "reserves," and over the African population that had been cordoned off into them. The spread of local trading in imported cash goods, the early introduction of a head-tax to be paid in cash, and other administrative measures, all helped to promote the supply of labor from the reserves to the "White Highlands" and of course, to the towns. The centrality of their concern for a cheap labor supply is indicated by the fact that even as late as the 1920's there were no less than three Government Committees or Commissions investigating "the labor problem."

Thereafter labor was not in such short supply; the consolidation of the market economy and increasing land shortage in the reserves were sufficient to guarantee all the labor that was required. But in the earlier period a further measure had been necessary to ensure that Africans in fact migrated to sell their labor. Having used the market carrot and the administrative stick to bring them into the cash economy, it was also essential to head peasants off from the other possible source of cash income —cash crop production. And so it was an inevitable part of policy in the colonial period to impose restrictions—in all but a few areas or for a few favored individuals—physically preventing African farmers from growing almost all of the higher-priced cash crops. These restrictions in fact remained in force until the 1960's.

The consequence for the two dense areas of "reserves" which had yielded up the labor force was to cut them off from the possibilities of further agricultural development based on cash crops and improved agriculture techniques. By the later colonial period they were suffering from economic stagnation and deteriorating fertility due to rapidly rising population now frozen in by the existence of the "White Highlands" around them. This basic contradiction between the settlers with their monopoly of political power and economic opportunities, and the African workers and the impoverished peasants who remained in the reserves is fundamental to the conflicts which flared up in the period of the main nationalist struggle. It also represented a fundamental challenge to independent Kenya: whether the new political power would be used to change this structure. But before we go on to further explore that issue, it is necessary to examine other consequences of the settler economy which produce other contradictions apart from the basic cleavage between European settlers and African peasants and migrant laborers.

[9] See for instance, M.P.K. Sorrenson: *The Origins of European Settlement in Kenya,* (Oxford University Press, Nairobi, 1966); Elspeth Huxley: *White Man's Country,* (Chatto and Windus, London, 1953); C.G. Rosberg and J. Nottingham: *The Myth of 'Mau Mau',* (Frederick A. Praeger, New York, 1966).

Settler attempts to provide for themselves a "civilized" way of life, and the marketing and processing facilities that were necessary for some of the non-export crop they produced, such as dairy products and maize and wheat, as well as the general colonialist interests of overseas investors and traders—all these factors encouraged the build up of relatively sophisticated economic structures for the handling of agricultural products, for their processing and for the manufacture of a range of consumer goods and supplies. The industrial and commercial opportunities which thus offered themselves were partly seized by Europeans and by Asian immigrants, first brought in as labor for the Uganda railway, in simple manufacture as well as retail and wholesale trade—but also increasingly by large multi-national corporations. These developments were such that industry and construction (including public utilities) accounted for a quarter of the Monetary GDP by the mid-1950's—a proportion almost equal to that of the settler farm sector—and a labor force of some eighty thousand.

This element in the labor force was different in character from the usually migrant farm laborers and squatters. This small, more skilled working class was easier to organize and more urbanized—especially as the employers argued from the 1950's on that a stabilized work force(in place of temporary migrants who left their families back home) was more economic. One effect has been to increase urban wages; in 1953 only one-fourth of town workers earned over one hundred shillings per month; in 1969 only one-fourth earned below that amount. How far this has resulted in a real process of proletarianization is open to some dispute. Certainly a survey of 1953 indicated that 48 percent of Niarobi workers had been in their jobs less than a year. One analyst has concluded, on the basis of this kind of indicative data that even today "instead of speaking of a Kenyan proletariat, it seems more realistic to think in terms of a variety of peasant adaptations to the growth of the private enterprise money economy, in which working for wages on a small farm, a large farm or in a town is an alternative to cash cropping . . . (and that) the whole social and political focus of the greater part of the wage labor force remains in rural areas." [10] However, a survey in 1963 indicated over half of African middle-income workers had no land in the reserves. A more recent survey of migrants to towns also suggests that the character of urban employment and increasing individualization of land may be inducing a more confirmed urban involvement, for only 12.5 percent of these migrants characterized themselves as *temporary* urban workers and two-

[10] Leys, *op. cit.*

thirds of them reported no land in the rural areas.[11] The modified wages and industrial relations policies coupled with these rural processes of change, had another consequence: increasing urban unemployment. By the mid-1960's the hard-core unemployed (landless and jobless) were estimated at two hundred thousand, one-third of the employed labor force.

The rise of commercial and industrial enterprise also promoted the development of a set of contradictions within the colonial economy. In addition to settler influence in Kenya, "the big corporation has exercized a decisive influence there," and with the growth in the period before and after independence of a "centralized network of associations (projecting) the voice of corporations more forcefully," [12] a shift has occurred in the character of the political economy from a purely settler colony to a neocolony dominated by international capital. At an early stage business interests tended to coincide with those of the settlers—for the latter provided the market for the former and both wanted to ensure the availability of cheap labor. Later, industry developed a potentially conflicting concern for a higher, family wage, for a stable labor force and for the continued expansion of the market (through African cash crop production if need be). Their more flexible view of political arrangements—so long as stability allowed business to continue they needed few entrenched powers—made them more ready to ditch die-hard settler claims in favor of a decolonization deal with "reasonable" African leaders. It is perhaps these kinds of forces, operating chiefly of course within the metropolis, which explain why a British Conservative Government was prepared to ride roughshod over settler protests (for the first time in sixty years) in moving to independence. These confiicts between the business interests associated with international capital, concerned merely with guaranteeing political conditions conducive to continued extraction, and the agricultural (and other indigenous) capitalists concerned with more entrenched interests—a contradiction not without its parallel in other settler colonies like Rhodesia—also have their continuing effect on development calculations today.

One additional feature to note is the characteristically uneven impact of the colonial economy. Labor was drawn out at highly differing rates from different parts of the country. The land pressures as a result of the settler presence near to the reserves, were far more intense in certain areas and the opportunities presented by missionary education, social services,

[11] H. Kempel: *Labour Migration into Urban Centres and Urban Unemployment in Kenya,* (Unpublished Ph.D. thesis, University of Wisconsin, Madison, 1970).

[12] Both phrases are quoted from an interesting recent study, Alice H. Amsden: *International Firms and Labour in Kenya, 1945–70,* (Frank Cass, London, 1971).

and the limited possibilities of cash production also varied. The ethnic dimensions of Kenya politics have to be seen against this framework of uneven development as well as the geographical distribution of its population.

Economic Differences and Ethnic Divisions in Kenya

Kenya's four main tribal groups—the Kikuyu (over two million) and Kamba in the center, and the Luo and Luhya in the west—each numbered over a million at the time of the 1969 census. These four major groups together with the somewhat smaller Kisii and Meru/Embu peoples, all of them settled agriculturalists concentrated in the two main population clusters noted earlier, account for 75 percent of the total population. Some thirty-four other smaller "tribes" recorded by the census-takers make up the rest—only two of them, the Minjikenda at the Coast and the formerly pastoral Kipsigis perched atop the Rift Valley wall, total half a million. In the three provinces—Central, Nyanza and West—where the largest groups are mainly concentrated, almost all of the agricultural land is classified as "high potential," whereas this is true of only a tiny fraction of even the agricultural land in the other provinces. Thus the former areas have been the site of all the past and recent advances in peasant agriculture; and the concentration of population has allowed for a much denser provision of education and other social amenities in these areas. It must also be noted that although these "tribes" represent sizeable groups sharing a common cultural and linguistic heritage, none of them represented a single political unit in the pre-colonial period. So Kenya did not contain any state systems which—like the kingdoms of Uganda—might retain a degree of separateness during the colonial period and after. Moreover, this segmented character of the traditional politics—together with the demand for much closer control of the population which stemmed from the settler economy's need for labor and for undisputed hegemony—led the colonial government to develop an alternative administrative system to the pattern of so-called Indirect Rule characteristic to Tanganyika. This legacy of an authoritarian, and hierarchial Provincial Administration stretching directly down from the center of government to appointed "sub-chiefs" at the locational level (the smallest administrative area) is one of the most distinctive institutional features of political life in Kenya.

Within this pattern of more or less uniform administrative arrangements, there were much more significant and differentiating socio-economic processes at work. Even between different groups in the more fertile, concentrated clusters some very important variations in the patterns of change must be recognized. Although each of the main groups suffered some alienation of land, and were contained in prescribed "Reserves" from which migrant labor was forced out, and although each of these areas has developed a commodity producing peasant economy in more recent years, the nature and extent of the impact and the responses were markedly different. The most traumatic effects were felt by the Kikuyu.

In contrast, the western areas were not so hemmed in by the European settlement. They were not in the same antagonistic proximity; they supplied a smaller proportion of the labor force and usually had slightly more elbowroom at home. However, in pockets in these non-Kikuyu areas, for instance among the Maragoli (a Luhya sub-group) and in parts of Kisii and Ukambani, very dense populations led to heavy labor migration, very fragmented and mainly subsistence farming, often coupled with decreasing fertility and some protest politics against authoritarian colonial government attempts to enforce conservation. Some of these densely populated localities have not had the ecological potential nor the land distribution patterns to benefit over much from cash crop expansion and remain backwaters of growing impoverishment, incapable within the present structures of production of either economic transformation, or even the political pressure for change from a polarized class structure. More generally in the western areas, changes did not reach such critical levels as a result of the comparative remoteness of the settler presence, of having slightly more room for an expanding population and of only limited early cash crop development. Perhaps due to its more restricted fertility potential, the traditional production relations in much of the western agricultural zone have not yet given way completely to the introduction of capitalist property relations. In addition, there has not been the same boom in peasant production that has occurred in the Central Province during the 1960's. Politically, the severe pressures from colonially-induced change occasioned a more elite kind of politics concerned with issues like education and job opportunities which allowed for alliances with non-indigenous groups like the missions. Even the organizational bases from which a more radical figure like Oginga Odinga emerged in the later colonial period—the Luo Thrift & Trading Corporation and the semi-traditional Luo Union—were more concerned with representing the interests of the educated petty bourgeoisie or of the distant town-based workers from the area.

Meanwhile, the central areas of Kenya had reached a flash point by the 1960's. Some land in southern Kikuyu had been actually taken away for settlers; but what became more generally frustrating was the closing off of any geographical spread of a population that was expanding. The White Highlands and Niarobi surrounded them on several sides; forest reserves above them on the slopes of the Aberdares and Mount Kenya closed the people in on themselves. Politically they were constrained by the colonial administrative system's replacement of the more democratic age-sets which cut across the more confining and authoritarian kinship system. The basic kin group—the *mbari* (sub-clan) in which land rights were vested—also began to disintegrate as tensions within the group increased with population, with no possibility of release through expansion. As land became scarce it was permanently farmed and overcultivated and continually further fragmented. The land pressure, the decreasing fertility of continuous subsistence production and the prohibition on cash crops achieved the primary settler aim of forcing labor, mainly those with the most marginal rights in or access to land, into town and the White Highlands. One estimate suggests that "by 1948 a quarter of the then million Kikuyu were living as laborers or squatters outside the confines of their inefficient reserves," [13] while those in Nairobi made up 60 percent of the city's African population.

But the pressures within the Kikuyu Reserves had other consequences, especially after the 1930's when the labor migration began to outpace the settler economy's needs. Impoverishment, landlessness, and general economic insecurity made worse by the disruption of indigenous social structures, affected the majority of the Kikuyu both within and outside the reserves. An emerging rural class structure increased the contradictions in the society. For with the breakdown in the *mbari* system, especially in the Kiambu district closest to Nairobi, and thus increasingly individualistic property relations, a Kikuyu "gentry" began to emerge—"chiefs, headmen, tribal elders, teachers in mission schools, and minor government officials bought the land of the less fortunate or less educated members of the community." [14]

The Mau Mau Revolt

One persistent strand in Kikuyu politics has been the political role of the better-off, educated elements—from the 1920's when an improvement-oriented Kikuyu Association was formed, and again during the State of Emergency that was declared in 1952 to combat the so-called "Mau Mau" revolt when they were seen in the ranks of the loyalist Kikuyu "homeguard." According to one colonial official's estimate "the 10 percent actively anti-Mau Mau are on the whole from the landed and wealthy classes." [15] But even the more radical opposition to colonial rule that

[13] Donald Barnett and Karari Njama: *Mau Mau from Within,* (Monthly Review Press, New York, 1965).

[14] M.P.K. Sorrenson: *Land Reform in the Kikuyu Country,* (Oxford University Press, Nairobi, 1967), p. 40.

[15] Provincial Commissioner, Nyeri, quoted by Sorrenson, *ibid,* p. 107.

formed the other strand in the political movements—represented from the 1920's until the Emergency by the Kikuyu Central Association (KCA)—was mainly an organization of "influentials." These were non-establishment persons and some of the more aware urban elites. It was not until the late 1940's, that the nationally focused and legal Kenya African Union (KAU) made possible more mass involvement. From this period, in the two Kikuyu districts to the north of Kiambu, Murang'a and Nyeri, the clandestine KCA (outlawed in 1939) continued to organize through a secret oath and took on a more mass character. This tendency was very much strengthened when the growing political unrest made the settlers decide to repatriate many thousands of Kikuyu squatters and farm laborers, and even urban workers to the already overcrowded reserves. The revolt broke out partly because these landless had little choice but to take to the forest or in some other way fight for their survival.

Thus the so-called Mau Mau was a political movement spearheaded by a landless minority with some organizational links with more radical urban workers, relying in guerrilla fashion on the support of the mass of small peasants who made up the bulk of the population. The class dimension of the conflict is underlined by the social origins of their main opponents, the settlers and the Kikuyu gentry (who were often the main target of violence), and also by the counter measures which the colonial authorities took once the revolt was contained militarily. Recognizing that land was at the root of the situation, the colonialists set about institutionalizing the growing individualism by consolidating the fragmented holdings and registering freehold titles, intending thereby to create a rural middle class from among the loyalists, which would be "too busy on their land to worry about political agitation." [16] This cynical program of social engineering was completed after 1960 when as part of the decolonization arrangements, peasants in central Kenya were freely allowed to plant coffee and some landless and others were resettled on former European mixed farms in order to "take the steam out of the land issue." [17] The resulting social structure is not bipolarized, as was originally envisaged, but is three-tiered. A small landed gentry persists but is now "merged with the new political elite"; [18] the mass of small farmers have the relative security of an assured title even if their plot is tiny and they have some cash crop income; while the "landlessness of the rebels (has

[16] Quote from Special Commissioner for Land Consolidation in Sorrenson, *ibid,* p. 117.

[17] The phrase was originally Kenyatta's but has become part of the political vocabulary of Kenya, for instance, Oginga Odinga: *Not Yet Uhuru,* (Heinemann, London, 1967), p. 258.

[18] Sorrenson: *Land Reform . . ., op. cit.,* p. 251.

been) confirmed."[19] Thus the class alliances within the Kikuyu population have shifted so that all strata except a growing but still small minority of desparate, landless *mutarukire* (literally, in Kikuyu, "the ragged ones") are basically supportive of the status quo. This realignment was evident in 1966 when Bildad Kaggia tried unsuccessfully to seek re-election, after joining the new opposition Kenya's People's Union (KPU), on the basis of the same slogans about land distribution that he had raised as one of the old guard radicals of KAU a generation before.

Other consequences of the emergency on the ensuing political formations should be noted. Of course, the KAU leaders were imprisoned, and KAU and all other African political movements throughout the country were banned in 1952 and only allowed again in 1957 if organized on a district-wide basis, and not at all for some time after that among the Kikuyu. In place of KAU with mass support in central Kenya and some tentative organization elsewhere in the country, there thus grew up a new pattern of African politics. Local, and thus tribal organizations were formed usually as the personal constituency of a new generation of political leaders. Although these "baronial" figures formed alliances on a national level out of which two parties, the Kenya African National Union (KANU) and the Kenya African Democratic Union (KADU), separated out and then later combined, the pattern of a loose band of often competing leaders reflecting a confederation of local machines remains the bacis character of the dominant party, KANU.

Politics and Class in Kenya

A new, younger and generally more educated generation of leaders emerged in the late 1950's—men like Tom Mboya, a Luo but with a Nairobi trade union base; the more traditional but yet radical Luo, Oginga Odinga; Daniel Arap Moi, the present Vice President and a representative of one of the pastoral Kalenjin peoples of the Rift Valley; and Ronald Ngala from the Coast, the former leader of KADU and since 1965 comfortably absorbed in the KANU Government. Pre-Uhuru politics at the national level had also become the preserve of non-Kikuyu figures, especially Luo. As a new more educated generation of Kikuyu politicians like the academics Dr. Gikonyo Kiano (Syracuse) and Mwai Kibaki (London School of Economics) arrived on the scene, and then as the old guard was released, there were conflicts and uneasy, changing alliances between new and old leaders for control of local machines, and between bosses of different tribal groups. The Kikuyu political leaders and their supporters first allied with the Luo within KANU, to be opposed in the

[19] *ibid,* p.

immediate pre- and post-independence phase principally by representatives of the smaller groups in the Rift and Coast who were scared of missing out at all levels—in terms of positions of political power for themselves, elite status for the local educated group, and services for the people of the area—because of their inherited disadvantages vis-à-vis the larger, more advanced peoples. But after Uhuru and as the spoils were taken over, the dominant alliance between the Kikuyu and Luo elites turned to conflict for political preeminence and for bureaucratic preferment. The overt political break came in 1966 when a new KANU Constitution that proposed to push Odinga farther away from the center of power was hurried through and the opposition KPU was formed. This new party got most of its weight from Nyanza M.P.s and other Luo influentials, together with a few Kamba, and gained its only popular support in the subsequent "Little General Election" in these areas. A few "maverick" M.P.s mainly from very backward areas also supported the party for a time, but clearly had no articulate or organized backing for their position. Of course, the KPU stance was not merely a personal expression of pro-Odinga influence, nor solely an attempt to develop an anti-Kikuyu tribal alliance. The party did represent elements which had been attempting to put forward a radical critique of the KANU Government's development policies and to appeal to the class interests of the poorer peasants and workers. However, the realities of Kenya politics—its fragmented local organization and an essentially ethnic rather than class consciousness, plus tight administrative curbs imposed by the government on their activities—meant that the party was not able to get any significant support outside Nyanza Province and parts of Ukambani nor to build an effective central organization.

It would be too simplistic to explain reactions among different ethnic groups to these events in purely tribal terms unrelated to issues of class. Evidence from the Little General Election suggests that Kaggia and other KPU elements were only able to enlist the support, against strong government pressure, from the desperate landless elements, while the small and rich peasants tended to back the establishment. Among the Luo some political leaders (Mboya particularly) stayed in KANU and few of the urban elites openly backed the opposition. It seems that KANU gained its small degree of popular support from better-off elements in the rural areas. A roughly similar situation occurred in the Kamba areas. These latter two areas, while supporting a fairly dense and settled agricultural population, have a more marginal potential. Moreover, resistance in these areas to the now generalized policy of land consolidation and registration, led to them being starved of agricultural credit and other services. Not only were there feelings of relative neglect in these areas, but the majority of peasants were still largely untransformed, with only a small proportion producing regularly for the market and more traditional land ties still in existence. In contrast with these areas where differentiated strata among the peasantries are inclined to take up different political stances, the peasantries in the more marginal areas where little development or differentiation seems to have occurred are scarcely involved in organized political activity at all, and any overt articulation of political opinion tends to be confined to their local elites.

In the last few years (since about 1968), a number of additional trends have emphasized the ethnic factor in politics in a way that has further obscured the class dimension. First, the Kikuyu–Lou conflict further intensified at central political levels, and in competition for elite posts as jobs became scarcer. It became acute and also more clear-cut with Mboya's assassination and the government violence against subsequent demonstrations in Kisumu (the center of Nyanza) against Kenyatta, which led to the banning of KPU and detention of its leaders in 1969. Luo of all strata felt threatened, the elites included; they were in turn seen, by definition, as a threat to the state, so that they were pushed out of the influence positions—not one, for instance, remained in the paramilitary, counter-insurgency general service unit of the police. The Kikuyu establishment also encouraged tribal fears so that they could close ranks, thus blurring class differences and even the significant conflict between Kiambu leadership and those from other Kikuyu districts. More recently, a new political leadership not formally associated with KPU nor including any of the Luo who stayed in the KANU government, emerged in the Nyanza Province and was given an opportunity by the 1969 election to consolidate a local and national base. In this period the Kikuyu, or perhaps more accurately the Kiambu, leadership has tried to exert its hegemony against elements from one of the other large tribes—the Kamba. The army chief and the chief justice were persuaded to resign office, and some Kamba farming near Kikuyu areas have been pressured out.

The shift in this competition and conflict during the 1960's away from an alliance of elites from the larger tribes towards Kikuyu supremacy is in part a response to objective economic circumstances. The structure of the Kenya economy, with its large farms, manufacturing executive posts, and widespread trading opportunities, provides for the possibility of satisfying the ambitions of a more considerable elite than many African countries. However, unstemmable pressures for education have led to a rapid expansion of those aspiring to elite membership. This was satisfied in the 1960's by Africanization of the civil service and provision of loans to buy settler farms and to start businesses. As these opportunities were taken up, competition for elite entry became sharper. By the later 1960's this pressure also led to attempts to move into new sectors—labor permits aimed to ensure that no non-citizen was employed except in skilled fields where there were no citizens available; trade licensing similarly forced non-citizens out of more and more fields of small business. This of course operated to the disadvantage of the Asian business class, and thus gave rise to some racial antagonisms, fears, and a mass Asian exodus in 1970. So far, there has been no similar pressure on the European community. The large corporations are quite ready to Africanize posts so long as they do not lose control of policy and profits. The exodus of many settlers at the time of independence has meant that the threshold where pressures—for further Africanization of the large farms, or the expansion of settlement schemes for landless or small peasants—would be felt by the remaining settlers has still to be reached. In these sectors of the economy there is still slack that can be taken up. Elsewhere, as regards land availability for peasants, employment opportunities for manual or clerical workers, and for elite posts and small trading opportunities, there is increasing pressure and competition. However, the nature of Kenya politics in the pre- and post-independence period suggests that such economic conflicts are more likely to be expressed in the language of tribalism than by means of a conscious cross-cutting struggle on class lines.

The State Apparatus in Kenya

Any intensive exploration of the nature of Kenya politics must focus on the state machinery rather than merely the parties. The colonial state in Kenya was distinctive in that it accommodated the interests of a settler population and was not simply an agency acting on behalf of general mercantile interests in the metropolis. This settler involvement had two notable political consequences. First, through various channels—a more established legislature, non-official membership of the executive, informal pressure group politicking—there was a significant access to decision-making power especially in resource allocation by local residents. Secondly, the degree of control over the rural African population, and the urban and rural workers, was tighter and more restrictive. The degree of this administrative control was further intensified during the emergency: for instance the number of administration officers doubled between 1951 and 1962.[20] In assessing the nature of contemporary, post-colonial politics and specifically in justifying our earlier assertion that the state in Africa generally tends to be a neo-colonial instrument of international capital in the hands of the locally privileged, the realities of power and control

[20] For this information and much other data on the political institutions see Cherry Gertzel: *The Politics of Independent Kenya, 1963–68,* (East Africa Publishing House, Nairobi, 1970), p. 25 *et passim.*

in the immediate post-colonial period offer a useful starting point. An assessment can be made of the degree to which formal structures have changed and of the precise influences to which the emerging structure respond.

In addition to the strength of the administration, certain other constitutional features of the colonial state have some carryover. Non-official representation on the executive had been a feature of colonial rule since the first World War, and a ministerial system had been in operation since the early 1950's. This fact supports the notion that the "transfer of power" that occurred in 1963 was not solely a devolution of authority from London to Nairobi, but a widening of the local elite represented at the center of power to include some African representatives. Another connected characteristic of the pre-Uhuru state was the existence of a reasonably articulate legislature, which did in fact become the platform for voicing the demands, and for the political maneuvering of the new African political elite in the period from 1968 to 1963. Observers have reached different conclusions about parliament in the post-independence period. According to one view it remains "a significant organ . . . performing a function that the party is not able to offer"; [21] others argue it has a "relatively weak position . . . as an institution in the Kenya political system." [22] It seems clear that the Kenya parliament receives more political attention than its counterpart institution in Tanzania, but while providing a visible public forum for intra-elite debate, it has offered only a very limited opportunity for the expression of interests and ideological outlooks different from those of the political elites themselves. This conclusion will become clearer as we go on to spell out the operation of other formal institutions and seek out the actual power holders in the decision-making process.

The formal steps in the process of decolonization and successive shifts in the power alliances are discernible in those cornerstones of British "parliamentary democracy"—the electoral system, and the consequent interrelation between parliament and cabinet. Kenya's suffrage was gradually widened following the first elections in 1957; as the racial composition of parliament broadened, elected leaders were incorporated into positions of full responsibility for the state machinery. Concurrently, a system emerged which in theory allowed for a popularly-elected, sovereign parliament from which the executive arm of government would emerge with majority party support. Similar systems arose elsewhere in ex-British Africa. Even though some metropolitan and settler interests had at first

[21] *ibid.*

[22] G. Hyden and Colin Leys: 'Elections and Election Studies in Single Party Systems—the Cases of Kenya and Tanzania', *British Journal of Political Science,* 1972.

seen the majority tribal representatives of KADU as more acceptable, and a fragmented regional constitution as a better safeguard of their interests, it was in fact the leaders of KANU who assumed state power following their substantial electoral victory in 1963. They won the Kikuyu, Luo, Kisii and Meru seats, and a good proportion of the Luhya and Kamba. However, direct British influence to restrict the new power holders to those ideologically acceptable (through the exclusion of more radical figures like Odinga) continued up to the eve of independence. But acceptability was guaranteed indirectly by the guided emergence in the late 1950's of a form of politics, "constitutional" and district-based, that favored an educated elite. This elite has been assessed by one Kenya scholar: "this younger generation of political leaders was essentially white collar, middle-class, self-interested, self-identified and basically tribalist in nature." [23]

In the immediate port-independence period there were some efforts, partly made through parliamentary pressure, to put forward a radical critique of the post-independence policies of the KANU government, and in fact this back-bench criticism became more marked after the more conservative KADU MPs crossed the floor in 1964. Spearheaded by leaders like Kaggia, who had resigned from government in 1964, with presumably tacit support from ministers like Odinga and Oneko, a group of KANU back-benchers did effectively challenge the official line. Both in parliament and in outside bodies such as the short-lived ideological party school, the Lumumba Institute, they attempted to provide an alternative power base. Their organizational effectiveness and their radicalism took a severe jolt when Pio Pinto, the ideologist and organizer of the radicals, was shot down by an assassin in 1965. In the year that followed the remaining radical forces were out-maneuvered and Odinga and other leaders were edged out of influence into a position where they decided to form a separate opposition, the KPU. Their attempts were unsuccessful in the Little General Election, which followed a retroactive constitutional measure forcing the new party representatives to seek re-election, and thereafter to pitch a popular appeal in class rather than ethnic terms. Since 1966, organized politics, both at parliamentary and other elite levels, and in the patron-client relations linking the elite to their local constituencies, have become more, not less, redolent of tribal chauvinism.

The most recent episode in the party-electoral-parliamentary life of

[23] John Okumu: 'Not Yet Uhuru?', *East African Journal,* (Nairobi), Vol. IV, No. 6, October, 1967, p. 15. For an interesting analysis of this dimension of Kenya's political sociology, see an unpublished paper by Ivory Robinson: 'The Petit Bourgeoisie—an Analysis of its Socio-economic Origins and its Contemporary Role in the Political Economy of Kenya', (Boston, 1970).

Kenya was the 1969 elections. The circumstances of the Mboya assassination had increased tribal cohesion and mutual antagonism and the banning of the KPU earlier that year meant that the elections took a quite different form from that originally intended. In an effort to make good the image of Kenya's "political freedom and stability" (which was seen to be the key to attracting investment) by permitting elections without running the risk of dividing KANU support and thus allowing opposition MP's through, a system of primary elections was proposed. With the banning of KPU, the elections were thus reduced to a set of primaries within the one party. These were completely open and an average of four candidates stood for each constituency, but the competition thus tended to be between individuals, rather than parties or programs. The net effect has been summarized by two observers:

> . . . there was substantial renewal of the incumbent political elite without any visible change in the relationship between that elite and either the rest of the population or the foreign sector of the economy. To the extent that the holding of the elections gave the government a respite by jettisoning MPs who had lost their local support, its chief result was to sustain the process of elite consolidation through the Africanisation of the foreign commercial and industrial sector which had begun with the land transfers of 1960–65, continued through the Africanisation of retail trade, and was now moving into the Africanisation of management in foreign commercial and industrial corporations, culminating in the system of 'partnership' between the latter and the Kenya government.[24]

While the immediate effect was seemingly to modify and consolidate the system, the same authors point to another possible long-term consequence —in contrast to the Tanzania elections which they claim did offer some choice while reinforcing a localized consciousness:

> . . . the experience of a frankly pork-barrel, clientelist exercise in manipulation in the context of rapidly crystallising patterns of social change and inequality that accompany the Kenya approach to development, may in due course help to raise the level of political consciousness of a growing number of voters.[25]

The representative institutions—a fragmented party organization, a working but hardly challenging parliament, and a manipulative electoral system—are thus able to influence the direction of policy very marginally and offer little prospect for popular involvement. We must then turn to the bureaucratic institutions of the state to see where formal power resides, and to discover what interests are there represented.

[24] Hyden and Leys, *op. cit.*, p.
[25] *ibid.*

In terms of prominence, the presidency must come first, for Jomo Kenyatta has invested the position with a prestige which no other actors nor institutions command. As a symbol of the struggle for independence, and as the one leader who has both a tribal base and a national image, his political position is unchallenged by any other leaders. This position is certainly used to consolidate the regime. Even KPU leaders like Odinga and Kaggia took the position that they were challenging KANU and not the "Old Man." As an executive president, president of the ruling party, chairman of its parilamentary committee, and with the powerful provincial administration responsible directly to a minister of state in his own office, his formal position is also formidable. However, his role is more as arbiter and the undisputed final authority, rather than as an initiator of policy like Nyerere in Tanzania. Still he sets a certain stamp on the direction of policy rather than acting as a merely "neutral" chairman. First, there is little doubt that he aims to preserve the status quo and his bourgeois views about property are reflected in the oft-repeated slogan that "people can't expect 'free things.' " Secondly, despite his long record of opposition to colonial government, he has always been and remains a member of the "Kiambu establishment," relying on such elements for almost all his closest associates, and extending his and the government's patronage to his home village, Gatunda, and the Kiambu district. He is then supremely well-cast as "the popular leader to whom will fall the dual role of stabilizing the regime and perpetuating the domination of the Presidency." [26] To quote Fanon further:

> "During the struggle for liberation the leader awakened the people and promised them a forward march, heroic and unmitigated. Today he uses every means to put them (the masses) to sleep, and three or four times a year asks them to remember the colonial period and look back on the long way they have come since then." [27]

Other members of the cabinet tend to be of two sorts—the "tribal figures," persons like Moi or Paul Ngei with long-standing local support or those who are at least brought in to balance the ethnic arithmetic, and the "bureaucrats." This latter group of university or ex-civil service types provide some measure of competence and intellectual weight. These latter ministers especially are socially and culturally very much in tune with their civil servants. There is no doubt that the colonial administrative legacy and the vast education "airlift" to the United Kingdom and the United States before independence have given the Kenya bureaucracy a degree of competence—and self-confidence not always found in Africa.

[26] Fanon, *op. cit.*, p. 133.
[27] *ibid.*, p. 136.

What is significant about the administration is not only its size and educational attainment, but the opportunities given it by the settler economy to acquire property interests, ex-settler farms, shops and other small businesses, domestic property and, increasingly, tourist enterprises. Indeea this conversion of a political-administrative elite into a property-owning *class* is encouraged by the provision of government loans and other official support. The manipulation of state instruments for personal ends is also illustrated by the fact that there were in the 1960's no less than three commissions looking into civil service salaries and benefits; all recommended increases. The kind of broader interests that accumulated policy prasures support can be gauged by the conclusions of a recent analysis of the taxation system which found it to be highly regressive.[28]

The administrators are thus part of the emerging African petty bourgeois and even bourgeois classes. In the official promotion of Africanization of business they have engaged in ethnic competition with Asian traders. As large farmers, they are still allied rather than in conflict with the remaining European settlers. As they move into areas like tourism they become more closely involved with large scale international capitalism.

It is by virtue of such a "natural" identity of interest and through informal contact that the state still reflects ex-colonial, but increasingly international, capitalist interests. Even though the state institutions are no longer settler-manned, the possibilities for the new forms of indirect influence are great. In fact, a number of parastatal, statutory and semigovernmental bodies are susceptible to the influence of imperialist economic interests: marketing boards still have settler members; the boss of the multinational brewery company is chairman of the national export council; three of the seven members of the recent Commission of Inquiry into the Public Service, although Kenyan (one naturalized) were executives or directors of international corporations. But it is necessary to recognize the existence of "entrenched sources of power other than the State." For international capitalism has brought "its institutions and ideology" . . . and has had, for instance, "tremendous influence on the personality of an African trade union movement" and has ensured that conflict between labor and capital have been fought out "on ground chosen by management: within the business rather than the political arena" [29]—tendencies which in turn are likely to dull the political consciousness of the urban workers. The shared interest among foreign capital, settlers and the new elite is supported by education and other cultural similarities, (Kenya's privileged are English-speaking, golf-playing, sports-jacketed subur-

[28] John Nellis: 'The Tax Structure in Kenya', *Universities of Eastern Africa Social Science Conference Paper,* (Kampala, 1971).

[29] Amsden, *op. cit.*

banites whatever their race) as well as a common ideology of acquisitive individualism. This ideological outlook is emphasized by an effective foreign-owned press and an entrenched public relations sector which exert a significant influence on public information and thinking. But more generally the influence of foreign capitalist interests is at once a reason for, and a product of, the central position accorded them by current development strategy; so "although they do not have access to the tools of coercion, they could 'buy' it in situations of crisis."[30]

One other consequence of Kenya's policies of system maintenance for her political structures should be noted before we turn finally to an examination of the development strategy itself. For, like the settler economy, a development path based on restricted opportunities for cash crop production for export and the encouragement of foreign business requires control. Here the continued strength and centrality of the provincial administration is a vital tool. This body of professional administrators with their social science degrees and their pith helmets play a dominating role throughout the provinces and districts. Their functions have extended beyond those of their colonial predecessors: they now chair district development committees, agricultural boards and land committees and promote self-help activities. In these roles they are not only often in conflict with fellow government officers from specialist ministries but also with MPs and other local politicians who are anxious to get access to the developmental spoils and who resent the commissioners' status as representatives of the head of state. Indeed, one of the few concrete changes suggested by a special committee of KANU to recommend measures to strengthen the party was that "Ministers . . . be the sole representatives of the President in all state functions . . . instead of Administrative Officials." But the role of the administration remains essentially one of "maintaining law and order" in the face of growing inequality and the desperation of landless and unemployed school leavers. The administration is not, then, developmental, and as such its continued dominance of politics at the local level seems a necessary component of the present policies.

Kenya's Development Performance

Looking at Kenya's development performance, there is no doubt that measured by conventional macro-economic indicators, Kenya has shown rapid growth since independence, averaging a 6 percent annual increase in GDP during the 1960's This increase has been achieved in agriculture by significant but not dramatic expansion in the two main export areas—

[30] Shem E. Migot-Adholla: 'Ideology and National Development—the Case of Kenya', *Ufahamu,* (Los Angeles), Vol. II, No. 1, Spring 1971.

coffee (at least in the early part of the period) and tea, and in the meat products and basic grains produced for local (or rather East African) consumption. Industry developed relatively slowly in this period as compared with Tanzania, but in commercial and servicing sectors and especially tourism there were very marked increases. This minor boom has still not led to any major structural transformation of the economy nor been based fundamentally on major expansions of productive capacity in either agriculture or industry. Rather it has been confined to the tertiary sector. The basic strategy underlying these changes of the last decade has consisted in the government promoting an agrarian revolution. Its programs include the industrialization of land tenure, the removal of colonial restrictions on peasant cash crop production and the provision, on a commercial basis, of a high level of services pioneered in settler heydays. This has selectively (in high potential areas and among better-off peasants) allowed for increased production and also gradually transformed much of the peasantry into a small property-owning class. The resulting increases in incomes, together with government incentives (such as tax holidays and profit repatriation and compensation guarantees) have been used to encourage foreign private investment in industry, in some areas of commerce, and in tourism. In attracting this foreign investment, Nairobi's inherited status has contributed as a peripheral center of the East Africa region, with a fairly developed infrastructure and servicing facilities, an attractive environment and the country's efforts to maintain political stability at all costs. As Union Carbide and Firestone build factories and TWA and Hilton put up hotels, these corporations also acquire a stake in the status quo.

The recent Development Plan (1970–1974), while sticking to the same basic formula of government-backed rural development, infrastructural creation and political control as efforts to support private investment in the modern sectors, reflects some changes of emphasis. The new plan put an increased emphasis on state initiative—"the achievement of the basic goal of an economy 60 percent larger in 1974 than in 1967 will be obtained through a greatly expanded government spending program. . . ." [31] And in this sense, the designation of the Kenya system as "state capitalism" may seem to have some justification. The term may also reflect the plan's intention to see greater "collaboration between foreign firms and the government," which has been evidenced in the recent and unresisted acquisition by government of shares in banks, oil companies and other international corporations. But we should be clear as to what these trends add up to: there is no intention to cut down the role of foreign investment

[31] Republic of Kenya: *Development Plan, 1970–74,* (Government Printer, Nairobi, 1970), p. 1.

nor to reorient the economy to internal as opposed to external stimuli. Indeed the plan calls for "more active and coordinated efforts to be made to attract foreign investment."

The increased role of the state thus grows out of a desire to promote conditions favorable to continued subservience of the economy. The continued need for government to promote a growing market and servicing facilities through rural and infrastructural development is recognized—as is the crucial importance of tight political control. This latter is rendered all the more necessary because of growing tensions due to the lopsided nature of development—increasing landlessness of a minority, a drift to the towns of well over 6 percent per year, unemployment swelled by school-leavers including now those with secondary level, all occurring against a background of a 3 percent increase in population. There have been increased expenditures on security forces and the composition of the higher command has been manipulated to ensure loyalty to the ruling establishment. More positively, foreign experts, aid agencies and the more enlightened bureaucrats and politicians have all urged on the government "reformist" policies designed to reduce possible social tensions. Programs of population control are mounted; a government-employers-trade union agreement for a voluntary 10 percent increase in employment; a greater emphasis on rural development and its broader spread; some talk, at least, of mild income redistribution through taxation and other measures; the announcement of new settlements to mop up some of the landless—these are some of the measures designed to make the system work more rationally. The government investment program is moreover designed in part to promote boom conditions for other forms of investment which can no longer rely on mere expansion of primary production for export to provide the necessary market growth. The actual take-over of shares can also be looked at as a device for ensuring greater government responsiveness to foreign capital and a means whereby the international corporations not only obtain guarantees of goodwill but find some of their own collateral replaced by public funds and thus liberated for new investments. Thus a system is developing, which even if termed "state capitalism" does not denote a new mode of production, an alternative to the colonial economic structure, but merely a modification of the patterns of foreign involvement and the forging of more effective links between the state apparatus, the Kenyans who now man it, and foreign capital.

In concluding this discussion of the emerging politico-economic patterns in Kenya it is important to recognize that they are in process of flux. The links with imperialism take on different forms, and new contradictions emerge. In the colonial period, the conflicting interests were seemingly racial—until nationalist resistance made evident secondary conflicts between settler interests and those of genuinely international capital. In the post-independence period, a new alliance of interests of settlers and foreign capital with the locally privileged emerged, led to, and was in turn supported by, some extension of benefits to sections of the peasantry. Some of the limits of this strategy not only in the increasing inequalities but even in maintaining growth and the stability of the foreign-settler-elite alliance are now beginning to emerge; the boom in coffee could not go on and was becoming embarrassing in the face of international quota limits, so some new engine (and a somewhat artificial one) is sought. Changes in property relations do lead to some increased production and temporary stabilization, but ultimately they will lead to the increasing desperation of the landless; so, too, unrestricted educational advance buys political support for a time but creates its own tensions as urban unemployment mounts. Concessions to the now-independent East African partners keep markets for Kenya produce open against import substitution, but only for a time. And as reformist policies to remove some of the more blatant inequalities and tensions are put forward by the more far-sighted local and foreign interests, these may entail conflict with the interests of existing settlers or local farmers who do not want to give up land or have ceilings placed on holdings, or of others who aspire to join the privileged. More directly, the wage and labor policies coupled with the capital intensive nature of foreign investment negate reformist measures to combat unemployment.

These prognostications suggest that continued elite cleavages (and those involving the aspirant elites) can certainly be expected; increasing tensions among certain desperate minorities (landless, school-leavers, a few poor, involuted, densely populated communities) can also be expected to develop. But these are not immediately likely to aggregate into a major revolutionary class struggle until the proletariat and the lumpen elements have become more significant. Even then some new political initiative would be necessary to provide both a radical consciousness which can sweep aside the ethnic mystification which has surrounded most of Kenya's political activity since Uhuru, and an organizational framework to channel such class forces into effective action.

Development of Tanzania's Economic Structures

The most striking characteristic of Tanzania's post-independence development has been the country's efforts to reverse those trends that are so evident in Kenya, toward the growing penetration of international capitalism and toward class formation. The explanation of Tanzania's commitment to an alternative, socialist, self-reliant course is, however, difficult to isolate. At first glance, the society contains, albeit in a more muted form, many of those elements that we discerned in Kenya: a settler presence, the emergence of rich peasants, traders and other petty bourgeois strata through cash crop production, uneven economic development of economic and educational opportunities superimposed on an even more ethnically diverse population, and a colonial state which was handed over intact to a group of educated Tanzanians at independence. In fact, the colonial economy that grew up in Tanzania was an uneasy amalgam of Kenya's settler pattern and that of promoting peasant cash crop production which characterized Uganda and other African colonies. The emphasis between these somewhat contradictory paths fluctuated back and forth. The Germans certainly encouraged the development of both plantation and settler agriculture, and indeed there were more Europeans in Tanganyika in 1907 than in Kenya at that time.[32] Their presence was sufficient to give them political power—enough, for instance to overcome the colonial administration's efforts to promote peasant cash crops as an economic antidote to the Maji Maji peasant rising of 1905 to 1907. The expulsion of the Germans in the First World War changed the direction of colonial economic strategy; British rule, Tanganyika's mandate status under the League of Nation (later UN) and a resultant "open-doors" policy to settlers of non-British nationality, and the uncertainty about the future of the colony, all inhibited further settlement, at least until the late 1940's and early 1950's. At that time, a policy of "multiracialism," which politically meant separate representation of each race, was used to support the removal of racial reservation of land units, thus opening the way to the rational use (by settlers, of course) of all available land. This issue was one of the rallying points of the nationalist struggle of the later 1950's, which by 1958 had not only won the concession of ultimate independence under African rule but had halted further expansion of the settler areas for good. Despite this mixed history, the sisal estates principally, but also, the coffee, tea and tobacco plantations and mixed farms of the European settlers—occupying altogether two and one-half million acres of alienated land (1 percent of the land area)—were still responsible for half of all the agricultural exports at the time of independence and employed a labor force of some 150,000.

Yet the settler sector was different in important respects from that in Kenya—apart from the much smaller relative size of the land alienated and of the settler population. The land consisted of scattered pockets along the northeastern border, at the eastern end of the central railway line and in the southern highlands. The settlers were a more heteroge-

[32] This and other information on the pre-1914 period is found in John Iliffe: *Tanganyika under German Rule*, (Cambridge University Press, Cambridge, 1968).

neous mix of nationalities, so that as a set of interests they were in every way less coherent and were never able to gain the same dominance. Equally, the impact of the settler presence, both in constraining nearby African communities and in underdeveloping the labor source areas, was more diffused than in Kenya where all the immediate consequences were most starkly visited on one group, the Kikuyu. There have certainly been local groups who have suffered land shortages through being boxed in by European agriculture—"serious land deficiency" was already reported in the Usambara mountains and around Kilimanjaro by 1913.[33] Such constraining "iron bands" were on occasion the basis for protest movements, of which the Meru Citizens' Union action over the Meru Lands Case in the early 1950's was only the most dramatic.[34] However, it was not these but other areas which as a result of supplying the labor force for the plantations and farms endured the induced backwardness. The bulk of the labor migration was in fact from the more remote parts of the country. Initially, the Nyamwezi, and their neighbors who straddled the main central trade routes and who had provided the porters for the slave-ivory trade, were looked to as one of the principal sources of labor. They are still the third and fourth largest amongst the population of Dar es Salaam —some six hundred miles distant. The building of the railways through these more western areas was thus a source of concern as well as a benefit to the German settlers—because it "may make it more profitable for the African to produce for the market and stay at home." [35]

The position of the settlers was in fact never strong enough to impose a total ban on peasant production of export crops as in Kenya. Indeed, labor supplies dried up from some of the traditional source areas as cash crops were introduced—cotton around the Lake at an early date, coffee and rice in Rungwe, tobacco and coffee in Songea in the 1940's and later pyrethrum and tea in Njombe. However, the spread of cash crops occurred only fitfully, and some areas like Kigoma and Singida regions retain to this day an inherited backwardness, largely as a result of the absence of an accepted market crop. Coffee was the first peasant crop, introduced in the German period in Kilimanjaro and West Lake. Cotton, in the Eastern Province and to the South of Lake Victoria, was mainly a post-World War I development. The ten or so districts (out of sixty) that were given over to these two crops were responsible for over half of the

[33] ibid, p. 206.

[34] For detail, see Earle Seaton and Kirilo Japhet: *The Meru Lands Case,* (East Africa Publishing House, Nairobi, 1966) and A. Nelson: *The Freemen of Meru,* (Oxford University Press, Nairobi, 1967).

[35] Letter from the German East Africa Planters Association, Berlin to the Governor, February 7, 1910.

marketed African agricultural production at Uhuru. Other crops—pyrethrum, tobacco, tea, cashews in the south, rice wheat—have affected development in other parts of the country mainly in the last generation.

This mixed pattern of settler agriculture and its resulting labor migration with very uneven peasant involvement in the external market economy has naturally produced a complex and regionally varied set of processes of socio-economic differentiation. But before attempting a crude summation of the inherited structure, we must also register the generally limited economic involvement of capitalist forces in Tanganyika even as compared with its neighbor.

This comparative neglect was largely a product of British policy. Up to 1914, the expansion of agriculture, the infrastructural development (especially of railways), and the provision of some training for Africans to produce the clerks needed, were all as advanced as elsewhere. Between the wars, however, there was hardly any investment in transport, agricultural programs or other capital projects, while the number of Africans in primary school in 1947 was much the same as in 1922.[36] It is hard not to accept the assessment of Tanganyika's colonialism as one where the "colonists did not use Tanganyika as an outlet for capital investment . . . [and] they were not very interested in selling manufactured goods . . . [but] were mostly interested in taking out certain raw materials . . .".[37] This tendency was further enhanced as such industrial and commercial developments as the Tanganyikan economy might have been able to sustain were in fact centered in Kenya, the "peripheral-center" of the East African economy. The measure of the relative neglect can be seen in the fact that manufacturing industry was responsible for only 3 percent of GNP, as opposed to 12 percent in Kenya at Uhuru. Even in 1970 less than half the children of school age had the opportunity to attend even primary grades, as opposed to almost two-thirds in Kenya. The much larger size of the country and the scattered nature of the population also makes the lack of infrastructural development more crucial.

The fearful limitations of industry, transport, and manpower have daunting consequences for attempts to build a self-reliant economy. Perversely, however, this relative backwardness might not have been without its positive implications for socialist possibilities. The small stake that imperialism had in Tanzania may account for its relative ease in obtaining independence and in getting away with a socialist policy of nationaliza-

[36] R.A. Chilivumbo: *Tansania—One Party State,* (Unpublished Ph.D. thesis, University of California, Los Angeles, 1967) quotes total enrolment figures of 100,000 (approx.) in 1922 and 115,025 in 1947.

[37] M.J. Yaffey: 'Self Reliance and Foreign Trade', *Uchumi,* (Journal of the Economics Society of Tanzania), Vol. I, No. 1, 1970.

tions after 1967. Equally, the tiny size and relatively unsophisticated nature of the petty bourgeoisie has been offered as one reason for the lack of serious intra-elite conflict and for the passivity of the privileged elements following the Arusha curbs on their economic status.

Class and Ethnic Differences in Tanzania

The colonial period thus left Tanzania with a class structure with a combination of those features found in the two neighboring countries—foreign capital in the rural as well as urban sector, and a small sector of capitalist farmers and a class of agricultural laborers; a largely urban petty bourgeoisie of officials, teachers and small traders; and a set of "peasantries" ranging from highly stratified ones in areas of long standing cash crop production or recent pioneering settlement, but little differentiated in other regions. Post-independence changes have modified this structure in some regards. The decline of the settler sector, due to the departure of European "gentlemen farmers" and the declining market for sisal, have further reduced the agricultural labor force, from 216,000 in 1961 to 110,000 in 1970, in comparison with that in Kenya. The doubling of marketed agricultural output which occurred in the 1960's, mainly in crops other than the traditional "big three" of sisal, cotton and coffee, probably succeeded in further differentiating the peasantry. Although as one outline of the picture suggests, this is very limited at the extremes, for only 14,000 (0.3 percent) employers and 150,000 full-time employees (2.7 percent) could be identified out of nearly five million persons gainfully occupied in agriculture.[38] The Africanization of official posts and some expansion of urban employment, together with sizeable increases in wage rates, have produced an increase in the number of Africans earning over two hundred shillings per month (roughly thirty dollars) from 8 percent in 1961 to 60 percent in 1970.

This necessarily brief overview of the class structure of Tanzania certainly does not suggest the presence of any fundamental cleavages, nor of desperate elements sufficiently large, organized or conscious to have been the spontaneous spearhead of the socialist opening, nor of social forces that can provide that inexorable push which could guarantee its success. The social structure is perhaps largely different from that of Kenya and others in Africa only in the limited involvement of foreign capital and in the small extent of indigenous privilege—features which facilitate socialist advance only in reducing the direct obstacles. The Tanzanian

[38] These figures are derived from 1967 Census figures in an unpublished paper by M. Gottlieb: 'Footnote to the Debate on Differentiation', (Economic Research Bureau, Dar es Salaam, 1971).

people thus deserve, even more than the Chinese, Mao's description of a "tabula rasa" on which anything can still be written.

Likewise, if we turn to the ethnic character of the population, there is little to provide social forces or conditions which could explain the move towards a socialist alternative—although there is at least an absence of those conflicts which blur consciousness of class difference in Kenya. A first glance at the make-up of the population makes even the prospect of national unity seem unlikely. The geographical features of the country are such that most of its people are widely scattered around its borders rather than clustered in the center as tends to be the case in Kenya and Uganda. Much of the center of the country is too dry for settled agriculture (although one finds there some semi-pastoral people) or is occupied by tsetse thus inhibiting any human or livestock habitation. Moreover the population is made up of a very large number of culturally distinct groups—some 120 "tribes" have been recorded by the census-takers (even though the term has no generally agreed, objective, defining characteristic). These groups include semi-nomadic pastoralists, others who are scarcely beyond the hunting and gathering stage, but also farming communities whose grandfathers planted export crops and whose children *all* go to school.

Closer inspection, however, indicates there are some positive aspects to the make-up of the population and even to its diverse ethnic character. There has been an absence of those "natural" cleavages which have sparked off conflict in the neighboring countries. Apart from some ethnographically and historically interesting but numerically insignificant Nilotic, Cushitic and even click-speaking peoples in the Northern areas, almost all of the different ethnic groups speak some Bantu language. Although this fact helps to avoid one potential cleavage which operates in Uganda, it has little positive cultural or political significance, except in making it easy for most people to acquire fluency in the national language, Swahili. However, due to other factors, the specter of a single ethnic group assuming complete dominance, because of its relative size, economic or educational opportunities, and/or its strategic location, is precluded. The largest single group, the Sukuma living south of Lake Victoria are far distant from the capital, only mildly prosperous, and somewhat introspective politically and culturally. The most prosperous groups—the coffee growing Haya, Chagga and Nyakyusa, are relatively small, located on the borders, and never formed a single state system. However, the unevenness of educational chances does create a situation where these groups are heavily represented amongst the bureaucratic and other elites, which allows some play for nepotism and cliquism at the highest levels. The Zaramo and related coastal people who form the biggest single component of Dar es Salaam's population have not had the leadership or size which might make them appear as a potentially dominating group. Indeed, the very mixed character of the capital's ethnic make-up, where no groups apart from the Zaramo claim more than 5 percent of the total, is in marked contrast to Nairobi and cities where the existence of a few sizeable clusters helps to promote a local cultural identity and a pattern of political conflict between these blocs.

The absence of factors likely to encourage ethnic factionalism in the politics of the chief towns and of the national arena is made much more significant when seen in combination with the influence of the Swahili language and culture. The language developed at the coast from a basic Bantu structure, being enriched by the addition of many Arabic and other imported words. It has the virtues of being essentially an urban and thus sophisticated language, and a great capacity for adaptation and development. Although it is associated in some sense with that small group of coastal dwellers of mixed Arab-African descent who define themselves ethnically as WaSwahili, it is also more inclusive and provides not only a vehicle for communication but a basis for cultural assimilition for most of the urban dwellers. Other elements of a common culture—certain styles of dress, diet, the "Swahili" multi-family house, and certain values connected with Islam—allow for the possibility of town-dwellers being absorbed in to a trans-tribal, "national" society. The deliberate encouragement of the language in political life (all election meetings must legally be conducted in Swahili) and in education (as the medium of instruction in primary schools throughout the country) has been a significant aspect of development policy since Uhuru.

However, one potential basis for factional cleavage is associated with Swahili; as a broader, cultural phenomenon it is associated with the Moslem faith, and even in some minds with Arab influence. Coupled with the historical accident that formal education, usually associated with Christianity, has been more widespread amongst up-country peoples, with their consequent over-representation in the ranks of the eilte, there is a slight tendency for government personnel and others in authority to stand outside this culture and be lukewarm about its development. Although such religious-cultural-ethnic factionalism has occasionally been the basis of local political conflicts, careful tactics by Jules Nyerere and other leaders have prevented this issue becoming the basis for national cleavages when on a few occasions they could have so emerged.

In addition to its integrating function, Swahili may also contribute to some degree to the development of mass consciousness. As one Swahili scholar put it, "Tanzania is the only country in Africa where the leaders can speak to the people" (in anything but a European language translated into the vernacular). Besides the obvious organizational and mobilizational advantages, this ease of communication allows for the possibility of that control from below which is increasingly seen as an essential ingredient of the development of socialism. Moreover, the obverse of the fact that the elite is weighted towards the up-country, Christian-educated elements implies that Swahili is to a degree a "working class culture"; it keeps the man in the street in touch with political life, can give him a degree of self-confidence in dealing with the elites, who are often guilty of linguistic crudities, and offers some basis for worker consciousness.

These then are some of the given characteristics that explain why the ethnic factor has not been as central an issue in Tanzania political life as in Kenya. The very disparate and fragmented nature of the population and the basis for a national culture in Swahili are part of Tanzania's fortunate inheritance. But note should be taken also of conscious policy measures undertaken by the national movement and the independence government to avoid politics taking an ethnic form. Nyerere himself had the advantage of coming from one of the very smallest peoples, the Zanaki, and he has taken care to ensure the leadership group (the cabinet and ruling party circles) includes representatives of the major tribes, of Moslem as well as Christian, and of the non-African people. Attempts to manipulate ethnic symbols or apparent local grievances have often been dealt with severely—before independence, the head of the TANU Elders Section was dismissed for drawing attention to Moslem under-representation; appeals on a tribal, racial or religious basis were specifically outlawed when the competitive election system was introduced in 1965. Some effort has been made to promote greater educational equality by allowing the same proportion of secondary school entrants for each region, although far more needs to be done if poorer areas are to catch up. The same kind of calculations were behind a decision to divide a newly set up, self-help project pump-priming "Regional Development Fund" equally among the seventeen administrative regions.

Through these and other measures, efforts have been made by the Tanzanian leadership to capitalize on the inherited advantages bestowed by the geo-political and ethnic make-up in order to avoid major cleavages. This absence of conflict has in turn made possible a degree of organizational effectiveness of national institutions, especially the single political party TANU, although its homogeneity and its capabilities can easily be over-estimated. Another consequence is that at least the Tanzania leaders have not had to face as their central concern issues about the very legitimacy of the emerging nation-state and the continued existence of the regime. Again, advantage has been taken of this situation which made it possible to focus on the connected issues of the dangers of class formation and the working out of an alternative to a neo-colonialist development strategy. Moreover, the avoidance of a pattern where ethnic symbols become the basis for political loyalties has in turn made possible the development of a more class-based consciousness; and the use of Swahili and the existence of an unchallenged party with a truly national character provide vehicles for the further development of a socialist consciousness.

One further way in which the dampening of potential ethnic conflicts connects with the efforts to follow a socialist path, relates to the policy with regard to the immigrant races, especially the sizeable Asian community. In Tanzania, as elsewhere in East Africa, there was some latent racial animosity particularly against the Asian middlemen and shopkeepers with whom many Africans had to deal daily, and consequent pressures for some kind of Africanization of trade. However, the leadership has resisted any attempts to take over retail trade (except for a short-lived attempt to develop consumer cooperative shops in the main towns under Israeli advice), and as late as 1971 President Nyerere was stating that it was premature to nationalize this petty trading sector. More especially, the government has not succumbed to pressures to Africanize trade by measures—credit and training facilities, restrictive licensing etc.—to replace Asian traders by aspiring African small businessmen, as has been done to a significant extent in Kenya. The calculation seems to have been one of encouraging racial tolerance and allowing the Asian shopkeeper and small trader to continue to provide a reasonably cheap and efficient service for the time being. Thus avoided is the possible entrenchment of a large African petty bourgeois element—one that because it is indigenous and because of its possible political links would be a more stubborn obstacle to eventual socialization. However, measures have been taken, through the nationalization of import-export and larger scale wholesaling and of some processing industries, and by the Building Acquisition Act of 1971 which virtually abolished landlordism in urban housing, against the more privileged members of the resident bourgeoisie most of whom belong to the immigrant races. There remains, however, a continuing problem of trying to ensure that popular radicalism does not take a purely racial form which would then be manipulated for personal benefit of members of the African elite anxious to assume the opportunities for advancement in the trading sector.

A similar problem, involving the form in which aspirations of sections of the population are aggregated and articulated, can be mentioned here. While Tanzania has avoided the Kenya-type of situation where the local demand for resources is viewed as a competitive, bargaining process which reinforces ethnic politics, it is not totally immune from localist pressures on central government to obtain services. This parochial tendency is to some extent reinforced by the system of representation through the one-party election system and the elected organs of TANU itself. The result is that political processes, which in many ways have healthy democratic functions, yet foster a consciousness which is mainly parochial and concerned with placing demands on central authorities;[39] even though this it not compounded into tribal or regional competition at the national level, it inhibits the possible development of a concern with the realities of national development in the face of imperialism, and of the existing class structure.

These qualifications notwithstanding, the degree of harmony and organizational integration achieved in Tanzania is still one of its most significant characteristics and does provide something of an opening which can make a more radical policy initiative at least viable. But it is necessary to note one debilitating aspect of this situation for the prospects of socialist construction. The welding together of an unchallenged, single national movement was done through and at the expense of any clear definition of long-run development goals; all classes and strata where involved and all expected to benefit from independence. As Nyerere himself has pointed out in talking about the problems of building socialism in an ex-colonial country.

> "There was a certain price to pay for the unity that was achieved: This lack of ideological content during the independence struggle often served to maintain unity among the anticolonialist forces, or to prevent a diversion of energies into the difficult questions of socialist education . . . But it can present a serious problem in the post-independence period . . ."[40]

The Role of the Party in Tanzania

Casual observers may be tempted to see Tanzania's socialist policies as a product of a strong, united and committed party and in turn look to TANU as the disciplined, ideological instrument which can spearhead their implementation. But as the above quotation from Nyerere suggests, TANU is not that kind of party. It was a broad national front and still retains the organizational and ideological limitations associated with its origins. Although some mention of socialist aims was written into the party's constitution in 1962, the same time that Nyerere's first pronouncement on "Ujamaa" appeared, even many of the leaders remained ideo-

[39] See in this connection Hyden and Leys, *op. cit.* and John S. Saul: 'Background to the 1970 Elections' in L. Cliffe and J.S. Saul (Eds.): *Socialism in Tanzania,* Vol. I—Politics, (East African Publishing House, Nairobi, 1972).

[40] From the Introduction to Julius K. Nyerere; *op. cit.*

logically uncommitted, so that Nyerere could still complain in 1970 that there were only a handful of socialists in TANU. This lack of clarity among the party activists is of course derived from the structure and social character of the party as it emerged in the colonial period.

Compared with other nationalist parties in Africa, TANU had some rather unique features. It was first and foremost virtually unchallenged; it was indeed a "nationalist movement from which no section (of the population) is excluded." [41] For socialist tasks, this had the benefits of providing some genuine mass (i.e. both peasant and urban worker) backing, but the drawback that the more privileged were also quite at home in the party. Indeed, because the growth of this organization was in part spontaneous, the activists in the early days where those who had both the time, education, and private means independent of government employ, to allow them to get involved in politics—often the local big farmers or small traders in a district. The spontaniety of the initial growth at the local level also had another consequence on the party's character; different district organizations grew up around different issues and drew on particular social categories in the area for their leadership and their support base.

However, these different local characteristics do not mean that TANU is similar to KANU in that it is merely a loose confederal umbrella for various local political machines. One of the most significant legacies of the proto-nationalist phase was to provide TANU with a "central focus," that is a rationally based movement with a coherent central nucleus. Thus, although the first branches came into being as a result of local initiatives, they were at once looking towards the center, and in fact from 1958 onwards the national headquarters was strong enough to send out their own organizing secretaries from Dar es Salaam to the districts. It was this fact, together with the geo-ethnic features we have noted earlier which precluded the emergence of tribal blocs within the party or of local machines owing allegiance to some particular personality. Some powerful personalities did emerge but not on the basis of purely local support; thus at a later stage even when such a key figure as Oscar Kambona, the party's Secretary General from its earliest days, resigned from government, the regime had merely lost the support of an individual not of a whole region.

To stress that TANU did in fact have a national organization and was not as fragmented or as weak as the ruling parties which inherited power in Kenya or Uganda, is not to imply that it was capable of exercising a

[41] Julius K. Nyerere: 'Democracy and the Party System', (1963) reprinted in *Uhura na Umoja—Freedom and Unity,* (Oxford University Press, Dar es Salaam, 1966).

leverage over policy independent of formal government institutions.[42] Indeed, the specifically party organs were considerably weakened immediately before and after independence, in part because party activists were brought into government positions, (like those of the new, "political," regional and area commissioners created to replace the colonial provincial and district commissioners) and in part because popular involvement dropped off as ordinary supporters felt that the nationalist movement's task was accomplished.

Since that time, several structural changes have been aimed at making party institutions more of a functioning reality—both in improving its organizational effectiveness and strengthening its representative character. At the lowest level these two imperatives have gone together with the formation of party cells grouping the members (and even non-members) of each set of ten houses together under an elected leader. This grass-roots structure is given more weight as it is tied not only to a party "branch" at the next highest level but also to local development planning machinery and to local authorities. This semi-fusion of party and state bodies is in fact a feature of the administrative setup all the way from the ward through district to the region. At all these levels the main appointed administrator is also the secretary of the corresponding TANU organization. At the national level, too, there has been a considerable change; more qualified personnel have been taken on and new sections of the party have been set up in the last three or four years to deal with political education and ujamaa villages. For all this, the party is not yet an apparatus capable of generating independent policy programs nor of keeping the much more powerful government and parastatal bureaucracies up to the ideological mark. This is only in part due to sheer lack of personnel; for in trying, as one commentator put it, "to correct the administrative chaos of the party, in 1966 (Nyerere) transferred a senior, and very non-political civil servant to the Party." [43] This hardly helped the party in the more essential task of developing an ideological clarity and commitment. As some of the problems of implementing the socialist policies became more obvious, this need has been recognized by more conscious elements and the party itself has officially stated that "the time has now come for the Party to take the reins and lead all the people's ac-

[42] For further discussion of the capabilities of TANU see H. Bienen: *Tanzania—Party Transformation and Economic Development,* (Princeton University Press, Princeton, 1969), 2nd edition, and for a differing view, L. Cliffe: 'Socialist Transformation and Party Development', *Africa Political Review,* (Dar es Salaam), Vol. I, No. 1, June, 1970.

[43] R.C. Pratt: 'The Cabinet and Presidential Leadership in Tanzania, 1961–66', in Cliffe and Saul, *op. cit.*

tivities."[44] How far it does so, will depend on the extent to which it can change its own character.

Perhaps more progress has been registered in making the party an instrument for participation. A functioning system of elected party committees and conferences has been set up from the grassroots level to the National Executive Committee (N.E.C.), the main decision making body of the party, and the composition of the smaller Central Committee was made more representative in 1969. The most imaginative new departure has been the establishment of a "democratic" one party state in which the party is the umbrella for competitive elections between aspirants for seats in Parliament, local government and other offices.[45] Despite these impressive strides towards that mass participation which is recognized as essential for ensuring socialist advance, there remain limitations in terms of the interests that are represented and the consciousness that is promoted. First, not only through local party organs but through a local development front of cooperatives, development committees and local authorities, opportunities are provided for popular participation and mobilization. But in practice the very elective nature of these bodies in the context of emerging class differences at the local level, often means a clientist system grows up out of which the better-off peasants, traders and the other economic "middlemen" emerge as spokesmen. The obvious solution to such distorted patterns of representation is the development of a broader consciousness of differentiation and class solidarity to overcome the fragmented basis of local politics and to make ordinary peasants better able to defend their interests. Yet an opportunity for such political education was missed during the second elections under the one party democratic system in 1970. Although this was the occasion for mass involvement, it was largely symbolic; and certain features of the system—particularly the personal and localized nature of each contest—probably only encouraged a fragmented perspective of the political process, even though the whole election was far less manipulative than the 1969 Kenya election.

Tanzania's efforts to build socialism must ultimately depend on finding some solution to these problems of participation in a manner that will ensure that control of policy is really in the hands of the workers and peasants. That such solutions are not yet available raises two issues that we must go on to explore. First, we must see what elements in the political process provided the springs for the socialist initiatives that have been taken, if mass involvement is as yet so limited. Secondly, in examining the problem of carrying out these socialist policies, we will be up against

[44] TANU Guidelines, *op. cit.*

[45] For details of the system, see L. Cliffe: *One Party Democracy—the Tanzania General Elections, 1965,* (East African Publishing House, Nairobi, 1967).

the central contradiction of current Tanzania politics: in the absence of a strong party and/or a mobilized peasant-worker movement, implementation is in the hands of a privileged bureaucratic stratum who may objectively have least to gain from a policy of socialism and self-reliance.

Nyerere and Tanzania's Commitment to Socialism

In fact, in seeking to explain the origin of the socialist directions the influence of one man—President Julius Nyerere—is centrally important. The possibilities that Nyerere saw and pursued for a peaceful negotiated decolonization and the principled non-racialism of his position—together with a style which operates through reasoned argument wherever possible—gave him the image of a "moderate" in the pre-independence phase. But a few of his early writings and the obvious integrity of his political stance gave some indication of the possibility that "African Socialism" might have more than rhetorical significance in Tanzania. Indeed, as he has pointed out himself in a report to the party on ten years of independence, some progressive measures were taken before the fuller commitment to a socialist path following the Arusha Declaration in 1967. Land was taken under ultimate national control, cooperative marketing bodies were promoted apace, taxes made more progressive and the line was held on elite business involvement and on the grosser forms of neocolonial influence. During these years, his own clear and simple commitment to egalitarian values and his incisive reaction to the actual development trend—a distorting and unsuccessful reliance on attracting aid, the limited spread of a few major projects, and the growing self-interest of the elite—decided him on a dramatic shift in policy emphasis. Slowly maturing plans for a commission to define "Tanzania's socialism," with the danger therein of coming up with the lowest common denominator, were shelved and a couple of months of up-country campaigning against "privilege" culminated in the TANU N.E.C. being asked to endorse the Arusha Declaration.

In thus equating the major policy shift represented by the Arusha Declaration with the thinking essentially of one man, we are of course attributing to him a commanding position in the decision-making process in Tanzania. He is an executive president and head of a ruling party which does retain some independent influence. Rural development and regional administration, foreign affairs and the control of civil service personnel are all under ministers of state within his own office (although his own state house staff remains relatively limited in its scope and capability). But in addition to these formal levers of power in his own hands, his position is in practice made much stronger by the political realities of Tanzania. No other political figure has an independent political base and few of them are even known to the public. Increasingly, the cabinet is becoming a committee of the president's own choosing rather than a group of notables whose influence has to be recognized. The possibilities of over-centralization and a system of personal rule which might thus result are mitigated by his own concern to preserve some collegial character to the leadership. Cabinet does, it seems, discuss and arrive at decisions by concensus rather than by voting; committees and commissions are set up to go into problems in which there could otherwise have been personal intervention from above. But another aspect of his style of leadership makes Nyerere encourage not only sharing of power but more popular involvement—partly in the sense of his wanting to develop a tradition of decision according to "due process," a certain "socialist legality," so that it is said that he has gone along with certain constitutionally reached decisions to which he did not necessarily agree. More recently, he and other leaders have avoided interfering directly too often, in part because of a realization that certain bureaucratic and other related tendencies can best be righted by pressuring from below rather than countermanding directives from above. However, it should not be assumed that Nyerere is a completely free agent, at least up to the point where he is prepared to take the initiative. A more accurate picture of his position would first recognize that neither his position nor the whole body of his policies is likely to be directly opposed. His ability to commit the state machinery to new policies without necessarily getting prior approval from his colleagues continues to grow. In any event, he is the source of much of the new policy thinking. Beyond this, he has to recognize that the party, and even to some extent government, has enough independent leverage to propose different initiatives or at least blunt some of his own. But the chief constraints on the socialist policies whose general terms he is enunciating lie not in the possibility of their formal rejection, but in the obstacles involved in translating general policy statements into concrete action programs and in implementing them—the problems of bureaucracy.

Obstacles to Socialist Development in Tanzania

At independence, only about one tenth of the senior civil service posts were held by citizens; by 1970 localization had reached almost 90 percent and moreover the size of the service had doubled. A large set of parastatal organizations was created as a result of nationalization of industries finance and trade; the state also became involved in tourism and crop marketing. Thus, the bureaucracy is becoming sizeable, but it is also a relatively young phenomenon. Most influential are the few more highly educated members of the pre-independence period—the "Makerere" generation; some of the more able political activists of the nationalist period have also assumed prominence. For the rest, positions have been filled by young men trained in the crash program for "higher-level manpower" mounted since independence. Recruitment into the bureaucracy is almost entirely on the basis of education, and an education which for almost all but the most recent graduates was a colonial one—which leaves them alienated from the life of ordinary people in the village or factory, unhappily suspended between two cultures, and often imbued with values of authoritarianism, contempt for manual work and elitism. These attitudes are also emphasized by the objective realities of their position—a guaranteed position (due to careful manpower planning to prevent overproduction) which in turn guarantees an income and life style totally different from their compatriots. As we shall document later, this "bureaucratic bourgeoisie" is obviously well-placed, in the absence of strong party direction, of a mobilized population, or of a cadre of strong and clear political leaders, to have a defining influence over the detailed programs whose working out and implementation is of necessity left to them. Moreover, their cultural stance and their own aspirations—even though their privileges have been curbed to a level much lower than those of neighboring elites—are hardly likely to make them enthusiastic implementors of a revolutionary policy. In order to see how central the issue of the bureaucracy is, it is necessary now to explore more fully the content of Tanzania's development strategy. The Arusha Declaration and the related policy statements do in fact add up to an explicit and coherent "strategy" —that is a statement of commitment to socialist values together with the broad outline of sets of policies designed to achieve these goals, these long-run action programs being in turn based on an analysis of Tanzania's realities. The Declaration itself, and even more so the TANU Guidelines (*Mwongozo*) which were promulgated in February 1971 in the wake of the invasion of Guinea and the Uganda coup, show an increasing concern with the privileges and inequalities associated with a process of internal class formation and see the country's dependence on the international capitalist system as the crucial obstacle to the development of a classless society, or indeed to any development.

The immediate move which followed was the nationalization of the almost entirely foreign-owned, industrial, financial and commercial companies and the sisal estates which constituted the "commanding heights of the economy." This immediately had the effect of halving that proportion of the country's "surplus" which was being extracted, making available for investment an annual sum far in excess of the levels of foreign public investment. But more crucial than the actual takeover—of an industrial base which scarcely existed—was the decision that state enterprise rather than the whim or profit prospects of foreign investors would set the direction for future industrial development. The task of defining an alternative industrial strategy and of working out appropriate employment, investment, and pricing policies for the nationalized enterprises, and the necessary forms of organizational control which can indeed ensure that both the national interest and the aspirations of the workers are served—these are tasks whose importance is recognized but still await solution. But not only are such detailed proposals held up, the actual programs of development followed by parastatal officials, almost invariably involving foreign private enterprise, often inhibit their working out.

The Declaration also had implications for the predominant rural sector of the economy. Self-reliance meant in fact a greater emphasis on rural development (through a broad-based mobilization of the energies of the people and not capital intensive settlement schemes) as a means of economic advancement not dependent on scarce foreign capital. At the same time such a self-reliant initiative could no longer be on the basis solely of production of a few food and industrial crops for the international capitalist market—on relative terms always moving to the country's disadvantage. President Nyerere later followed up the socialist implications of the rural emphasis in his policy statement "Socialism & Rural Development." He proposed that peasant energies should be mobilized through the creation of "ujamaa communities," cooperative villages in which "people would live and work together for the benefit of all." This pattern—as compared to Kenya's strategy of trying to institutionalize and activate an improved, individualistic peasant mode of production—was put forward as the only alternative to a process whereby technical innovation and economic expansion were leading to a process of class formation in the rural areas. Since the program has gotten underway, there has been an imrepressive response on the part of many peasants, especially in the poorer but less crowded areas; at the end of 1971 it was estimated that almost 10 percent of the rural population had, provisionally at least, grouped themselves into two thousand embryonic ujamaa villages. Again the inappropriate cultural outlook of bureaucrats has blunted some of the logic of this rural strategy and strenuous efforts had to be made by the president to stress that the program is to be based on "persuasion not force." There is also something of a "formalized" definition of an ujamaa group, and an emphasis on "villagization" rather than on changing the relationships of production. In this area, too, one of the most severe limitations of the party is manifest not just in the unavailability of any rural cadres on the necessary scale and with the necessary sensitivity to the ujamaa policy, but also in the social character of TANU's local units. These are often dominated by richer peasants and small traders who can be expected to drag their feet or distort the ujamaa program to their own benefit, if not directly circumvent it.

The TANU leadership was aware of the general problem of elite entrenchment and of the specific need to change the style and character of the bureaucratic stratum in order that it be an effective instrument for implementing socialist policies. Education was seen as a key weapon in this strategy of elite transformation, and in fact this was the first area of policy in which Nyerere elaborated further the implications of Arusha. His policy proposals on "Education for Self Reliance" were destined to attack the basic problem of the "elite" character of the inherited educational system. Specifically, there was a fundamental change in the approach to primary education through a recognition of the fact that for almost 90 percent of school children the primary school was no longer either a preparation for further schooling nor for a clerical or other paid job. It must therefore fulfill its responsibility to the majority and provide them with a useful grounding for the life that would in fact face them—making their own living, hopefully in Ujamaa communities, in the rural areas. The specific changes are thus designed to link formal education with the basic production processes, especially agriculture, and provide the appropriate technical and literary skills and an orientation toward, not away from rural life.

At higher levels the problem is somewhat different. A carefully planned expansion of secondary and further education to match actual manpower needs means that once a student has gained entry he has by definition become a prospective member of this "elite." The aim then becomes one of producing a new generation of government and parastatal officials, meeting the urgent demands for qualified personnel, and understanding the country's problems and the historical imperative for a new direction in development: this requires an elite not dedicated to its own self-interest. To this end, political education has been introduced at all levels including the university, the emphasis of the syllabus in other subjects has been modified, agriculture is just being introduced into the secondary schools, some productive work is now part of the school timetable and generally greater involvement with the society at large is sought. Such changes, requiring a totally different outlook on the part of teachers and administrators brought up in the colonial cultural environment, does not occur without some struggle. The president has in fact talked about a "cultural revolution," and students in schools and the university are beginning to challenge the old educational establishment, but are meeting with resistance.

The development of a new political culture among the next generation is only one of several political tactics designed to make possible the new development path. Political education directed towards existing party and government leaders has become an established fact of life since Arusha. With the declaration of the TANU Guidelines, the central importance of programs to develop a political consciousness has been further stressed. One of the immediate provisions of the Arusha Declaration was for "leadership conditions" which in effect prohibited any party or other public official from having any business interests. Despite some blunting of the actual regulations at the edges, this provision will effectively seal off the possibility of the elite becoming a "class" in the classical, property-owning (and thus self-perpetuating) sense. But the Arusha Declaration also realized that however the elite was restricted in its self-interest and remolded by political education, the only long-run guarantee of development benefitting the workers and peasants was for these classes to have effective power.

The Declaration recognized the need for TANU to become a "party of workers and peasants" and the Guidelines have taken the logic further by calling for a whole new style of work in all political and economic institutions to curb "commandism" and to make a reality of involving people in the running of organizations and in the solution of their own problems. There has also been a growing realization that the party is the one institution which not only can provide the means for such involvement but must also provide the ideological direction and control over other institutions whose commitment to socialist values cannot be assumed. Some of the resulting discussion has been phrased in conventional terms of the need for a "vanguard," but the challenge which faces TANU is how to combine some capability to provide a socialist lead with a continuing mass involvement. And here one comes up against one of the most intractable problems of Tanzania's future development: the contradiction between the clear necessity for a change in the role of the party to guarantee further socialist advance, and the present mixed social character of the party, itself susceptible to those bureaucratic and petty bourgeois interests that can impede such development.

Conclusions

It was earlier suggested that Kenya and Tanzania faced similar problems of "neo-colonial underdevelopment." In both cases, local capital is not able, and foreign capital is not willing, to transform their weak crop exporting economies, and the political elites are not prepared, and the masses are not mobilized to change the inherited social and economic structures. Kenya, despite the added aggravation of European settlement and the violent rebellion against it, was not able to sustain an assault on the system. The enforced isolation of the peasant revolt and its localized nature, together with successful colonial reformist tactics to change the balance of class forces by land reform and to foster a more amenable generation of political leaders, probably are the major factors explaining why it was that the "nationalism stops short, falters and dies away on the day that independence is proclaimed."[46] As economic growth is unlikely to be sustained on the present strategy, and as social injustice and deprivation are escalating, new contradictions are emerging. These will take time to mature, however, and the potential for change that they contain will not be realized without new departures in ideology and political organization.

The leadership in Tanzania woke up to the dangers of such trends and has offered a rational blueprint for an alternative development strategy. This new plan could economically reduce foreign domination and reliance and allow for a more productive use of the surplus; politically it aims to reorient the elite to serve the masses of the people and at the same time subject them to control from below, with the party playing the crucial educative and guiding role. Certain characteristics of Tanzania's social structure and of its political life did allow a sufficient opening for such a policy initiative by a committed and clear-sighted leadership. Some success has been achieved in implementing this program—notably in limiting the role of foreign capital, forcing some changes in income structure and consumption on the privileged, with the result that national investment, largely self-financed, has reached about 25 percent of GNP. But some of the difficulties of pushing through such a strategy in the absence of a well-organized and ideologically clear revolutionary movement or of a strong goundswell of popular social forces are becoming apparent. We have in fact seen how the bureaucracy drags its feet and even distorts policies; and there are some signs of growing unease among the ranks of the elite at income and tax squeezes and at efforts to challenge their authoritarian bureaucratic style. Though recognized, the need for a change in the character, structure and role of the party cannot occur spontaneously or without resistance. The small size of the urban working class, plus the largely indirect form of exploitation of the peasantry by adverse world prices working at a distance and a residue of localism in their consciousness, means there are few readily available political forces to support a sustained revolutionary trend—even though political education was stepped up to support the 1971 policy to develop a people's militia. There are some indications of a growing radicalism among an active minority of the educated youth, and some factory workers' committees and

[46] Fanon, *op. cit.*, p. 163.

ujamaa committees are beginning to flex the verbal muscle given to them by the new Guidelines. However, whether these forces will be given time and opportunity to emerge to the point of real effectiveness against bureaucratic inertia and strength is a crucial issue in assessing future prospects for socialist advance in Tanzania. This question becomes infinitely more vital when one recognizes that Tanzania's embryonic radical forces have ultimately to contend not only with their own elite but with that whole array of international forces that is termed imperialism. It was probably the very insignificance of Tanzania to international monopoly capital that allowed for the process of nationalization with so little direct reaction. Foreign interests have, however, fought a significant rear guard action over compensation conditions, parastatal management contracts, terms of future partnership with state enterprise and prices of Tanzania exports. They have thus to retain considerable influence over the economy. In this connection, the business orthodoxy of the bureaucracy in the parastatal organizations, the absence of a clear long-run industrial strategy outlining future priorities, and the hook-up with the East African Community and thus with the corporations dominant in the other two economies, greatly reduce Tanzania's ability to resist these outside pressures. And to the extent that Tanzania does succeed in developing its own productive capacity and limiting its involvement in the international economy, more overt political pressures can be expected—especially as Tanzania, because of its geography as well as its commitment, plays such a leading role in the liberation struggle in Southern Africa. Indeed, there have already been minor acts of sabotage, foreign-encouraged subversion, border incidents and incursions by the Portuguese and by a South African-backed Malawi. This situation of being bounded on the south by hostile white racist regimes; unsympathetic, and even (as with Uganda after the 1971 coup) potentially hostile, neo-colonies to the north present a further economic threat. A country as poor and small as Tanzania cannot hope to build up a separate industrial base, to create "socialism in one country." Thus the brave attempts being made in Tanzania to build self-reliance and socialism can only be partial. Their success will depend in large measure on the struggle for liberation from imperialism that is going on in the white-dominated South, in the neo-colonial states of independent Africa, and in fact throughout the world.

Zambia

THE POLITICAL ECONOMY OF ZAMBIA

by

Dennis Dresang

Introduction

The tasks that must be accomplished by the leadership in Zambia, as in most new states, comprise an extraordinarily heavy burden. At the same time, a new political order and national identity must be established, expectations for significant improvement in living standards must be satisfied, and the remnants of external control must be severed. Zambia does not have the option of meeting these challenges sequentially or incrementally, as was done in most Western countries.[1] All of these goals are of equal and immediate urgency. Their solutions are also interdependent and ideally the efforts to solve these problems would bring balanced success. More likely, the pattern will be unbalanced and emphasize stability rather than development. The specific characteristics of the challenges confronting Zambia's leaders and the way in which those problems are being handled provides a useful focus for this discussion.

National identity

The direct antecedent of the present state of Zambia is the colonial territory of Northern Rhodesia. Colonial rule was imposed over this area by Cecil Rhodes's British South Africa Company. This company held a charter with the British government that provided it British protection from the threats of other commercial firms and foreign countries and in return it was to act as an agent of the British government. Thus, although the British South Africa Company was fundamentally a business organization interested in making a profit, it was also charged with the responsibility of governing.

[1] Lucien Pye, *Aspects of Political Development* (Boston: Little, Brown and Company, 1966), pp. 62–67.

Much to the dismay of the stockholders, the tasks of governance north of the Zambezi consumed more energy and resources than did the tasks of economic exploitation. The absence of significant economic activity during the first years of colonial rule was not so much due to the belligerence and active resistance of the Africans indigenous to the area as it was to the early assessment that there were few, if any, sources of wealth and that the area was not healthy for whites.

Despite the fact that the company came to an early conclusion that little revenue was likely to accrue from operations north of the Zambezi, the charter obtained from the British government committed the company to establish and maintain an administrative presence in the area. Furthermore, Cecil Rhodes saw Northern Rhodesia as strategic to his goal of constructing a surface transportation route through British-held territories from the Cape of Good Hope to Cairo. With these considerations in mind, the Company made plans to establish a minimal and inexpensive administrative presence in the area and to concentrate investment for development in the territory to the south where profits were more certain.[2]

Initially Northern Rhodesia was administered as two separate entities, North-Western Rhodesia and North-Eastern Rhodesia. Because of the varying patterns of European competition for the control of Central Africa, the British government had to grant two different charters to the B.S.A. Company for North-Western Rhodesia and for North-Eastern Rhodesia and Nyasaland. At the time, separate administrations also made sense because of the routes for communications. The North-West was reached by travelling through or to the west of Bulawayo, while the North-East was approached by the Shire and the Zambezi Rivers.

The company began its administration over North-Western Rhodesia in 1897, when R. T. Coryndon crossed the Zambezi with a secretary and a police force of five men and established a headquarters at Mongu. By the end of 1899 there were stations at Mongu, Sesheke, Kazungula, Kalomo, Monze and Victoria Falls and the headquarters was moved to Kalomo, which was more centrally located than Mongu.

[2] For accounts of the British South Africa Company rule over Northern Rhodesia, see: Michael Gelfand, *Northern Rhodesia in the Days of the Charter: A Medical and Social Study. 1878–1924* (Oxford: Basil Blackwell and Mott, Ltd., 1961); L. H. Gann, *The Birth of a Plural Society: The Development of Northern Rhodesia Under the British South Africa Company, 1894–1914* (Manchester: Manchester University Press, 1958); L. H. Gann, *A History of Northern Rhodesia: Early Days to 1953* (London: Chatto and Windus, 1964); Richard Hall, *Zambia* (New York: Praeger, 1965); A. J. Hanna, *The Beginnings of Nyasaland and North-Eastern Rhodesia 1859–1895* (Oxford: Oxford University Press, 1956); and A. J. Wills, *An Introduction to the History of Central Africa,* 2nd ed. (Oxford: Oxford University Press, 1967).

North-Eastern Rhodesia, under an agreement reached by the British government and the British South Africa Company in 1891, was under the administrative control of Her Majesty's Commissioner for Nyasaland, Harry Johnston, but was to be developed and exploited by the B.S.A. Company. In 1891, the only administrative presence in North-Eastern Rhodesia was a station at Chiengi near Lake Mweru and occasional court sessions at Fife, Fwambo and Abercorn near the Tanganyika border. By 1900 there were stations at Fort Rosebery, Kazembo and Kalungwishi.

The tasks of establishing colonial rule over the two territories varied considerably. In the North-West, the B.S.A. Company acquired mineral and administrative rights over most of the area by concluding a treaty with the Litunga of the Barotse Kingdom. The other societies in the territory were small and fragmented. The commencement of colonialism here did not require military operations.

In North-Eastern Rhodesia, however, there was inter-tribal warfare and Arab slave-trading that the Company was committed to end by the terms of its charter, and had to end before peaceful rule and economic exploitation could take place.[3] Treaties had not been concluded with the Bemba and the Ngoni, both of which were in a position to resist the imposition of company rule and cause the company to bear heavy military expenditures. The Bemba had benefited from an alliance with the Arab slave-traders and became militarily powerful. The alliance, however, did not include united resistance to European rule. Company expeditions succeeded in expelling Arab slave-traders from the area and the Bemba then submitted in a piecemeal fashion, some after conflict and some through agreement, to company rule.[4] The Ngoni were the last people in this part of Africa to present armed resistance to the establishment of colonial rule. It was only after several bloody battles in 1897 and 1898 that Chief Mpezeni finally surrendered and the Ngoni were subjected.[5]

In 1911, the two territories were amalgamated into one administrative unit, Northern Rhodesia. This was done in an effort to cut administrative expenditures. At the time of amalgamation, for instance, the two territories had a combined annual income of £95,000 and combined expenses of £149,000. The deficit had to be covered from profits made elsewhere by the Company, and this caused discontent among the shareholders. Another reason for the amalgamation was that the B.S.A. Company-financed railroad that extended north from the Cape of Good Hope through the center of South Africa and Southern Rhodesia was continued

[3] L. H. Gann, *A History of Northern Rhodesia,* pp. 22–24, 91 and 92.

[4] *Ibid.,* pp. 83–85.

[5] J. A. Barnes, *Politics in a Changing Society: The Fort Jameson Ngoni* (Oxford: Oxford University Press, 1954).

across the Zambezi and through Northern Rhodesia. The railroad reached the Congo border in 1909. With the railroad completed, the accessibility factor that was part of the rationale for separate administrations was no longer important.

The amalgamation of the two territories did not result in a surplus of income over expenditure. Between 1914 and 1924 the company had to absorb losses averaging £130,000 a year, and by 1924 company operations in Northern Rhodesia had accumulated a deficit of £1.5 million.[6] Faced with these costs and without any immediate prospect of a favorable alteration in the situation, the company understandably sought to rid itself of administrative responsibility for Northern Rhodesia.

The white settlers in the territory were also anxious to see company rule come to an end. Shortly after World War I, the company made plans to levy an income tax on the settlers. This prompted the settlers to petition the company and the British government to reform the system of administrative rule in Northern Rhodesia so that taxpayers could be certain their money was being used with care and discretion and was not being collected in order to secure a big profit margin for a commercial company.[7]

Negotiations between the company and the British government began in 1921 and culminated in the Northern Rhodesia Order in Council of 1924. According to the agreement, the territory was declared a British protectorate and a crown colony form of government was established to administer it. The company did not go uncompensated for its role in pacifying and administering Northern Rhodesia. The Order in Council provided that the company would receive one-half of all net revenue resulting from the sale of lands in what had been North-Western Rhodesia and would retain mineral rights in the territory forever.[8]

The British government received from the British South Africa Company a territory with arbitrary and artificial boundaries. Northern Rhodesia included widely different and disparate societies and cultures. There was no common sense of identity that was held by the inhabitants of

[6] Northern Rhodesia, Legislative Council, *Legislative Council Debates,* Third Session, Sixth Council, May 25, 1939. (This figure does not include any part of the Company's commercial activities nor the receipts from the Victoria Falls Concession.)

[7] Kenneth Bradley, "Company Days: The Rule of the British South Africa Company in Northern Rhodesia," *Northern Rhodesia Journal* V (1961): 446–452; and Wills, *History of Central Africa,* pp. 241–249.

[8] The end of "forever" was October 24, 1964. For an account of how the new Republic of Zambia ended the Company's mineral rights see Hall, *Zambia,* pp. 230–234.

Northern Rhodesia, and colonial administrators were not concerned about establishing one. Throughout company and colonial office rule, the goals of those in positions of formal authority were to maintain law and order and to support the economic activities and the missionary work of Europeans in Northern Rhodesia. Africans were considered very much like the soil, rivers, climate and other natural resources of the area. They were given features of the environment and presented both problems and opportunities for accomplishing the tasks of imperial rule. No effort was made to integrate the various communities indigenous to the territory into a single, cohesive society, and thus the leaders of Zambia, like the British government, assumed governance over a largely fragmented and artificial state.

The economic motivations of colonialism not only failed to make colonial officials concerned about establishing a congruence between national loyalties and state boundaries, but these motivations led to the introduction of alien communities into the territory. The single most important cause for the presence of Europeans in Northern Rhodesia, and Zambia, is the development of the copper mining industry. Two breakthroughs in 1923 made it possible for Northern Rhodesia to rise from being one of the poorest territories in the British empire to one of the wealthiest. One breakthrough was the discovery by mining engineers of rich sulfide ores one hundred feet below the surface in the area near the Katanga border. The other was a technological breakthrough, in which the "flotation method" of concentration was developed for the exploitation of sulfides.[9] Coincident to these events, the world demand for copper was significantly increased because of growth in the automotive, electrical, and light industries.

Relieved of its administrative responsibilities, the B.S.A. Company was able to concentrate its capital and its energies on taking advantage of this opportunity. It revised its concession policy which had limited the size of economic enterprises, and began to encourage the activities of large, powerful organizations on what became known as the Copperbelt. By 1929, the various mining companies merged into two strong groups. The

[9] For general historical surveys of copper mining in Zambia, see Kenneth Bradley, *Copper Venture* (Ndola: Selection Trust Ltd., 1953); Sir R. L. Prain, "The Copperbelt of Northern Rhodesia," *Journal of the Royal Society of Arts* (February, 1955): 196–216; L. H. Gann, "The Northern Rhodesian Copper Industry and the World of Copper: 1923–1952," *Rhodes-Livingstone Journal* 18 (1955): 1–18; and, for a detailed analysis see Robert E. Baldwin, *Economic Development and Export Growth: A Study of Northern Rhodesia, 1920–1960* (Berkeley: University of California Press, 1966).

Rhodesia Anglo-American Corporation controlled the operations at Nkana, Bwana Mkubwa and Nchanga. The Rhodesia Selection Trust controlled Roan Antelope and Mufulira.

The policy of the colonial administration toward the development of the mining industry was to give it the latitude and the assistance it needed to work the mines most profitably. Due to the shortage of government capital, the companies had to provide their own infrastructural and social facilities. Government approval was given for the establishment of American-styled "company towns" on the Copperbelt. More active governmental assistance was given in the recruitment of inexpensive African labor and of European workers with the necessary mining skills.

With the growth of copper mining, individuals from Europe and southern Africa were attracted to Zambia both for working in the mines themselves and for providing supporting goods and services. In 1928 and 1929, the colonial administration and the mining companies publicized the opportunities available for commercial farmers in Northern Rhodesia. Land policies were adopted assuring Europeans of the most favorable land.[10] A loan program was introduced to help finance the improvement of farming facilities and an agricultural research station was opened.

When African farmers increased their production of maize, cattle and other commodities and threatened the competitive position of European farmers, the government regulated the market in order to maintain a favored position for Europeans. The establishment of the Maize Control Board in 1936 illustrates the relevant forces at work. In 1930, Africans sold about 30,000 bags of maize. Responding to the increased incentives of the expanding Copperbelt markets, African farmers sold 100,000 bags in 1935. This increase was accomplished without government encouragement or assistance. During the same period, European production rose from 168,000 to 211,000.[11] Increased African production did not concern European farmers as long as the demand for maize exceeded the supply, but with the slump that began in the copper industry in 1932 because of the world depression, European farmers began to fear that African competition would be economically disastrous for them. This sentiment found support in the government,[12] and in 1936 the Maize Control Board was established. The board was given the power to purchase and sell all maize

[10] Gann, *A History of Northern Rhodesia,* pp. 213–214.

[11] Northern Rhodesia, Department of Agriculture, *Report of the Maize Sub-Committee of the Northern Rhodesia Agricultural Advisory Board* (Lusaka: Government Printer, 1950), paragraph 72.

[12] See, for instance, Northern Rhodesia, Department of Agriculture, *Annual Report for the Year 1931* (Lusaka: Government Printer, 1932): 16.

at fixed prices. It set a domestic price which was above that on the world market and allocated one-quarter of the domestic needs to African producers and three-quarters to Europeans. If one group did not fill its quota, the other could do so. Any excess production was sold on the world market. In his discussion of the Maize Control Board, Robert Baldwin points out:

> The measure was a typical device for price stabilization under conditions of a declining market. Like all such measures, it penalized those producers whose market share was expanding. The Northern Rhodesia copper companies were in a similar position with respect to the international copper cartel. Unlike African farmers, however, the copper companies could (and did) refuse to accept their allotted quota.[13]

Given this kind of support and the existence of economic opportunities, European population in Northern Rhodesia grew rapidly. In 1904, there were only 850 Europeans in the territory. This grew to 3,634 in 1921 and then jumped to 13,846 in 1931. After a slight decline during the Depression, the number increased steadily to 53,000 in 1954 and to almost 70,000 in 1964, at the time of independence. Very few of these ever identified themselves as citizens of Northern Rhodesia/Zambia and virtually all maintained a distinct cultural identity as Europeans.

Asians, too, were attracted to Northern Rhodesia. Almost all migrated from South Africa and Southern Rhodesia and established themselves as small businessmen and retail traders. Although the Asian community in Zambia is not as large as the one in East Africa (there were only about ten thousand Asians in Zambia in 1966), they were important because of their predominance in business positions in the economy. Asians did not farm, were not employed in the mines, and were not admitted into the civil service. They were traders and, to a smaller extent, professionals. Like Europeans, Asians maintained a distinct cultural identity and few became citizens.

In sum, at the time of independence, October 24, 1964, Zambia consisted of a number of culturally and ethnically distinct groups who were not tied together by a common national loyalty. Europeans and Asians could, and did, identify other countries, thousands of miles from Zambian borders, as their homes. Africans were divided by different languages, historical traditions and styles of living. The struggle for independence was the first significant effort to unify these disparate groups and the importance of the current slogan, "One Zambia, One Nation," reflects

[13] Baldwin, *Economic Development,* p. 152.

the continued desire to establish a strong and viable national identity and national loyalty.

Political process

Whereas the legacy of colonialism is the major reason for the absence of national integration in Zambia, the struggle for independence has had the effect of disrupting former political processes and of requiring the establishment of new rules of the game. The nationalist movement was fundamentally a demand for the political independence of Northern Rhodesia/Zambia. As such, the major targets of the movement were the institutions and the procedures of the colonial government. The leaders of the struggle for independence attacked the legitimacy of the way in which individuals were recruited to positions of authority, the manner in which policies were formulated and administered, and the fundamental goal of white domination over the indigenous population that pervaded the whole colonial political system. In that the nationalist movement was successful in destroying the structure and dynamics of the existing political order, it made necessary the establishment and acceptance of new institutions and procedures.

The essence of a colonial society is that an alien, culturally distinct minority has established itself in a position of political, economic and social predominance. The resources of political power, economic wealth and social prestige are all the property of this ruling minority. Control over and access to these resources are jealously guarded by the group in power for fear that the possession of one resource may lead to its use in securing the others and thus challenge the existing order. The political ability to allocate public funds, for instance, can be exercised in a way to redistribute societal wealth in order to advantage the group with a predominance of political power. The Maize Control Board represented an instance in which Europeans used their political power to preserve their economic position. Similarly, Africans were kept from attaining high levels of education, earning high salaries, exercising significant authority, and becoming accepted or assimilated into European society.[14]

Kenneth D. Kaunda, who became the first president of Zambia, related an experience he had which dramatically illustrates the elitism and distinctness that the European community tried to maintain. He once went to the District Commissioner of Broken Hill with a small request. When he was shown inside the D.C.'s office, he said "Good morning," in English.

[14] Leo Kuper and M. G. Smith, eds., *Pluralism in Africa* (Berkeley: University of California Press, 1969); J. S. Furnivall, *Colonial Policy and Practice* (London: Cambridge University Press, 1948).

> The D.C. turned to the head clerk and said: "Tell this man in Bemba to say, 'Good morning, Sir.' " Throughout that interview the D.C. insisted on his head clerk interpreting everything he said into Bemba while I spoke in English.[15]

In large part, the nationalist movement was built on the particularistic and general grievances Africans felt from being subjugated in such a comprehensive manner in their own country. There were both idealistic and very practical reasons for wanting to destroy the colonial order.

The event that precipitated the struggle for independence was the creation of the Federation of Rhodesia and Nyasaland. The Federation was not introduced until 1954, although the idea of a close union between Northern and Southern Rhodesia had been considered for almost three decades. Previous moves to amalgamate or federate the two Rhodesias had failed primarily because of two sets of conflicting interests.[16] While the white settlers in Northern Rhodesia were anxious to have the degree of independence from the British government enjoyed by the Southern Rhodesians and were willing to recognize their economic and cultural ties to the south, they were not willing to share the revenue earned from copper mining. Whites in Southern Rhodesia, on the other hand, welcomed the increase in funds that would accrue from a federal arrangement, but were not willing to sacrifice the self-government status that Southern Rhodesia enjoyed within the British Empire. If a federation meant that the colonial office would exert more than the perfunctory supervision than it had over Southern Rhodesia, it would have been unacceptable to whites in that colony.

The advent of independence after World War II in British colonies in Asia and West Africa brought the white settlers together on the need for federation. Europeans in Northern Rhodesia and Nyasaland were in the most vulnerable position because of their smaller numbers and because of the presence of meaningful colonial office rule. It was much more likely that they would follow the pattern of Ghana and Nigeria than was the case for Southern Rhodesia. Thus, the disadvantages to the Northern Rhodesia whites of sharing copper revenue were considered less costly than the possibility of African majority rule. The primary goal of the Federation was to make secure white domination in central Africa and

[15] Kenneth D. Kaunda, *Zambia Shall Be Free* (London: Heinemann, 1962), p. 17.

[16] For discussions of the Federation of Rhodesia and Nyasaland, see: Patrick Keatley, *The Politics of Partnership* (Baltimore: Penguin, 1963); eds., Colin Leys and Cranford Pratt, *A New Deal in Central Africa* (New York: Praeger, 1960); T. R. M. Creighton, *Anatomy of Partnership* (London: Faber and Faber, 1960); and Robert I. Rotberg, *The Rise of Nationalism in Central Africa* (Cambridge: Harvard University Press, 1965).

to attain dominion status within the Commonwealth. This would have placed the Federation in a position similar to South Africa, before her severence of Commonwealth membership. The provisions of the Federation preserved Southern Rhodesia's special status and made the federal government essentially responsible for matters affecting the European communities and the three territorial governments responsible for African affairs.

The Federation was established over opposition voiced by Africans. Although justification for the Federation publicly emphasized the economic advantages, Africans perceived that the primary motive was to make white rule secure and permanent. It was this opposition that sparked the inauguration of the struggle for independence in what was to become Zambia and Malawi.

The first organized opposition by Northern Rhodesia Africans to the settlers' agitation for self-government and closer association with Southern Rhodesia was the Federation of African Societies. This was a body that brought together a number of African welfare societies, farmers' organizations, shop assistants' associations and the like. The formation of the Federation of African Societies took place on May 18, 1946 under the leadership of Dauti Yamba, a schoolmaster, and George Kaluwa, a trader and farmer in Mazabuka.[17] For the most part, the activities of this organization consisted of formulating resolutions and communicating them as representing the collective will of Africans in Northern Rhodesia to the governor. These tactics were not effective and the anxiety stirred by their failure prompted the establishment of the African National Congress in August, 1951.

Harry Nkumbula, who remained president of the African National Congress (ANC) until it was outlawed when Zambia became a one-party state, was elected as the leader of the new organization. Nkumbula was widely respected for his efforts to secure rights for Africans in Northern Rhodesia and was considered to be the most forceful and courageous leader available for the fight against the establishment of the Federation of Rhodesia and Nyasaland. Nkumbula was not satisfied with just forwarding resolutions to the governor. He extended the organization of the ANC from its base of African societies and solicited widespread individual support. The major accomplishment of ANC leadership prior to the establishment of the Federation was that they were able to make a credible claim for representing African opinion. However, little was done other than expanding ANC membership and articulating African opposi-

[17] Mulford, *Zambia,* pp. 13–17.

tion to the Federation. No working relationship was established with the African trade union movement. No strikes, boycotts, demonstrations or any other activity to disrupt social and economic life were seriously attempted. When the Federation was established, ANC and the movement it represented became demoralized and disenchanted with the tactics and approaches that had been used.

At the 1953 conference of ANC, a group of militant leaders were elected for the positions below the presidency. One of these militants was Kenneth D. Kaunda, who was elected secretary-general. In the first years of the Federation, ANC began organizing activity designed to dramatize African discontent and to disrupt normal activities in Northern Rhodesia. A close and cooperative relationship was established with the unions on the Copperbelt. In 1956 "rolling strikes" were organized, i.e., just as a strike at one mine ended, another was started somewhere else. Africans were encouraged to break certain laws and to disregard the authority of district officers and other colonial officials in the interest of attaining independence. Europeans became alarmed at these developments and in 1957 began working in earnest to sever all ties with the colonial office and secure dominion status for the Federation.[18]

Part of the impact of the nationalist movement was that it assaulted the legitimacy of white rule over the African majority and sought to undermine the political institutions and processes of colonialism. This necessitated new symbols and new rules of the game for the post-colonial political system. The split that occurred in the nationalist movement had an important effect on the nature of the symbols and rules that were created. The split made it quite clear that African unity could not be taken for granted. The willingness of one element of the nationalist movement to collaborate with the European settlers contributed to a belief in the post-colonial period that any opposition is a serious threat because it might invite external involvement in domestic politics.

The division in the nationalist movement grew out of the frustration at failing to prevent the formation of the Federation and a disagreement over how much militancy was required to attain the goal of African independence. According to David Mulford, the difference in the leadership styles of Harry Nkumbula and Kenneth Kaunda became dramatically evident after they both emerged from their first prison experiences. They were both imprisoned in January, 1955, for possessing copies of a banned publication, *Africa and the Colonial World*. After serving two months at hard labor, Kaunda resumed his political activity with increased fervor

[18] *Ibid.*, pp. 36–55.

and dedication, whereas Nkumbula emerged as an unenthusiastic and moderate nationalist.[19] In their speeches to the 1956 annual conference of ANC, Nkumbula defended a pledge which he had made to co-operate with the colonial authorities and Kaunda argued that militant action was urgently needed to thwart the federal government's goal to achieve dominion status by 1960.

By 1958, the tension between Nkumbula and the militant members of ANC was very severe. Nkumbula felt that his position was threatened and dismissed a number of district and branch officials who opposed his moderate posture. Nkumbula even supplied information to the police about the financial affairs of certain branches within the party and about the activities of some ANC officers. Militants were unable to unlodge Nkumbula from his position as President of ANC and felt too constrained by his leadership, and so in October, 1958, Kaunda, Simon Kapwepwe, Munu Kayambwa Sipalo, and others formed another political party, the Zambia African National Congress (ZANC). ZANC was successful in securing the support of local ANC organizations in Luapula and Northern Provines, areas on the Copperbelt, and some of the leaders in the Eastern and Central Provinces. ANC retained its strongest support in the Southern Province.[20]

The first issue that demonstrated the different approaches taken by ANC and ZANC involved participation in territorial elections held in 1959. ZANC boycotted the elections, claiming that the definition of the electorate and constituencies was so designed as to preserve white rule. ANC, however, participated in the elections. Colonial officials were disturbed by ZANC's success in persuading large numbers of Africans to boycott the election and feared a spread of the violence accompanying the independence struggle in neighboring Nyasaland to Northern Rhodesia, and so ZANC was banned on March 11, 1959. The leaders of the party were rusticated[21] to remote areas of the territory the following day. ANC, which had been cooperative and was not considered a likely vehicle for the spread of violence, was not included in these restrictions.

The present ruling party in Zambia, the United National Independence Party (UNIP), was formed while the ZANC leadership was in rustication. A major purpose in forming UNIP was to unify all elements of the nationalist movement. ANC continued to splinter after the division between Kaunda and Nkumbula and the party continued to weaken under Nkumbula's moderate leadership. When UNIP was established, it consisted of

[19] *Ibid.*, p. 62.

[20] *Ibid.*, p. 69.

[21] Rustication is a type of imprisonment in which the individual is confined to a certain geographic area, rather than put in a prison building.

a number of groups that had severed their ties with Nkumbula and of the supporters of ZANC, which continued to be banned. Nkumbula did not join the new movement and maintained ANC as a separate entity. In January, 1960, after Kaunda, Sipalo and Kapwepwe had been released, they assumed the same leadership positions in UNIP that they had held in ZANC.

Two tasks occupied the attention of UNIP from January, 1960 until Independence was attained in October, 1964. One was the campaign to win as many adherents to UNIP as possible and the other was the struggle to secure the secession of Northern Rhodesia from the Federation and then the independence of an African-ruled Zambia. These goals were related and their attainment depended on developments outside as well as inside Northern Rhodesia/Zambia. As UNIP came ever closer to accomplishing these tasks, ANC and the white settlers felt increasingly threatened and desperate. In implicit and explicit ways, ANC and the United Federal Party (UFP), representing the white settlers, worked together and formed an alliance. The willingness of ANC to enter such an alliance during a period when critical decisions were being made regarding the freedom of Africans in Central Africa incurred a wrath and distrust for ANC that has continued to this day.

When Kaunda assumed leadership of UNIP in January, 1960, he launched a serious effort to acquire mass support for the party. People throughout Northern Rhodesia, in rural as well as urban areas, were contacted and encouraged to join the party. The models Kaunda followed in this recruitment campaign were the Labour Party in England and the Convention People's Party in Ghana. As was the case with the latter, party membership was considered a total and almost religious kind of commitment. The rolls of UNIP supporters grew rapidly in all parts of the country except the Southern Province, which maintained its support for ANC. Given the intensity with which individuals held their party allegiances, clashes and violence were not infrequent between UNIP and ANC in areas where both parties had a significant following. Furthermore, the demand by UNIP was for positive, if not enthusiastic support. Apathy or withdrawal were not acceptable. The conflict, for instance, between UNIP and religious groups like the Lumpa Church[22] and the Jehovah's Witnesses, who did not want to participate in secular politics, was as intense as the struggle between the two political parties.

Kaunda not only sought African support for UNIP, but also welcomed

[22] Andrew Roberts, "The Lumpa Church of Alice Lenshina," eds., R. I. Rotberg and A. A. Mazrui, *Protest and Power in Black Africa* (New York: Oxford University Press, 1970), pp. 513–569.

Europeans to join and to work for the party. Kaunda assured Europeans that UNIP was working towards the establishment of a multi-racial society in which Africans and non-Africans could live together in harmony. Despite his hard and sincere efforts, however, he was only able to attract a small minority of Europeans. Whereas in the elections just preceding independence UNIP received over two-thirds of the votes cast by Africans (this does not include twenty-four constituencies where UNIP won without a contest), it received only one-third of the ballots cast by Europeans.

The goals of breaking up the Federation and securing independence for Zambia under a majority-rule system of government were accomplished with considerable assistance from developments outside of Northern Rhodesia. The demise of the entire British Empire was very evident by the 1960's and other colonies had already become independent states ruled by indigenous, not alien, peoples. Prime Minister Harold Macmillan publicly acknowledged that the "winds of change" indicated that the movements for independence throughout the British colonies were likely to succeed. Of particular relevance to Northern Rhodesia were developments in Nyasaland. In response to the violence in 1959 caused by the nationalist movement there, the British government sent a commission headed by Mr. Justice Devlin to determine the causes and implications of the disturbances. The Devlin Report noted the almost universal opposition by Africans to the Federation and referred to Nyasaland as a police state.[23] The clear implications of the Devlin findings were that the Federation would be much better off without Nyasaland and vice versa. Following the publication of this report, the Monckton Commission was established to assess the viability of the Federation. This commission, too, found sincere and widespread opposition by Africans in the northern territories towards the Federation. The report issued by the Monckton Commission in October, 1960, stated that maintenance of the Federation in its existing form was possible only through force and suggested the British government make serious consideration of altering the structure of the Federation and/or allowing territories to secede.[24]

Whites in Northern Rhodesia and the federal government protested strongly to the British government that these two commissions were in serious error. UNIP's leadership, of course, pursued the logic of the reports and pressed for a break-up of the Federation. From late 1960 to mid-1962, the British government first made promises to satisfy UNIP,

[23] Great Britain, Colonial Office, *Report of the Nyasaland Commission of Inquiry,* Cmnd. 814, (London: H.M.S.O., July, 1959).

[24] Great Britian, *Report of the Advisory Commission on the Review of the Constitution of Rhodesia and Nyasaland,* Cmnd. 1148, (London: H.M.S., October, 1960).

then the white settlers, and then UNIP again. UNIP was obliged to use mass resistance and disturbances, including violence, to demonstrate its power and the soundness of the Monckton Commission's warning that the Federation could survive, even on a short-term basis, only if it used force.[25] The final response of the British was to hold elections in 1962 under an arrangement designed to test the popular strength of the various parties and to force one-third of the candidates to secure votes from both Africans and Europeans. The electoral arrangements were so complicated and the racial tensions so high, that only the former purpose of the elections was accomplished. The device to force some candidates to secure multi-racial support failed miserably.[26]

Despite the fact that UNIP received over 76 percent of the votes cast, the constituencies were so defined that UNIP won only fourteen seats. ANC won seven seats and UFP won sixteen seats in the Legislative Council. No party had a clear majority and so a ruling coalition had to be formed. ANC was heavily courted by both of the other two parties. The alliance between ANC and UFP in the campaign did not carry over to the post-election situation. UNIP had clearly demonstrated that it was the dominant party and would rule in a one-man-one-vote electoral system. In an effort to recapture a more favorable image among the African voters and at the price of receiving half of the cabinet positions, ANC agreed to join UNIP in a ruling coalition. Kaunda made it clear that he considered the coalition an abominable and temporary necessity and began working immediately for another election under a constitution that provided for majority rule and for independence.

Bowing to the strength of the nationalist movements, the British government announced its acceptance of Nyasaland's right to secede from the Federation and seek its own independence in December, 1962. The Northern Rhodesia Legislative Council demanded the same right in February, 1963 and received formal assurances of that right on March 29. Elections were held under a new constitution in January, 1964. The only

[25] Rotberg, *Rise of Nationalism,* pp. 310–316; Mulford, *Zambia,* pp. 197–210.

[26] The device used to force candidates to secure votes from members of all racial groups was to allocate one-third of the seats in the Legislative Council to special national constituencies. In order to be considered duly elected from one of these constituencies, a candidate had to win at least 12½% or 400 votes (whichever was the less) cast by the members of each race. (Voters were divided into the Upper Roll, almost entirely European, and the Lower Roll, entirely African. This division was used in calculating whether the racial requirements were met by candidates in national constituencies.) If more than one candidate met the requirements, the winner was the one who had the highest average of the percentage of votes received from each roll. For a more detailed discussion of this complex system, see: Mulford, *Zambia,* pp. 178–210.

concession UNIP leadership made to the one-man-one-vote principle was the creation of ten seats in the legislative assembly that would be reserved for Europeans. In the 1964 elections, UNIP again tried hard to run European candidates that might win. However, it lost all ten of the reserved seats. Of the remaining legislative contests, UNIP won fifty-five (twenty-four of them unopposed) and ANC won ten. At the end of January, an all-UNIP cabinet assumed control and on October 24, 1964, Zambia became an independent country.

Although Zambia became independent with formal institutions of government, a constitution and a body of laws and regulations, no assumption could be made that these would actually guide the behavior of men in the political arena. The independence struggle involved an attack on the legitimacy of many of these same institutions. The principles of rule by and for a culturally distinct minority were replaced with the ideals of egalitarianism and a widespread distribution of wealth. This change in the *raison d'etre* of government requires new institutions and procedures and new uses of existing structures. The effects of the split in the independence movement, moreover, tempered the principles of democratic participation in the political process with a suspicion of opposition parties and a belief that stability requires extensive and enthusiastic unity. In short, when Zambia was created, an institutionalized political process was a goal, not an existing trait of the political system.

Economic conditions

The citizens of Zambia expect their standard of living to improve now that independence has been attained. In part this expectation is the result of promises made by those who mobilized support for the nationalist movement. In part a less explicit thinking process is involved. Africans who saw the life styles of Europeans and then realized that Europeans were no longer in power could reasonably anticipate that there would be a reallocation of Zambia's wealth to provide for the welfare and comfort of Africans. Whatever the causes, Zambian leaders are aware of the need to satisfy existing expectations for improving the quality of material living.

Unlike many new states, Zambia has the potential for becoming a very wealthy nation and for making her people comfortable. The present economic strength of Zambia is derived from copper. Zambian copper production has accounted for about 13 percent of the total world production. Over 90 percent of Zambia's export earnings and 60 percent of government revenues are directly attributable to the copper industry. Other mining activities are not well developed, but there are known deposits of coal, tin, tungsten, precious gems and other minerals. Few secondary industries have been established to utilize this mineral wealth, but there is potential development of this sector as well. Hydroelectric power can be harnessed to support these industries and to supply private consumers. The construction of the Kafue Dam in 1971 was a major step towards self-sufficiency in the production of electric power.

Zambia also has the resources for the growth of a highly productive agricultural industry. In the first years after independence, self-sufficiency was attained in the production of sugar, maize and some dairy and poultry products. Most of Zambia's foodstuffs could be produced within the country. In addition, cash crops like tobacco, cotton, soy beans and confectionary nuts are grown and represent activities that could be expanded. Magnificent waterfalls, and large numbers of game have attracted the establishment of a tourist industry that is far from reaching an optimal size.

Despite the resources for a healthy and diversified economy, Zambia has had an economy that, although fairly prosperous, is precariously unbalanced. If copper prices should suddenly fall, the effects on Zambia would be disastrous. In the immediate years after Independence, development efforts using funds from copper have not resulted in the establishment of new revenue-earning activities. Instead, there was a phenomenal growth of the construction industry as the government sought to provide for needed infrastructure and for government buildings. Also, to remedy the severe shortage of skilled and educated personnel in Zambia (at the time of Independence, there were only 1200 Zambians with a secondary school certificate and 104 with a college diploma), the government increased its real expenditures for education by 66 percent between 1963 and 1966. Although economic and social infrastructure are essential, they do not directly produce national income. The cost of their development and maintenance, in fact, make even more critical the growth of diverse sources of revenue.

The configuration of the Zambian economy is imbalanced in other dimensions as well. One of the most dramatic imbalances is regional. By far, the most developed, advantaged area of Zambia is the area adjacent to the railroad constructed by the British South Africa Company in the beginning of this century. The railroad runs in a north-south direction through the central part of the country, from Livingstone to the Copperbelt. Parallel and adjacent to the railroad is one of the few all-weather roads in the country. Along the "line of rail," as this area is referred to, are the commercial activity and, of course, the mining industry. In addition, the large farms owned for the most part by white settlers are located in this area. Proximity to the railroad is valuable to farmers to get produce to markets with minimal transportation costs.

Regional imbalance is not only marked by the concentration of cash nexus economic activity along the line of rail and subsistence agriculture elsewhere in Zambia, but there are also differences in regional resources.

The provinces best endowed for agriculture are the Southern, Central, Copperbelt and Eastern Provinces. Luapula Province has an abundance of lakes and rivers, and fish are an important natural resource. The North-western Province is one of the least developed in the country, although there are known rich copper deposits and the area is very appropriate for growing pineapples. Western and Northern Provinces are the least well endowed. The natural environment does not lend itself well to agricultural development and there are no known mineral resources of any significant value.

Because provinces are identified not only with different economic needs and resources but also with different linguistic and ethnic groups, regional imbalance takes on added political significance. When the level of wealth or the amount of governmental development activity varies from province to province, individuals often fail to distinguish between regional differences and ethnic differences. A relatively low allocation of development resources to a given province is frequently regarded as prejudicial treatment of the ethnic group identified with that province.

The imbalance in levels of wealth between racial groups is also of political significance. The action taken by the colonial government to protect the high income status of Europeans and the special economic role of Asians were discussed earlier. Ironically, it is the group of Africans who are more wealthy than the bulk of Zambians who express the most concern about income differentials among the racial communities. The Zambian mine workers and civil servants, whose salaries place them in a relatively envious position, are most cognizant of the luxurious living of Europeans in Zambia. The definition of injustice ascribed to many in this situation is primarily that Africans should enjoy the same comforts as their European colleagues. Of secondary consideration is the goal of equal distribution of national wealth to all citizens.

President Kaunda is aware of the complex nature of the demands made upon the political system to ensure improved living standards for Zambians. He has pleaded with mine workers, civil servants and others employed in urban areas not to forget their poorer rural brethren when demanding higher wages and more material benefits. The President is also aware of regionally-based demands and of the necessity of reducing existing sectorial imbalance. Identifying the problems and challenges, while important, is only the first step in the difficult process of finding solutions.

External dependence

Colonial rule involves more than just political control. The major dimension of colonialism is economic exploitation. The pattern of economic development that takes place during the colonial period is designed to extract wealth from the subjugated territory. Any improvement in the welfare of indigenous people that may result is best regarded as a side effect.

Zambia's most important industry illustrates the ties to external economies that were established during the colonial era. Until recently, the mines in Zambia were controlled by two groups of companies.[28] The largest of these two was Anglo American Corporation. Despite its name, this company was owned primarily by South Africans and the managerial staff in Zambia was predominantly South African. British and, especially, American involvement in Anglo American has been insignificant. The other company was Roan Selection Trust, Limited, which was almost entirely owned by Americans, particularly American Metal Climax, Inc. which held 43 percent of the stock. Almost all of the managers of RST were British.

Ownership and managerial control constitute only part of the pattern of dependency. Copper mining requires machinery, chemicals and other supplies. These are available only outside of Zambia and usually from sources owned at least partially by the external shareholders of the copper companies. Furthermore, copper is shipped from Zambia as refined ore. Very few copper products are made in Zambia and so there is a very heavy reliance on the demands of external markets and there is a loss of revenue that might be earned if Zambia exported finished copper products instead of ending the processing at the electrolytic stage. Skilled labor, in addition to managerial staffs, provides another area of dependence until Zambia can supply her own mining engineers and technicians.

The kind of external ties evident in the copper industry are important in other sectors of the economy too. The vast bulk of investment in the manufacturing sector has originated from subsidiaries of overseas firms. Many of these firms had headquarters in Rhodesia and South Africa.[28] The Asian predominance in retail trade has been mentioned. Profits earned by these merchants and traders were rarely reinvested in Zambia, but instead were used to finance economic activity in other countries.

Geographical and historical factors are also important in understanding Zambia's lack of economic independence. Again, those factors relevant to copper are the most critical.[29] Copper is a bulk commodity and, as a landlocked country, surface transportation facilities are of vital importance

[27] The introduction of state control will be discussed below.

[28] Charles Elliott, "The Zambian Economy," *East Africa Journal* (December, 1968): 13.

[29] For an excellent discussion of these factors, see Richard L. Sklar, "Zambia's Response to U.D.I.," *Mawazo,* vol. 1, (June, 1968), pp. 11–32.

in getting the copper to consumers. The only major means of surface transportation to the sea has been the railway that runs through Rhodesia to the ports of Beira and Lourenço Marques in Mozambique. Alternate routes and facilities by rail through the Congo and Angola and by road through Tanzania are extremely limited in the traffic they can bear. Before the Kafue Dam was finished, Zambia relied on the power generated at the Kariba Dam facilities for electricity. The Kariba Dam is located on the Zambezi River, which forms the boundary between Zambia and Rhodesia, but the power station is located on the Rhodesian bank. Electricity is essential for operating the pumps that keep the mines from being flooded, as well, of course, for satisfying more familiar needs. High grade coal, also necessary for the mining industry, has been imported from Wankie in Rhodesia and, until the construction of a pipeline from Zambia through Tanzania was completed in 1968, petroleum products entered Zambia from the south.

What is clear from this survey is that Zambia is not only heavily dependent on other societies for essential goods and services, but also that this dependence is tied to the southern part of the continent. The effects of the Unilateral Declaration of Independence (UDI) by the white minority government in Rhodesia made this pattern of dependence dramatically clear. Zambia is firmly committed to the replacement of incumbent regimes in Southern Africa with governments based on the black majorities in those societies. However, Zambia is constrained because of the necessity to use facilities located in the south.

Since UDI occurred in November, 1965, Zambia has pursued with the highest sense of urgency the development of alternative supplies and facilities to those tying the country to the regimes in the south. The attainment of this goal, however, will not make Zambia self-sufficient and insulate the Zambian economy from the dynamics and structures of economies outside her borders. All societies are affected by the behavior of other societies. At issue here is a situation in which Zambia is so restricted by the decisions of a small group of investors and governments that there are few, if any, policy options that Zambia can realistically pursue. Diversifying patterns of reliance will have the effect of presenting Zambian decision-makers with more alternatives and of altering relations with external economic factors from a state of dependency to a state of interdependency.

The legacy of British colonialism is also responsible for non-economic constraints on the direction of Zambian policy. Although the British did not pursue a policy of cultural assimilation similar to the French and Portuguese, they did introduce elements of Western, particularly British, culture into Zambian society. The nature of colonialism tried to instill into Africans the notion that Western values and styles of living were superior to all others. Modernization and progress are identified as Westernization.

The practical effects of this cultural dimension to colonialism was the introduction of modest amounts of Western education and the use of English as a *lingua franca.* The combination of these has made Zambia dependent primarily on personnel from English-speaking parts of the world to provide the expertise needed to maintain public services and to attain development goals. The education that was available for Africans in Northern Rhodesia was sufficient to impart a desire for changing Zambian society so that the technology and prosperity of the West might be attained. However, educational facilities were so meager that Zambia became independent with a paucity of indigenous manpower with a high level of skills and training. The small number of Zambians with secondary school and college education was mentioned above. Furthermore, no efforts were even contemplated for allowing Africans into positions of significant responsibility until 1959.[30]

To secure personnel with needed skills and experience, Zambia had to provide opportunities for her citizens to obtain an education while in the short run relying on personnel from outside the country. Like most new states, Zambia has sought to avoid dependence on any single major power in the world. That goal is partially compromised in that the source of English-speaking personnel is limited primarily to England and the United States. In 1968, over 80 percent of the approximately 3,600 expatriate personnel in the public bureaucracy were British. Not only is the linguistic element important here, but also the generous technical assistance programs available to Zambia from Great Britain.[31] Increasingly, Canada is looked to as a country that is not a major world power but still provides a source of personnel that will not have a language difficulty. India could be another such source, were it not for domestic problems in Africa regarding Asian communities.

As discussed above, the cost of securing political independence was the destruction of existing symbols and institutions and the construction of a new order, the definition of new purposes. The generation of consensus for fundamental changes is not easy and constitutes one of the major challenges confronting Zambian leadership. Similarly, obtaining economic and cultural independence requires sacrifices as the transition is made

[30] Dennis L. Dresang, "The Civil Service in Zambia," *Government in Zambia,* ed., William Tordoff (London: Heinemann, forthcoming).

[31] For a discussion of Zambianization, see Dennis L. Dresang, *The Zambia Civil Service: Entrepreneurialism and Development Administration* (Nairobi: East Africa Publishing House, forthcoming).

from old to new. The allocation of scarce resources for the construction of facilities to replace existing ones that can be considered adequate seems like wasteful duplication. Yet, the costs are borne and considered worthwhile. At stake are symbols and options. The dynamics of the national identity crisis make the symbols of independence in all areas important. The demands for tangible and material evidence of changes in the political system prompt leaders to seek ways of enhancing their capacity to control the pattern of development and the fate of their country. The accomplishment of this task requires more real control over the economy than Zambia had at the time of independence.

National integration

When groups that feel alienated from a political system have a geographic base and when national loyalties are not firmly established, a likely demand for political change will be secession. Efforts at secession are not probable when groups do not identify a region of the country as their home. During the discussions in the late 1950's and early 1960's regarding constitutional changes in Central Africa, a demand was made by the traditional leadership of the Lozi that Barotseland, the southwestern area of Northern Rhodesia/Zambia, be excluded from an independent Zambia and recognized as a separate state. The argument used by the Litunga (King of the Lozi) was that Barotseland had always had a special legal status within the British Empire by virtue of a treaty concluded in 1900 between the Litunga Lewanika and the British South Africa Company, representing the Crown of England. Although Barotseland had always been administered as a part of Northern Rhodesia, technically it was a separate protectorate. Barotseland's special status was also recognized in the constitution of the Federation.

Apart from the legal justification for the Litunga's claim for separate independence, it was quite clear that the leadership of UNIP did not envision any special position for the traditional leaders in the post-colonial political order. Positions of authority were to be acquired through success in electoral contests and not through claims of heredity or historical tradition. UNIP did not press for the abolishment of chieftainships or other traditional offices, but neither did they recognize any significant authority attached to these positions.

In response to the Litunga's demands for secession, Lozis active in UNIP, including such prominent figures as Munu Sipalo, Arthur Wina, Sikota Wina and Nalumino Mundia, formed the Barotse Anti-Secession Movement (BASMO). This organization worked both in the urban areas and in Barotseland to isolate the Litunga and to win support among the

Lozis for UNIP and what it represented. UNIP pressured the colonial administration to ensure that campaigning and elections would be held in Barotseland as in other parts of Northern Rhodesia and the confrontation between the Litunga and UNIP was settled at the ballot boxes. In the 1962 elections, UNIP was opposed by the Barotse National Party, which had the clear but implicit support of the Litunga. UNIP won all of the seats. Although the Litunga and his supporters continued to press for separate independence, the British government refused to recognize these claims. UNIP continued to demonstrate the support it had among the voters in Barotseland by winning local elections and the 1964 contests for parliamentary representatives.

Although occasional threats have been made since independence by Lozi and other leaders that they will lead a secessionist movement, no serious attempts have been made. Recent warnings of action to withdraw certain areas from the Zambian political system do not reflect a concern for the role of traditional leadership. Rather, they reflect the weakness of national loyalties and the strength of ethno-regionalism in Zambia politics.

The congruence between regional economic differences and ethnic identities was mentioned above. Other differences also exist and help to reinforce these divisions. The Lozi had an advantage in available educational facilities with the early establishment by the Paris Missionary Society of the Barotse National School. Differences in educational opportunities and the stereotypes held by Europeans of the various African peoples in Northern Rhodesia led to differential patterns of recruitment. Bemba, for instance, were considered to be most capable of hard work and were recruited for the underground mining work. Nyanja-speaking peoples from the Eastern Province and Nyasaland were regarded as most appropriate for clerical and white-collar employment. Tonga were employed as policemen.

The contemporary ethnic groupings in the political arena do not coincide with all the different African communities that existed in the precolonial period. Rather, these cleavages divide groups according to objective regional differences and subjective stereotypes. The major ethno-regional groups in Zambia are: 1) the Lozi—this includes many non-Lozi groups located in Western (formerly Barotse) Province; 2) the Bemba—most of the population in the Northern and Luapula Provinces, which includes Bemba, Bisa, Mambwe, Kazembe-Lunda and others; 3) the Nyanja—the Chewa, Tumbuka, Ngoni and other Nyanja-speaking peoples who are primarily from the Eastern Province; 4) the Tonga—most of the people from the Southern Province, including the Ila and a number of smaller ethnic groups in that area; and 5) the smaller groups of the rural areas of the Northwestern, Central and Copperbelt Provinces, such as the Lunda-Ndembu, Soli, Lenje, Lamba, Lala, Lovale and Kaonde. It is important to remember that these groups are relevant when discussing politics at the national level. Ethnicity, in particular, is situational and at a lower level of politics, a different definition of cleavages would be required.

The possibility that any given ethno-regional group might achieve a position of dominance and then disadvantage other groups has been a matter of major concern in post-colonial Zambian politics. The arena for competition has been both within UNIP and between UNIP and other political parties. ANC has always had as its base of support the Southern Province. One other opposition party, the United Party (UP), which has been banned since August, 1968 and has never been able to contest an election, was commonly regarded as based primarily on Lozi discontent with the policies of the UNIP government. In this regard, the ANC victories in the Western Province in the 1968 general elections relied almost entirely on the use of the organization and leadership of the banned United Party.[32] All of the ANC candidates in that province were former UP members. A visible linkage between UP and ANC was provided when Nalumino Mundia, who had been expelled from the UNIP Cabinet in 1967 on charges of corruption and had subsequently become president of UP, was made deputy president of ANC.

Three periods can be distinguished in analyzing ethno-regional politics within UNIP. In the first period, from the inception of UNIP to the Mulungushi Conference in August, 1967, a conscious effort was made to ensure the representation of all ethno-regional groups in the ruling organs of the party. Although individuals changed positions, at any given time the background of the members of the party committees demonstrated a careful balancing of ethnic backgrounds, party service and levels of education. The ideal combination of political representativeness and intellectual excellence was approximated to give the party and the government both legitimacy and competence.

In August, 1967, the party held a National Conference at Mulungushi to, among other things, hold elections for positions on the Central Committee. Seven of the eleven elective posts on the committee were contested and President Kaunda, who was unopposed, scrupulously avoided demonstrating what his preferences might be. In the contests for the seven posts, alliances were formed by the various ethno-regional groups.

[32] Robert Molteno and Ian Scott, "The Zambian General Elections," *Africa Report* (January, 1961): 42–47.

The results were that the Bemba and Tonga candidates won and the Lozi and Nyanja candidates lost.[33] The Bemba-Tonga alliance takes on added significance when it is recalled that the Tonga within UNIP could not claim strong support from the people of their province. The Tonga in the Southern Province have always supported ANC. Therefore, Tonga who attained national offices in UNIP depended almost entirely upon Bemba support for their positions.

During the period ushered in by the 1967 Mulungushi Conference, the strife within UNIP was of critical proportions. The absence of an institutionalized political process exacerbated the conflict, for in that there was little adherence to "rules of the game," those who were disappointed with the results of the Mulungushi elections refused to accept them as legitimate.

Charges were made inside and outside the party that the government was dominated by the Bemba. In its publication *The Mirror,* the United Party included an article entitled "Tribalism in Zambia; Who Are Encouraging It?" which argued:

> . . . There are 73 tribes in Zambia and their interests must be balanced. But look at this arrangement: The President, The Vice President, The Chairman of the Public Service Commission—which deals with Promotions of civil Servants; Teaching Service Commission—which deals with Promotions of Teachers; Police Service Commission—which deals with Promotions of Police; University Council of Zambia and Judiciary Service Commission belong to one tribe. The Commissioner of Police and the Secretary of the Cabinet belong to the same tribe. These are the people governing the country and all the other ministries and departments are merely branches in some form or other of the above. The same tribe has majority of Permanent and Under Secretaries than any other tribe (sic). It has more people in the foreign service than any other tribe. It has more Directors in Charge of Departments and Semi-Government Organizations such as the Zambia Railways, Zambia Broadcasting Services and the Commissioner of Traffic Departments, etc., etc.
>
> What is all this about? Does it mean that they are the most dedicated ones than other tribes? (sic) It is also estimated that the same tribe has nearly 150 people in the executive and higher positions of office in the Public Service. The Tongas, the Ngonis, and the Lozis next range between 30 and 50 people each in similar positions. Can anybody explain why?[34]

[33] Robert I. Rotberg, "Tribalism and Politics in Zambia," *Africa Report* (December, 1967): 29–36; and Thomas Rasmussen, "Political Competition and One-party Dominance in Zambia," *The Journal of Modern African Studies* 7 (1969): 407–424.

[34] "Tribalism in Zambia; Who Are Encouraging It?" *The Mirror* 1 (March, 1968): 3.

Except for the classification of President Kaunda as Bemba (his parents were from Malawi, although he was raised in Bembaland), the catalog presented by UP was highly accurate and was of great concern to other peoples in Zambia.

Whereas many Lozis in UNIP responded to the Mulungushi elections by supporting UP, local UNIP officials in the Eastern Province were active in forming a movement referred to as "Umodzi Kamwawa" (Unity in the East). Threats were voiced of secession if the imbalance was not redressed. Vice-President Kapwepwe, Bemba, was fully aware that he was feared and rejected by non-Bemba groups who believed that he spearheaded a movement for complete Bemba control. Munu Sipalo, Lozi, on the other hand, encountered hostile demonstrations when he toured the Northern Province. President Kaunda was openly and visibly upset by these developments. He even "resigned"[35] in reaction to a heated debate at a meeting of UNIP's National Council in which charges of tribalism were traded. After receiving pledges of unity and cooperation, he rescinded his resignation nine hours later.

A third phase of ethno-regional politics began when Vice-President Kapwepwe resigned in August, 1969, claiming that he was not accepted throughout Zambia as the legitimate vice-president and that because of hatred of him Bemba people were being discriminated against. President Kaunda succeeded in getting Kapwepwe to withdraw his resignation for at least a year and at the same time suspended the constitution of UNIP and appointed his own committees and officials. The dominant characteristic of this third phase is that the president has attempted to restore the balance and the unity that existed prior to the 1967 Mulungushi Conference. Stability and progress in Zambia, according to the president, requires cohesion and discipline in UNIP, not the fragmentation and strife that has characterized the party.

Obviously, the ethno-regional group that stands the most to lose by the president's intents is the Bemba. Their fears were in part confirmed when in November, 1970, the president asked Vice-President Kapwepwe to step down and appointed Mainza Chona, who is Tonga and a close and loyal associate of the president, in his place. The Bemba hold on top positions throughout the government deteriorated steadily from 1970 to 1972. The virtual monopoly on senior posts in government commissions was broken. Whereas 30 percent of the Zambians who were Heads of Departments in 1968 were Bemba, in 1972 less than one-fifth were Bemba.

[35] There is some debate regarding the legal effect of President Kaunda's resignation. Although the term used by the President and by the Zambian press may not be legally precise, the intent of his action was to leave office.

Table 1 demonstrates the trend among those directing government ministries.

TABLE 1

COMPARISON OF ETHNO-REGIONAL IDENTITY OF SENIOR GOVERNMENT OFFICIALS, 1968 and 1972
(percent)

	TOTAL AFRICAN POPULATION	CABINET MINISTERS		PERMANENT SECRETARIES		TOTAL	
		1968	1972	1968	1972	1968	1972
Bemba	31.4	26.7	21.7	31.6	12.5	30.6	17.0
Nyanja	19.4	20.0	13.0	26.3	41.7	22.2	27.7
Tonga	13.0	13.3	17.4	15.0	4.2	13.9	10.6
Lozi	12.6	26.7	13.0	15.0	20.8	22.2	17.0
Others	23.6	13.3	34.8	10.5	20.8	11.1	27.7
	N=4,100,000	N=17	N=23	N=19	N=24	N=36	N=47

The response to these events by Bemba Members of Parliament, among others, was a series of charges of discrimination and corruption and a call to establish a new political party. After some hesitation, Kapwepwe launched the United Progressive Party (UPP) in August, 1971. The UPP had a Bemba base, although it tried to broaden that base by articulating the grievances of those unhappy with the slow pace of economic development and the direction of leadership in Zambia.[36] The UPP had little opportunity to test its ability to mobilize an electorate, however. Violent clashes ensued between UNIP and UPP supporters, over 200 UPP leaders and sympathizers were placed in detention, and finally the party was banned and Kapwepwe himself arrested. In the aftermath of these events President Kaunda departed from his intent to persuade Zambian voters to make the country a one-party state through the ballot box. In February, 1972 he declared that the country was going to be a one-party state and in December of that year the constitution was changed to implement that decision.

Although the rhetoric of ethno-regional politics is phrased in terms of tribal competition, it is important to be aware of the objective as well as the subjective dimensions to these divisions. Political conflict in Zambia is for the most part not motivated by irrational, primordial loyalties and

[36] Robert Molteno, "Zambia and the One-Party State," *East Africa Journal* 4 (February, 1972): 6–18.

sentiments. The objective variances define very real and significant implications for how power is distributed among these groups.

Economic development

One of the most salient issues in Zambian politics is the government's performance in promoting rapid economic development. The goals are to raise the general levels of welfare and education, to achieve sectorial and regional balance in the economy, and to prevent the development of wide gaps in levels of income. The attainment of these goals would place a heavy burden on any government. For Zambia, as a new state, the strain is particularly severe.

The capacity of the public bureaucracy to provide for rapid economic development has not been hampered by the lack of capital or natural resources, which have been important factors in other developing countries. The constraints have been due to the shortage of skilled and experienced personnel and to the absence of central control and co-ordination in the administrative process. The paucity of local manpower with all the needed expertise to promote economic development is only a short-term problem. The temporary void has been filled by employing personnel from outside the country. As educational and training programs make available more Zambians with abilities to perform the required tasks, non-Zambians will be replaced. The expatriates that have been hired rarely have the abilities and the experience that they are assumed to have, but they do partially fill the immediate needs created by the shortage of local expertise.

It will be more difficult to remove the constraints on development administration that are due to the absence of central direction and co-ordination. The basic unit of the administrative system is the department, an agency that specializes in one area of knowledge and field of activity. These specialized units enjoy a substantial amount of autonomy from any central source of authority. In part this autonomy is due to the power that accrues to them because of their expertise and the inability of those outside the department to fully understand all of the technical problems and opportunities that exist. Another reason for departmental autonomy is that the post-colonial bureaucracy is really a new organization that lacks the cohesive force of institutionalized norms or processes. In 1959, there were only nine ministries and twenty-six departments in the Northern Rhodesia bureaucracy. At the time of independence in 1964, there were seventy-six department-level units and fourteen ministries, plus the office of the president, which was essentially the same as a ministry. This proliferation of new structures has continued and in

1968 there were 102 departments and fifteen ministries plus the office of the president and the office of the vice-president. There has been a concomitant expansion of the number of civil servants from 5,873 in clerical positions and above in 1965 to 11,469 in 1968.

Most development programs require the input of more than one specialized agency for successful completion. Likewise, the attainment of balanced sectorial and regional growth patterns requires the joint efforts of a number of bureaucratic units. When departments are largely autonomous and their activities are not coordinated, development plans will not act as effective guides for bureaucratic behavior and a gap between plans and accomplishments is likely to occur. Ironically, those countries who need the efficiencies that come from planned economic growth are the countries least capable of formulating and implementing development plans effectively and efficiently.

To some extent, these limitations are offset by the actions of bureaucrats who perceive an opportunity for rapid upward mobility in an administrative system with a shortage of skilled personnel and with a low degree of institutionalization. These bureaucrats seek to become identified with successful development efforts and thus enhance their reputation and chances for a successful career. Given these motivations, they carefully assess the relevant variables and calculate what projects or programs are most worthwhile for their investment of time and energy and they provide a driving force to secure the various inputs needed for the effort to succeed. This small but important element within the bureaucracy is responsible for some dynamism and direction in development administration, but it does not avoid the waste and duplication that occurs in the absence of central control and co-ordination.[37]

Tables 2 and 3 provide an indication of the divergence between the plans for balanced sectorial growth and the actual imbalance in administrative activity. Table 2 shows how over a period of three years the allocation of funds for development gradually changed from an initial plan for balance among the major sectors to a pattern heavily emphasizing the development of economic infrastructure. The changes were primarily a response to initial miscalculation on the part of planners and to a cumulative effect in which success in this area made claims for more funds appear as an investment that was both necessary and safe. The increase in the absolute amount of money devoted for development in 1969 was due to an underestimation of costs initially and also to the effects of inflation.

[37] Dennis L. Dresang, "Entrepreneurialism and Development Administration," *Administrative Science Quarterly,* March, 1973.

TABLE 2. COMPARISON OF ESTIMATED EXPENDITURES BY SECTORS ACCORDING TO THE FIRST NATIONAL DEVELOPMENT PLAN AND THE CAPITAL FUND AS REPORTED IN THE 1969 BUDGET

	Development Plan		Capital Fund, 1969	
	K million	Percent	K million	Percent
Economic Infrastructure	165.0	29.2	467.9	55.0
Social Infrastructure	194.1	34.4	185.1	23.0
Productive Investment	188.3	33.6	162.0	19.0
Miscellaneous	16.2	2.8	35.4	3.0
TOTAL	563.6	100.0	849.9	100.0

Note: Absolute figures are given in millions of Kwacha. One Kwacha equals U.S. $1.40.

Sources: Republic of Zambia, *First National Development Plan, 1966 to 1970* (Lusaka: Government Printer, 1966) and *Estimates of Revenue and Expenditure (Including the Capital Fund and Constitutional and Statutory Expenditure) for the Year 1st January, 1969 to 31st December, 1969* (Lusaka: Government Printer, 1969).

Table 3 compares the total costs estimated for the development projects with the amount of money spent for these projects. There is a margin of error involved in using this comparison as an indicator of the progress attained in implementing these projects. Implementation includes more than the expenditure of funds and costs can be underestimated or perhaps even overestimated. However, it is instructive that the development plan itself provided that about two-thirds of the funds allocated would be spent by December, 1968. Of the K563.6 million initially planned for the whole Plan period, K159 million was to be spent between July, 1966 and July,

TABLE 3. COMPARISON OF ESTIMATED TOTAL COSTS AND EXPENDITURES ON DEVELOPMENT PROJECTS AS OF DECEMBER 31, 1968

	Estimated Total Cost K million	Estimated Expenditure July 1, 1966- Dec. 31, 1968 K million	Percentage of total Cost spent
Economic Infrastructure	467.9	159.3	34.0
Social Infrastructure	185.1	77.4	41.8
Productive Investment	162.0	36.9	22.7
Miscellaneous	35.4	0.1	25.4
TOTAL	849.9	282.7	33.3

Source: Zambia, *Estimates of Revenue and Expenditure for 1969*, pp. 57–90.

1967, K153.9 million was to be spent the second year, K140.7 million the third year, and K109.8 million the final year. As the data presented in the table indicates, however, only one-third of the allocated funds were spent by the end of 1968 and the revenue-earning sector ("productive investment") was particularly far behind schedule.

The pattern of expenditure for rural development, not including national projects such as central hospitals and roads linking Zambia to other countries, is a curious one. As can be seen in Table 4, there was a lack of balance between the various provinces, even when allowing for differences in population. An interesting feature of this imbalance is that, despite the apparent favored position of the Western Province, spokesmen from that province have been among the most vociferous of those complaining of the lack of development in their areas. In part, this is a dramatic reminder that government expenditures cannot be equated with developmental accomplishments. For instance, the largest item of expenditure in the Western Province has been the K1,292,660 spent prior to January 1, 1969 for an all-weather road from Lusaka to Mongu. The sandy soil of the Western Province has posed serious technical problems, and that road in 1969 was still far from completion. Furthermore, many resources must be poured into those areas off the line of rail before they will have the infrastructure and source of trained farmers, artisans and other personnel to start catching up with the more advantaged areas of the country. Thus, in spite of heavy expenditures, there are few visible results of development in the Western Province.

TABLE 4. EXPENDITURES FOR RURAL DEVELOPMENT BETWEEN JULY 1, 1966 AND DECEMBER 31, 1968
(in Kwacha)

Province	Kwacha
Northern Province	3,341,341
Copperbelt Province	2,534,285
Eastern Province	2,178,134
Central Province	1,682,806
Southern Province	2,020,559
Western Province	4,026,391
Luapula Province	1,899,370
Northwestern Province	939,302

Note: Included in these totals are expenditures for health, roads, schools, agriculture, fisheries, forestry, water affairs and community development. Excluded are expenses for staff housing and training and similar administrative infrastructure.

Source: Republic of Zambia, *Estimates of Revenue and Expenditure for the year 1st January, 1969 to 31st December, 1969,* pp. 80–90.

Regardless of the factual situation regarding expenditures or administrative constraints, there has been political discontent with the slow pace of development in Zambia. This discontent is based both on a general assessment and on the particularistic grievances of a region. One response to this unhappiness has been attempts to encourage people to work harder and to reform the administrative structure to make it more effective. The most serious attempt at administrative reforms was announced during the campaign for the December 1968 general elections and implemented in January, 1969.

The major assumption behind the 1969 reforms was that UNIP could provide the source of control needed to direct and co-ordinate bureaucratic activity. A closer union between the party and the public bureaucracy was attempted by: 1) encouraging civil servants to become active members of UNIP; 2) changing the position of head of the civil service from an administrative to a political post; 3) making permanent secretaries, the highest ranking civil servants, members of UNIP's national council; and 4) appointing political figures to supervise governmental activities in each district and province. To implement the last policy, a member of the cabinet was appointed in charge of each province and the portfolios of central ministries were consolidated so that there would be fewer ministries.

The disunity within UNIP dissuaded the president from fully implementing the reforms. As the new cabinet ministers for the provinces and the new district governors assumed their posts, it became evident that they were not going to provide a common style and direction of leadership. Some interpreted their mission to be ridding the country of ANC supporters and they launched a campaign of threats and intimidation and purged the governmental units in their jurisdiction of suspected ANC sympathizers. Others assumed they had little direct control over the personnel and policies of other government departments. In February, 1969, a cabinet circular was issued indicating that district governors and ministers in provinces did not have jurisdiction over civil servants and departmental activities, and several months later President Kaunda initiated his campaign to infuse more unity and discipline in the party.[38]

Economic Independence

Another response that has been made to the divergence between expectations and accomplishments in the pace of economic development has been a series of efforts to secure more control by Zambia over her own economy. The aim is to obtain discretion as to how those funds in foreign and pri-

[38] Republic of Zambia, Cabinet Office, *Cabinet Circular No. 13 of 1969.*

vate hands will be utilized and thereby enable the government to mobilize more resources for the attainment of national goals.

UDI played an important role in prompting the leadership in Zambia to free the economy from existing ties to the south. The disruption of the flow of essential supplies and the provision of transportation services that were occasioned by the hostile relations between Zambia and the Rhodesian regime made Zambia's dependence on the south painfully clear. Not only were there inconveniences and anxieties, but there were very tangible costs incurred in the aftermath of UDI. K84,000,000 alone was spent in government subsidies to transport petroleum products into the country between the time when the supply from Rhodesia was cut off and the pipeline through Tanzania was completed. The commitment to the construction of the K200,000,000 railway from the Copperbelt through Tanzania to the Indian Ocean became stronger and more urgent as the dependence on Rhodesia Railways became more resented. These projects, the construction of the Kafue Dam, the exploitation of Zambia's coal deposits, and the like would have been on the agenda for development efforts even if UDI had not occurred. The main impact of UDI was to give these projects the highest position of priority and urgency and to remove the option of completing the construction of these alternative facilities in a way that was more orderly and caused less disruption to the rest of the economy.

The Mulungushi economic reforms constitute the other major effort of securing more control over the economy. These reforms were implemented in three phases. The first phase was introduced in March, 1968 and consisted of three parts: 1) the government expanded its participation in the economy by securing over 51 percent ownership in twenty-three leading firms in the manufacturing, transportation and retail trade fields; 2) constraints were placed on the repatriation of profits made by foreign firms operating in Zambia; and 3) certain enterprises such as rural trading and sand gravel contracting were reserved for Zambian citizens. To help implement the last policy, credit was to be made more readily available to Zambian entrepreneurs and rationed to non-Zambians. Restricting trading activity to Zambian citizens in effect terminated the near monopoly that the Asian community held on this sector of the economy. Hundreds of Asians made application for Zambian citizenship immediately after the announcement of this policy so that they could retain their position, but few of these applications were processed by the end of 1968 when the policy of granting trading licenses to non-Zambians was formally terminated.

The second phase of the reforms was announced in August, 1969. The major thrust of this phase was the extension of government control to the mining sector. Anglo-American and RST were invited to sell the government 51 percent or more of the stocks of their Zambian mining operations and the government assumed control over all mining and prospecting rights in the country. Negotiations for exact terms of the government stock purchases in the mining industry were not completed until early 1970. The withdrawal of the two firms was not to be complete, although the Zambian government did assume ownership control. Continuity and minimal dislocation were highly valued in this critical industry.

The final sector in which the government assumed more direct control and ownership was the financial sector. In November, 1970, President Kaunda announced that the government would obtain majority ownership in all commercial banks and complete ownership of insurance firms. Both institutions in Zambia have been subsidiaries of foreign firms.

The probable cost of the Mulungushi reforms is a virtual absence of capital imports. Private investors from outside Zambia are not likely to consider investment there as safe or as attractive as in countries where the public sector is not so comprehensive. However, Zambia's major concern is that the profits earned in Zambia be used to further the welfare and development of Zambia. Pleas and threats to foreign firms that they should reinvest more of their profits in the country went unheeded prior to the Reforms. One large foreign concern, for instance, showed a profit of K9,384 in 1960, K5,142 of which was retained in the business and K4,242 of which was distributed as net dividends. In 1967 that company had a profit of K20,668. K5,312 was re-invested and K15,356 was distributed as net dividends.

Prospective Developments

The ethno-regional cleavages within UNIP and the political system as a whole are not likely to dissolve in the near future. Politics in societies more integrated than Zambia's are still affected by ethnic differences. The real and important differences in the policy needs of the various regions in Zambia provide a fundamental force for the persistence of this dimension of political competition. President Kaunda is working to establish a balanced representation of the major groups in the highest levels of government so that everyone will have a sense of participation. If symbols, rules and procedures can be institutionalized for the political process, competition can take place without threatening the stability or the boundaries of the state. The generation of lasting consensus for a particular political order and set of basic rules and principles, however, takes time and builds on the precedents established by the resolution of political conflicts. The challenges of institutionalizing the political process will continue to place a heavy burden on Zambian leadership for an indefinite future.

Events since independence suggest a growing importance of class formation in the political and social order. One source of emerging class divisions is the growing salaried middle class. Civil servants, teachers and white-collar workers in the private and semi-private sectors share a level of income and education that makes them objectively distinct from the bulk of Zambians. Their favored position in a land of general poverty, moreover, gives them important vested interests in their positions and the general status quo.

Similarly, there is an emerging group of Zambian entrepreneurs and businessmen. Although the Mulungushi economic reforms were justified in terms of African socialism and Kaunda's philosophy of humanism, the provisions for replacing Asian traders and for assisting aspirant Zambian businessmen has the effect of simply localizing a class rather than eliminating a class. As more and more Zambians become active as businessmen in the private sector and accumulate wealth, they, too, will constitute a distinct group with common interests in the nature of public policy and the political order.

The emergent classes that have been discussed have not demonstrated clearly that they in fact subjectively share a class identity as well as objective interests. There is little evidence that these groups have acted as a unit in the political arena. There is an abundance of evidence, however, regarding the activity of the laboring class.[39] One of the most serious and chronic problems confronting Zambian leaders has been to meet the demands and the strength of the labor unions, particularly those involved in copper mining. Wage demands have been regarded as responsible for the inflation that has taken place since independence and for the continuance of discrepancies between the welfare of those in urban areas and those in the rural areas. Continued increase in wages could seriously weaken Zambia's competitive position as a supplier of copper. High transport costs already cut into the profit margin. The government has found it very difficult to control the labor unions. Leadership that is willing to be co-operative with the government is undermined by wildcat strikes

[39] See, for instance: Robert H. Bates, "Input Structures, Output Functions, and Systems Capacity: A Study of the Mineworkers' Union of Zambia," *Journal of Politics* 32 (November, 1970): 898–928; A. L. Epstein, *Politics in an Urban African Community* (Manchester: Manchester University Press, 1958); and Elliot Berg and Jeffrey Butler, "Trade Unions"; *Political Parties and National Integration in Tropical Africa,* eds., James S. Coleman and Carl G. Rosberg, Jr. (Berkeley: University of California Press, 1964).

organized at lower levels.[40] Although there is Bemba predominance in some of the unions, workers in Zambia act to further their common interests, regardless of ethnic background, in ways that are indistinguishable from workers in other societies. Again, ethnicity is situational and has a lower degree of salience in the relations between workers and the rest of the political system than it does in political competition among workers. To some extent, the class unity of workers may further class formation in other sectors of society as others respond to the demands and the power of labor.

Another major dimension of political change is Zambia's relations with external political and economic forces. The response to UDI and the policies inaugurated as part of the Mulungushi economic reforms were important steps in moving Zambia from a position of dependence to interdependence in the international community.

The severence of former ties has not been complete and the policies have been pursued with a degree of moderation. The copper companies frustrated Zambia's attempt to control them through partial ownership and in 1973 President Kaunda announced that the government would secure complete ownership. Still, the companies' control over many of the supplies and services needed by the mining industry enables them to inflate the prices of these essentials and thereby continue to extract wealth from Zambia. The Zambian leadership is aware of the continued ties and the various devices used by foreign firms. Zambia is for the most part not the victim of clever trickery. Rather, the decision has been made to alter former structures and establish new relationships with as little disruption and as few costs as possible. In accordance with this policy, non-Zambians are more seriously constrained in their ability to exploit Zambian resources and Zambia recognizes a need to cooperate with foreign firms until internal resources and managerial experiences are adequate to sever ties more completely.

In foreign policy, despite the close relationships established to Western countries during the colonial period, Zambia has meticulously maintained a non-aligned posture. She has diversified sources of aid. The People's Republic of China has assisted Zambia in the construction of roads in the country and the railroad through Tanzania to the Indian Ocean. East European countries have provided technical assistance, a Yugoslavian consortium has been a major actor in the construction industry, and the smaller countries of Europe have increasingly become attractive as trade and aid partners because of their lack of identification with super-power

[40] Bates, "Mineworkers' Union of Zambia." See also his *Unions, Parties, and Political Development: A Study of Mineworkers in Zambia* (New Haven: Yale University Press, 1973).

rivalry. Both the United States and the Soviet Union have maintained a very low profile, in part with Zambia's encouragement.

President Kaunda has personally asserted a leadership role among the non-aligned states. He was active arranging the detente between Kenya and Somalia and offered himself as a mediator to the conflict between Biafra and Nigeria. Zambia, despite her own problems with national unity, was one of four African states to recognize Biafra. At the president's initiative, Lusaka was the site of an African summit meeting in 1969 on the problems in southern Africa and of a conference of non-aligned states in 1970. Zambia has also been active in the United Nations and in 1969 began a term as a member of the Security Council.

As a humanist and pan-Africanist and because of the significant implications for Zambia's security, President Kaunda is deeply concerned about the struggle of Africans in the southern part of the continent to free themselves of white minority rule.[41] Zambia shares boundaries with Angola, Mozambique, Namibia (Southwest Africa) and Zimbabwe (Rhodesia), all areas in which freedom fighters were active in guerrilla warfare. Zambian relations with Great Britain have been most hostile in matters regarding Zimbabwe and South Africa. To no avail, President Kaunda has opposed British inaction in the face of the control exercised by the white minority regime in Southern Rhodesia. Similarly, Great Britain ignored the protests of Zambia and other African states when resuming arms shipments to South Africa.

The support given by Zambia to the freedom fighters has essentially been limited to moral support and to the use of Zambian soil for transit and refuge. The existence of supply and training camps is a debated point. Although Zambia is not supplying troops or equipment, her present involvement makes her vulnerable to retributive attacks by the superior forces of Rhodesia and South Africa. Acts of espionage and sabotage within Zambia have already occurred and have been attributed to the white regimes in southern Africa. President Kaunda is keenly aware of the vulnerability of his country and has begun the establishment of a modest air defence system, including missiles, to help deter bombing raids. Efforts to make the country militarily secure can be little more than symbolic, especially if resources are to be made available for economic development. In a serious confrontation, Zambia would have to rely on the support of outside powers to maintain her security and survival.

[41] For discussions of the liberation movement in Southern Africa, see: Russell Warren Howe, "War in Southern Africa," *Foreign Affairs* 47 (October, 1969): 150–165, and Richard Hall, *The High Price of Principles* (New York: Africana Publishing Corporation, 1969).

Zambia's involvement in southern Africa demonstrates two principles which have been evident in domestic policy areas as well. One is that Zambia's leaders are not free to follow any course of action that they consider most desirable. Dependence on external economic, political, military and social systems is more extensive than the legal constructs of colonialism. Secondly, in making choices and deciding what costs to pay and what benefits to reap, national interests are placed ahead of ideals such as humanism and African socialism.

South Africa

SOUTH AFRICA: FORCED LABOR, INDUSTRIALIZATION, AND RACIAL DIFFERENTIATION

by

Martin Legassick

Introduction

Two processes are starkly evident in contemporary South Africa. The first is the rapid and long-sustained tempo of economic growth which has over some forty years transformed a colonial-type economy into a modern industrial nation: in the 1960's the country's real growth rate was surpassed only by Japan. The second is the marked disparity between white affluence and non-white poverty.[1] While whites, receiving some 74 percent of the national income with less than 19 percent of the population, enjoy one of the highest standards of living in the world, Africans, 69 percent of the population, receive only 19 percent of national income. Or, in other terms, the average *per capita* income of whites is something like thirteen times that of Africans. Indeed, the vast majority of Africans exist on an income below the minimum necessary for subsistence; even in Soweto, the largest African township situated on the Witwatersrand, area of most rapid growth, a recent survey showed that nearly 70 percent of the inhabitants were living below the poverty datum line. The disparities in actual income are matched in the provision of social services and

[1] Terminology represents an acute problem in writing on South Africa. "Black" in its current sense might be preferable to "non-white," despite its somatic inaccuracy; however I have used "non-white" in accord with Fanon's dictum that "it is the settler who has brought the native into existence and who perpetuates his existence." I use "Khoisan" for the peoples otherwise referred to as "Hottentots" and "Bushmen" and "Bantu-speaking" for those members of the South African population referred to as "Bantu," "natives," and "Africans," though I switch to "Coloured" and "Afros" respectively for these people in the modern era.

amenities; in terms of education, health facilities, housing, pensions, and recreation whites are served as well as any advanced industrial country and non-whites in grossly inadequate terms. Most startling of all, perhaps, are figures on infant mortality. While for whites the amount is negligible, surveys in African areas have given figures of two hundred to five hundred per thousand deaths in towns before the age of one year, and, in the rural areas, nearly half the children born die before the age of five.[2]

In addition to this, non-whites are subjected to a degree of control by the state unparalleled in all but the most totalitarian phases of Nazi Germany or Stalinist Russia. Not only are they rigidly restricted to inferior facilities in all public amenities down to benches and toilets, not only are they denied all the basic freedoms, of speech, assembly, publication, movement, associated with modern capitalist societies, but they are subject in their day-to-day lives to the regulation of almost every aspect of their existence. In recent decades, moreover, to the extent that non-whites and even some whites have contested the policies and nature of the South African regime, the system has been maintained by ruthless repression, based on a vast military machine, an ever more powerful secret police, and the use of the most refined and brutal forms of physical and mental torture of suspected opponents of the white-controlled state.

None of these features is unique to South Africa. The poverty of non-whites in South Africa is at least matched, and perhaps exceeded, in parts of Latin America and Asia. Disparities between rich and poor, and the controls that maintain them, can be found in many other societies past and present. Repression, secret police, and torture are hardly exceptional. Similar rates of economic growth have occurred, though comparatively rarely, elsewhere. Yet the ways in which South Africa can be fitted into a comparative study of social systems—and therefore the ways in which it is exceptional—have been obscured by the bulk of the voluminous commentary on that regime. It is the intention of this essay to outline, crudely and schematically, an alternative approach to the study of social dynamics in South Africa.[3]

[2] These figures and their sources can be found in *Industrialization, foreign capital and forced labour in South Africa* (United Nations, Unit on *Apartheid,* 1970, ST/PSCA/Ser A./10), a useful document, as are other United Nations publications on the area.

[3] Some of the ideas in this essay have been aired in other forms at seminars at the Institutes of Commonwealth Studies, London and Oxford, at the Royal Institute of International Affairs, and at the University of Sussex; I am grateful to the organizers of and participants in these seminars. I must also acknowledge my debt to discussions with, among others, Tony Atmore, Rick Johnstone, Ben Magubane Shula Marks, Henry Slater, Bob Sutcliffe, Stan Trapido and Harold Wolpe.

Much of the writing on South Africa has tended to situate its recent social changes into a model created with reference to the experience of "modernization" in Europe and America, with one addition. Industrialization, it is argued, is inevitably associated with progressive urbanization, progressive assessment of persons on criteria of achievement (merit) rather than ascription (birth), with equality of justice and opportunity, free social mobility, and even with a gradual "levelling" of political, social and economic inequalities. In South Africa, it is claimed, some modification of this model must allow for the existence of a "dual economy," of a pre-existing African "subsistence economy" which is only gradually being absorbed into the white-created "market economy." This persistence of the subsistence economy, conservative and offering no income opportunities, is used to explain the abundance of non-whites on the labor market and the low level of non-white wages.[4] Within the "market economy," and as the subsistence economy gradually disappears, it is maintained that the social consequences of industrialization should follow. If progressive "cooperation," "integration," and "interdependence" of black and white in the economic sphere is not followed by similar effects in the social and political spheres, then the cause is white racial attitudes. And such attitudes, the argument continues, are an archaic inheritance from earlier periods of South African history: from slavery, Calvinism, the competition of the frontier, and the group-consciousness of Afrikaners against both non-whites and the British.[5]

Several trends of contemporary social theory cast doubt on this analysis. As Barrington Moore's seminal writing has shown, there is no single model of social relationships consequent on industrialization, and the different

[4] See, for example, H. Hobart Houghton, *The South African Economy* (Oxford: 1964), pp. 19, 45, 67–71, 150, 159–160; *Oxford History of South Africa,* eds., L. M. Thompson and M. Wilson (Oxford: 1971), vol. 2, 1–48 *passim;* R. Horwitz, *The Political Economy of South Africa* (London: 1967), pp. 215–220, 238–9; van den Berghe, *South Africa: A Study in Conflict* (Berkeley: 1967), pp. 91–2, 95–6, 183–190. A key theoretical underpinning here is W. A. Lewis, "Economic Development with Unlimited Supplies of Labour," *Manchester School* 22 (1954), 26 (1958); for a critique of which see the important article by G. Arrighi, "Labour Supplies in Historical Perspective: A Study of the Proletarianization of the African Peasantry in Rhodesia," *Journal of Development Studies* (1970): 197–234.

[5] This argument may be found implicitly in the works quoted above and many others, though the key study for this theory is I. D. MacCrone, *Race Attitudes in South Africa,* (London: 1937). "Afrikaners" are the descendants of the pre-nineteenth-century Dutch, German and French colonists as distinct from British or Jewish South African whites of more recent immigration. Their homogeneity and group-consciousness has been greatly overstressed. As discussed below, the manifestation of this consciousness in "Afrikaner nationalism" has occurred at specific times for specific reasons, in a "populist" cross-class ideological form.

patterns of modernization are produced by different class relationships in preindustrial society.[6] Moreover neither in South Africa nor generally, in terms of the usual analysis, does a "dual economy" exist; in whatever forms, the furthest reaches of all so-called underdeveloped societies are influenced by the existence of the world capitalist economy. Indeed in this respect Barrington Moore's own analysis needs to be complemented and qualified. On the one hand, different societies have evolved autonomously and differently, with different patterns of class relationship; yet on the other hand, since the fifteenth century European expansion, the social systems and relationships of classes in the remainder of the world have been drastically altered by their incorporation into the world capitalist economy. The processes involved have been described as "uneven and combined development," as imperialism, as the "development of underdevelopment," but in each specific case they are reflected in, and their dynamics determined by, the nature of classes and their relationships in specific social systems.[7]

This is not to argue that the white racial attitudes which flow from an ideology of white racism are unimportant in South African society. It is to claim that neither such attitudes in themselves nor the "dual economy" explains either the contemporary structure or the unfolding dynamics of South African society. If South Africa is unique it is not because growing economic cooperation and integration have been impeded by competitive and racialist forces. It is because the forms of that "integration," of the incorporation of non-whites into the world capitalist economy, have been consistently shaped by white political power and manifested in a system of racial differentiation. It is not true that "social classes in the Marxian sense of relationship to the means of production . . . are not meaningful social realities in South Africa." [8] It is true that the system of racial differentiation masks the structure of class relationships through the dynamics of politico-military power. South African economic growth has not occurred, as many would claim, despite racialism; it has occurred through the creation of a system of forced labor based on white power and white racist ideology, and its fruits have been distributed in terms of this system. The international process of simultaneous development and underdevelopment is reproduced within South Africa itself, with the

[6] Barrington Moore, *The Social Origins of Dictatorship and Democracy* (Boston: 1966).

[7] See, *inter alia,* L. Trotsky, *Results and Prospects* (1906); V. I. Lenin, *Imperialism: the Highest Stage of Capitalism* (1917); A. G. Frank, *Capitalism and Underdevelopment in Latin America,* and the important critique of Frank in E. Laclau, "Feudalism and Capitalism in Latin America," *New Left Review* 67 (May-June 1971): 19–38.

[8] van den Berghe, *South Africa,* p. 267. Also *Ibid.,* pp. 62, 100, 179.

division basically coinciding with the division between white and non-white.

The World Commodity Market and Colonial Systems of Forced Labor

From the fifteenth century and the era of great sea voyages of "discovery," Western Europe began to forge direct relationships with the societies of Africa, Asia, Oceania and the Americas. "This was the commercial revolution, the creation of a world commodity market, the most important change in the history of mankind since the metallurgical revolution."[9] In some cases Europeans did not directly disturb the political systems of the societies they encountered. Although accompanied by piracy and plunder on a vast scale, the links established were those of trade. It was through the inherent inequalities of exchange in the trading relationships themselves that European development began to occur at the expense of colonial underdevelopment. At the other extreme, entire non-European populations were exterminated, directly or by new diseases: some twelve to fifteen million Indians by the Spanish *conquistadores* alone. In other cases—Australia or parts of North America—Europeans created new societies and economies on a virtual *tabula rasa*.[10]

In yet other situations Europeans, or those of European origin and with ties to the Western European economy, harnessed the labor-power of non-Europeans to create a surplus for themselves and for the metropolis. In some cases the exploited were "imported" to the new society, most often as slaves. In other cases, where the indigenous population had proved too numerous, and resistant to suffer extermination, their existing mode of production was harnessed (and transformed in the process in various ways) to the requirements of surplus-creation for Western Europe. In these cases, in other words, the expansion of Western Europe led to the creation of colonial economies of forced labor.[11]

Although the intuitive distinction between forced labor, of which chattel slavery is the extreme example, and free labor might appear obvious, the formulation of a generally applicable analytical definition is not that easy. For Marx the "free" laborer, the proletarian, is free in two senses. He

[9] E. Mandel, *Marxist Economic Theory* (London: 1968) vol. 1, p. 106.

[10] See P. Baran, *Political Economy of Growth* (New York: 1957), p. 141. This applies also to the pampas of, for example, Argentina and Uruguay. And even in such situations, e.g. the Northern states of America or the Queensland sugar industry (Mandel, *Marxist Economic Theory,* vol. 1, p. 288), slave or semi-slave labor was used.

[11] Moreover, as some recent writers have suggested, the rise of mercantile capitalism in Western Europe contributed to the intensification of serfdom and forced labor in Eastern Europe also—with, it should be noted, similar consequences in terms of racial ideologies.

is "freed" from access to the means of production, and hence is compelled to offer his labor-power for sale as a commodity. He is also freed from any kind of bondage, which is more significant in this context; he is "the untrammeled owner of his capacity for labor, i.e. of his person." [12] It is not *himself,* but his labor-power, which is the commodity. He is able to contract his labor for a limited period, to transfer it from one master to another, to move freely in search of the best market for his labor-power. Or, in other words, he is not subject to non-economic coercions.

Forced labor economies, however, are not only subject to a variety of forms of appropriation of the surplus (slavery, rent, tribute, share-cropping, debt-peonage, etc.). They are also characterised by a multitude of different forms of non-economic coercion. It might be possible however to group these roughly as *repressive* (organised physical repression) and *ideological.* In some instances the state itself is the prime enforcer of such non-economic coercion by means of legislation backed by ideology and enforced by its monopoly of the legitimate means of force. In other situations the role of the state itself may be weak in comparison with the repressive or ideological weapons in other hands: of local agents (the feudal lord, the slavemaster), of the colonial metropolis (generating an ethos of racism) or even through manipulation of the institutions of the direct producers themselves. "Particularly where the peasant society is preserved, there are all sorts of attempts to use traditional relationships and attitudes as the basis of the landlord's position." [13]

The difficulty arises in that the "classic" proletariat of Western Europe was not and is not entirely free from such non-economic coercions. The creation of this proletariat, for example, that "historical process of divorcing the producer from the means of production" which Marx called primitive accumulation, involved such measures. Enclosure of the common lands, evictions, restrictions on movement from country to town, conscription of labor, compulsions to work on "vagrants" and the "idle," restricted entry to occupations, maximum-wage legislation, criminal penalties for breach of contract all existed in Britain between the sixteenth

[12] K. Marx, *Capital,* vol. 1, p. 168; also, pp. 713–737 *passim.* Compare M. Dobb, *Studies in the Development of Capitalism* (London: 1963 ed.), pp. 35–37.

[13] Moore, *The Social Origins,* pp. 434–5, raises another problem, that "precommercial and preindustrial agrarian systems are not necessarily labor-repressive if there is a rough balance between the overlord's contribution to justice and security and the cultivator's contribution in the form of crops." This also raises the question of to what extent one can talk about "paternalism" in master-slave relations or systems of racial domination (see, for example, van den Berge, *South Africa*). Economically, however, the rate of exploitation is in principle measurable. The question is to what extent power and ideology, however apparently "benevolent," accentuate it.

and eighteenth centuries and some into the nineteenth. Moreover forms of non-economic restraint on the "freedom" of labor continue to exist under advanced monopoly capitalism in the forms of immigration laws, the role and policies of trade union bureaucracies, traditions of community cohesion, etc. One can only insist that the crucial question is the significance of such measures in the total mode of production, and that in this case differences in degree become differences of kind.

Why did such forced labor systems arise on the peripheries of the developing world commodity market after the fifteenth century? A full analysis of this would require extended argument, so the following crude analysis must suffice. In the first place, those wishing to produce commodities for the world market were economically subordinate to the merchants who carried their goods to the market and who preserved a monopoly allowing them to "buy cheap and sell dear."[14] Secondly, and consequently, they were not willing to pay wages sufficient to attract a relatively scarce and relatively unproductive labor supply.[15] The existence of colonists and the indigenous population did not in itself constitute an "abundant" supply of labor. Colonists, immigrants from the metropolis, preferred to engage in trade with the *indigenes* or to tap the natural resources, and tended to regard the "virgin land" actually occupied by the indigenous inhabitants as theirs of right to conquer. The indigenous inhabitants, controlling their own means of production, also preferred to continue a pattern of subsistence or to trade with the foreigners rather than work for them.[16] The "opportunity cost" or "effort price" of other forms of existence was, in other words, less than that of wage-labor.[17]

[14] Dobb, *Development of Capitalism,* pp. 88–9, 127ff. See also A. G. Frank, *Latin America: Underdevelopment or Revolution* (New York: 1969), pp. 128, 329; Laclau, "Feudalism," pp. 34–5; and Mandel, *Marxist Economic Theory,* Vol. I, pp. 82–86.

[15] This argument of "open resources" was expounded by H. J. Nieboer, *Slavery as an Industrial System* (The Hague: 1900). See also, in usual dazzlingly polemical style, K. Marx, *Capital,* vol. 1, Ch. 33, and W. Kloosterboer, *Involuntary Labour since the Abolition of Slavery* (Leiden: 1960); Mandel, *Marxist,* vol. 1, pp. 286–290; Leclau, "Feudalism and Capitalism," p. 35fn; Dobb, *Development of Capitalism,* pp. 37–70 who discusses the analogous question in conditions of Western against Eastern European feudalism. The debate in American history on the role of the expanding frontier as a "safety-valve" on class conflict is also relevant in this connection.

[16] "Subsistence" is an inaccurate and misleading term; a "redistributive" economy is more correct. Some French anthropologists are currently working towards a more precise Marxist analysis of such "classless" societies.

[17] These terms are used by G. Arrighi, "Labour Supplies," and in *The Political Economy of Rhodesia* (The Hague, 1967).

Hence a labor force which could not be attracted by economic means was obtained by non-economic coercion. The means by which this was obtained depended, of course, on the relative force in the hands of colonizers and indigenous inhabitants. Both where the indigenous population was exterminated, and where it was sufficiently powerful to resist separation from the means of production, the usual recourse was to slave labor, imported by means of slave trading with tropical Africa and elsewhere. Alternatively, or as a supplement, the force in the hands of the colonizers might be sufficient to extract some form of surplus from the indigenous inhabitants but insufficient to separate them completely from the means of production and create a proletariat or indigenous slaves. This latter, moreover, was a dynamic process. Trade with the indigenous inhabitants, partial conquest and appropriation of surplus, sharpened economic and political inequalities. Development in the European metropolis and partial development at its colonial epicenters (the points of commodity production and marketing) led to underdevelopment on the colonial peripheries. The balance of political power altered slowly but surely in favor of the colonizers so that a greater surplus could be extracted or the indigenous inhabitants separated from the means of production.

European expansion under mercantile colonialism and the creation of a world commodity market, thus generated systems of forced labor in a syndrome of *conquest*.[18] At all times such systems of forced labor have included an ideology of superiority among the master class; and since labor-control is made easier by physical and cultural differentiation between masters and forced laborers, such an ideology often had an explicitly racial-ethnic dimension. With the European expansion, where the masters were predominantly European and the forced laborers non-European, this ideology was generalized and internationalized as white racism. This is not to say that all such systems of forced labor resulted in rigid separation of the society into white masters and non-white forced laborers. Far from it. Indeed the resulting patterns of what is usually called "race relations" were diverse and complex, and the precise and varied causes of such patterns cannot be entered into here.[19] The degree of racial inter-

[18] This factor of conquest is stressed, though in a rather unsatisfactory form, in John Rex, *Race Relations in Sociological Theory* (London, 1970), especially Chapter II.

[19] A useful and Marxist-oriented introduction may be found in E. Genovese, *The World the Slaveholders Made* (New York: 1969) and *Slavery in the New World*, eds., E. Genovese and L. Foner (New York: 1969). Nor can such matters be considered without reference to the attitudes of "rulers" towards the "ruled," of exploiters towards the exploited, in Western and Eastern Europe—of English towards their poor or their Celtic "colonies" for example.

marriage or extramarital sexual intercourse, the possible roles and statuses achievable by non-whites, are important questions. Yet they neither caused the creation of colonial systems of forced labor nor have they significantly affected their dynamics. Take, for example, the Portuguese colonies of Angola and Mozambique as compared with South Africa. Between the seventeenth and nineteenth centuries one can trace certain comparable features in their political economies, although their patterns of race relations were different. In the twentieth century the ideology and pattern of race relations remains different, yet the evolution of their respective systems of forced labor can be analyzed with identical tools.

South Africa in the Era of Mercantile Colonialism, 1652–1875

The political economy of contemporary South Africa is largely a product of the period since the discovery and large-scale mining of diamonds (from 1870) and gold (from 1885). Yet it was by no means unaffected by the social structures which had developed in the two centuries since the Dutch East India Company had established in the Western Cape a seaport and refreshment station for its ships travelling to and from the mercantile exploitation of Asia. By 1700 this refreshment station had developed into a tiny colony of white settlement based on forced labor; and over the next two hundred years this settler population increased from some two thousand to about three hundred thousand and dispersed from the Western Cape to cover thinly and unevenly most of what is today South Africa. In the meantime, around the turn of the nineteenth century, political hegemony over Southern Africa's colonial economy became transferred from senescent Dutch mercantilism to the rising industrial power of Britain.

Under Dutch mercantile rule, a class of merchants developed in the port of Capetown who were the major colonial appropriators of surplus. The British abolished the formal monopolies of the Dutch era and initiated a period of "free trade imperialism" under which the merchant class, augmented by British immigration and British capital, enlarged its numbers, spread to new coastal towns, and increased its power. Through their ever increasing control over external and internal trade and credit, they were able to exert a substantial influence over other sections of the economy (agriculture, hunting etc.), and were very often landowners and land speculators as well.

Through most of this period South Africa was but weakly and peripherally engaged in the production of agricultural commodities for export to the European market: until the nineteenth century, cattle (for passing ships) and wine were the only such exports. However, as a result of the expansion of the British textile industry, production of wool became important in South Africa from the 1840's, to be joined soon thereafter by the production and export of sugar. In addition, surplus could be appropriated by the export of hunting produce (ivory, animal hides, ostrich feathers), an activity which probably reached its peak around the mid-nineteenth century.

Precolonial South Africa was inhabited by Khoisan and Bantu-speaking peoples who, with some exceptions, might be regarded as practising an Iron Age economy of mixed pastoralism and agriculture. They also engaged in some internal trade, based on a redistributive form of social organization, and with some limited and possibly indirect contact with external markets.[20] Their initial entry into the new colonial economy was through trade, exchanging cattle or the products of the hunt for European goods: only slowly and in comparatively small numbers did they become sufficiently separated from the means of production to be useful for agricultural production for the market. Hence, for the reasons outlined in the previous section, potential commercial farmers found a labor supply largely, though not entirely, by the *importation* of slaves or other types of bondsmen. Wine, wool, sugar were produced by labor deriving largely from such sources. Meanwhile the acquisition of cattle and products of the hunt for export formed a more or less separate economic sector. And, as unequal trade and exertion of superior colonial power weakened the indigenous societies, surplus appropriation by colonists from indigenous inhabitants not fully separated from the means of production constituted a third economic pattern. These three economic patterns merit elaboration.

Agricultural Production for Export

The military power of the Dutch was sufficient to expropriate initial land on which production could begin, and through the eighteenth century the commando system developed by the colonists was sufficiently strong, despite resistance, to continue this expropriation from the Khoisan peoples. Yet until the start of the nineteenth century the main labor supply was of slaves brought from Mozambique, Madagascar and the East and distributed in the Western Cape with usually ten to fifteen slaves per farm.[21] When the British took over the colony, importation of slaves and then slavery itself was gradually abolished. By this time, however, the Khoisan

[20] On precolonial South Africa see *Oxford History,* vol. 1, pp. 1–182; ed., L. M. Thompson, *African Societies in Southern Africa* (London: 1969). It cannot, however, be said that these provide an adequate account of the means and relations of production.

[21] By and large slaves imported from the East became house-slaves or slave-artisans.

peoples were deprived of access to land and could be used to supplement the forced labor supply; the "Caledon Code" of 1809, abolishing Khoi landownership outside mission stations and applying penalties to the Khoi for "vagrancy" for the first time, was a key measure in this respect.[22] With formal abolition slaves and Khoisan melded to form the "Cape Coloured" people, who were soon subjected to new forms of non-economic coercion. Modeled on legislation in the West Indies, the Masters and Servants Ordinance of 1841, strengthened in 1856 and 1873, made breach of contract a criminal offence. Other pass law measures and vagrancy laws were also passed, and convicts were used as laborers. Labor, however, was still scarce, and was brought in on contract at various times from Zanzibar, Mozambique and South West Africa, and was contemplated from even further afield.[23] Similarly, when it was discovered that the coastal lands of Natal were suitable for sugar plantations, the initial labor force was recruited in India on the basis of five-year indentures. Indeed, to this day a significant proportion of the work force for sugar, and to some extent that for the remainder of the agricultural sector, comes from outside the immediate South African area.[24]

This role of slavery or quasi-slavery did, however, extend beyond the *agricultural* export sector. In the eighteenth century the cattle-farmers dispersing from the Western Cape to the interior, for example, employed Khoi as herders and domestics. Although formally paid a wage in they were often tied to the farmer beyond the period for which they had contracted by his refusal to pay the wage, or by holding the family as hostage. And, later in the century and into the nineteenth, commandos raiding from the colonial sector began to seize and trade Khoisan and even Bantu-speaking children on a small scale. With the formation of independent states by white colonists in the interior after the Great Trek (1836) this practice was continued. Bantu-speaking prisoners of war were "apprenticed" to colonists, very often as domestics, and "war" may often have been stimulated to produce such quasi-slaves.

Moreover, although the bulk of the labor in this sector was either Khoisan or labor seized and imported from abroad or beyond the market influence of the colonial economy,[25] Bantu-speaking people were begin-

[22] This point emerges with particular clarity in W. M. Freund, "Society and Government in Dutch South Africa: the Cape and the Batavians, 1803–6" (Ph.D. Thesis, Yale, 1971).

[23] See *Oxford History*, vol. 2, pp. 117–123, 146–7, 156.

[24] M. H. Smith, *The Labour Resources of Natal* (Oxford: 1950), p. 42. I am grateful to Henry Slater for this reference.

[25] For the significance of the "market influence" of the economy see Arrighi, "Labour Supplies," p. 210.

ning to enter it without direct seizure by the mid-nineteenth century. In part, these were people displaced as the result of upheavals in the South African interior stemming from the formation of the Zulu state, people who very often had the intention of returning to their homes when conditions improved.[26] And in part they were those who, like the Khoi in the eighteenth century, were beginning to feel the less direct colonial pressures of trade imbalance and land expropriation.[27]

The Mercantile Trading Economy and Indigenous Societies

Initially Khoisan and Bantu-speakers were not employed as agricultural labor, but rather participated in the colonial economy through the sale of cattle and products of the hunt. In itself this trade tended to be unequal, exchanging productive assets for items of consumption in a situation where the overall economic power was in the hands of the metropolis and its colonial extension. This was the more true because colonists intervened in the initial direct trade between the Dutch East India Company and the indigenous peoples, taking surplus as middlemen, and using direct force to a greater extent. From trading they turned to raiding, particularly if the indigenous people tried to raise prices. From trading products of the hunt they turned to hunting on their own account on the territory of the indigenous peoples. From these activities they turned to the expropriation of the land of the Khoisan and, even where they were unable to forcibly expel the inhabitants, laid claim to it in the name of the colony.

Through the eighteenth century such colonists dispersed well ahead of the sphere of agricultural production. And, despite quite extensive resistance by the Khoisan-speaking peoples the combination of economic and political strength in the hands of the colonists essentially undermined the Khoi economy so that by 1809 they were completely separated from the means of production.[28] But in the nineteenth century the dynamics of this process began to change. In the first place, the commando system, the military basis of colonial power in the eighteenth century, was by no

[26] On these upheavals see J. D. Omer-Cooper, *The Zulu Aftermath* (London: 1966). The question of entry into the colonial labor force is touched on here and in other works, but has not been investigated fully.

[27] Of such groups the most important were the Mfengu (a community displaced by the upheavals) and the Xhosa in the Ciskei, and southern Sotho communities in the valley of the Caledon river.

[28] This is not strictly true. On the fringes of the colony and beyond its formal limits groups known as Kora, "Bastards," Nama, "Oorlams," Griqua preserved access to land, cattle and resources until after the mid-nineteenth century: see M. Legassick, "The Griqua, the Sotho-Tswana, and the missionaries, 1780–1840: the politics of a frontier zone" (Ph.D, UCLA, 1969).

means so effective against the Bantu-speakers which the colonial vanguard now encountered as it had been against the Khoisan. In the second place, the colonists at the frontiers who had been extending the network of colonial trade, land, and power, were gradually displaced in the nineteenth century by specialist itinerant traders (*smouse*), by British "gentlemen" who engaged in trading and hunting, and later by a network of country storekeepers. All these later groups had much closer connections with the colonial merchant class. Moreover, as the sphere of agricultural production for export extended from the 1840's and encouraged land speculation, the value of land increased and hence the pressure for expropriation on the indigenous inhabitants.

At this stage, it would seem, the eighteenth century vanguard, the hunter-trader-pastoralist, moved to the interior to set up separate states in areas where the indigenous population was comparatively thin or weakened for some reason. The main pressure on the Bantu-speaking people's political economy occurred elsewhere, where increase in the value of land and the activities of specialist traders were supplemented by British military power, more effective than the colonists' commando. By a variety of means, these pressures weakened the indigenous redistributive economy, or, more accurately, began to absorb it into the colonial economy by promoting class differentiation in Bantu-speaking societies. As in the case of the Khoisan, there was on the one hand the beginnings of a class of landless Africans, compelled to enter the agricultural forced labor sector, or at least to pay some form of rent-tribute to white or black landlords. On the other hand, those who had been able to accumulate wealth during the trading process, or by temporary employment in a wage-earning sector, could enter commercial farming on their own account; in the case of wool, this is what some were beginning to do.[29] Yet, it must be emphasized, this process was not advanced by the time of the discovery of diamonds and gold. Indeed around the peripheries of white settlement there remained a number of Bantu-speaking states who had retained ownership of their land and formal political autonomy: the peoples of the Transkei (Xhosa, Thembu, Mpondo, etc.), of Zululand, of the Zoutpansberg, of Lesotho, of Botswana, and to some extent the Swazi, the Lobedu, the Pedi. Despite the pressures on them, such peoples, by a combination of military resistance and careful diplomacy, preserved and adapted a cultural tradition whose roots were in pre-colonized South Africa. In the twentieth century the vitality of this tradition, still present and alive, would continue to form a major part of African opposition to white

[29] Important research on such groups is currently being carried out by, *inter alia,* Colin Bundy at Oxford, Henry Slater at Sussex, and Robert Ross at Cambridge.

supremacy; for Africans, if not for the Coloured or Indians, the forced labor economy has not involved the near-complete cultural disruption of slavery in the Americas.[30]

Surplus-extraction from Independent Indigenous Producers

Displaced from behind by specialized traders, unable on their own to make any impact on settlement of Bantu-speakers where this was dense, the descendants of the eighteenth-century hunter-trader-pastoralist scattered into the interior to seek more distant avenues for trade and hunting. They were followed closely by the land speculator and the trader, colonial or directly British, though much less closely by the full weight of British military power.[31] In this situation, land was secured initially in areas where the indigenous people were few or weakened; full-time labor was obtained initially by the seizure of "apprentices." If the colonists and others were strong enough to claim sovereignty over increasing tracts of land, they were less able to separate indigenous Bantu-speakers from the means of production, or to engage in production for the export market. Hence, in nineteenth century South Africa prior to the mining era, there developed a number of other forms of surplus appropriation.

Initially, for example, the interior settler communities (and the British colony of Natal) imposed a labor tax on the indigenous inhabitants, drawing a seasonal supply for domestic agricultural needs which did not preclude Bantu-speakers from production on their own account. Or, particularly on the large tracts whose ownership was gobbled up by land speculators, the existing occupiers of the land might be compelled to pay rent in kind or in money. Other methods of exploitation, which may have developed somewhat later, were the system of "half-shares," under which the indigenous occupiers received seed and implements and paid half of the crop they produced in tribute, and the system of labor tenancy by which indigenous occupiers worked for the landowner for, usually, ninety days per year. These forms were all in the broadest sense forced labor, but of a different kind from that performed by Cape Coloureds,

[30] I do not here intend to enter the controversy over "African survivals" in the black culture of the Americans which in many cases clearly exists. My point is that such "survivals," after the traumatic "shock" experience of enslavement and transportation (Cf. S. Elkins, *Slavery,* New York) are qualitatively different from a continuous repository of cultural tradition *in situ.*

[31] These brief remarks refer to the so-called "Great Trek" (1836)—although the dispersion of such people occurred both before and after this event. The causes and, more important, the contemporary as opposed to later ideological significance of the Great Trek, need, in the light of my own assessment, considerable reinvestigation.

Indians, or "apprentices." The system was, one might say, quasi-feudal rather than quasi-slavery.

Class differentiation occurred, too, in this economic sector. At one extreme were large-scale land companies, often owned by mercantile capital. At the other extreme were white *bywoners,* those whom the pressures of colonial development behind and inability to expropriate further land from Bantu-speakers ahead were reducing to landlessness and the payment of rent or tribute. In between these groups were white landowners anxious to increase the exploitation of their tenants insofar as they could do this without their decamping to other land, and insofar as they could gain access to new markets. And among the indigenous occupiers of the land, those occupying suitable areas and able to produce a surplus over and above the needs of subsistence and their rent tribute, were also aspirant commercial farmers, especially insofar as they could purchase land.

The economically dominant class during this period was the merchant class, composed of substantial investors in land as well as in trade. But if export-oriented and other farmers were often economically dependent on the merchants, they also shared in the power of the colonial state. One might speak indeed of an "alliance of merchants and farmers" as the ruling class at this time, an asymmetrical alliance, with farmers waging continual struggles to maintain their share of it, but an alliance no less. Through their share in this alliance the farmers had secured slave labor and the slave codes which accompanied it. They had secured the legislation which perpetuated the forced labor system beyond the era of slavery. Through the commando system, operating semi-autonomously from the colonial state, the vanguard of the colonists had secured cattle, products of the hunt, labor and land from the indigenous inhabitants. They had been able to penetrate sections of the interior. But, as the condition of the *bywoner* indicates, such a military-political institution was no longer sufficient for these purposes. Further conquest of still-autonomous African areas, more intensive exploitation of African producers on white-owned land, required greater politico-military power. Moreover, both in land under African and white ownership, a class of Africans was developing who could engage, and were engaging, like whites, in the commercial agricultural economy. On the other hand, through the varieties of forced labor, through the pressures on the indigenous economies, the political and economic forces which had sparked development and surplus appropriation for the largely white few had exacerbated underdevelopment for the largely non-white many.

No simple formula would suffice to describe the pattern of race relations in the mercantile colonial era. Initial colonization, and the power which was exerted to perpetuate the forced labor system and extend the area of colonial hegemony certainly hardened the existing generalized ideology of white racism. For a "white" to undertake manual labor was degrading. Yet who was "white" was socially rather than biologically defined; it is well-known that a large proportion of the South Africans descended from the pre-nineteenth century colonists have partly non-white "blood." Moreover, throughout this period non-whites in colonial society, whether of the Cape or the interior and whatever the proclaimed ideology of the rulers, had access to roles other than those of manual labor. The social change of the mining era bears no simple relationship to pre-existing racial attitudes, as many commentators assume, and is best discussed in terms of the immediate interests of the dominant social classes involved.

South Africa in the Mining Era, 1875–1924: Gold, Maize and Segregation

The discovery and mining of diamonds and gold produced qualitative transformations in the South African political economy. From supplying meager exports of wool and sugar, from furnishing a rather limited market for British manufactures, from having a largely strategic significance because of its situation on the sea route to the East, South Africa became the major supplier of the currency base of the international capitalist system: gold.[32] At the end of the nineteenth century, the "free trade imperialism" of the period of undisputed British industrial hegemony was being replaced by the scramble for economic and political territory characteristic of monopoly capitalism. In South Africa itself the ruling alliance of merchants and farmers was transformed into what one recent writer has termed the alliance of "gold and maize.[33] The country's economic and political focus shifted from the Cape and Natal to the interior: to Kimberley, where diamonds were produced, to the Transvaal, where the gold-bearing reefs of the Witwatersrand were situated, to the Orange Free State, where white farmers began to grapple with the problem of supplying maize to urban markets which were flooded with cheap imported grains.

Both mine owners and potential commercial farmers demanded an increased supply of labor, under conditions where most of the potential non-white labor force retained access to the means of production. In mining the problem of non-white labor costs was supreme. Technical

[32] This point is developed in recent unpublished work by Paul Trewelha, Tony Atmore, and Ben Magubane.

[33] S. Trapido, "South Africa in a Comparative Study of Industrialization," *Journal of Development Studies* 7 (1971).

and geological problems had produced, both in diamonds and gold, an industrial structure, whose ownership was highly concentrated and which required large-scale investment of foreign capital. Gold, at any rate, sold at a fixed price. Through direct taxation, railway rating policy, and other methods raising the cost of mining equipment, the Transvaal state took its share of the mining surplus for the benefit of farmers. The mine owners had to pay their skilled (and white) workers high wages to attract them to South Africa from abroad. And the white farming community, till then geared to production for European markets, to a very limited local market, or to subsistence, suddenly found themselves unable to compete with the American grain that was carried from the ports to the new urban mining centers along rail lines that bypassed them. Moreover, in the production of such foodstuffs as maize, the small emerging group of African farmers producing for the market, with their better knowledge of local conditions, intensive cultivation of small holdings, more frugal living, use of kin rather than coerced workers as a labor force, presented a potential economic threat to white farmers.

At the point of production, mine owners rapidly instituted forms of labor-coercion. From almost the earliest days of large-scale diamond mining the non-white workforce was housed in compounds, barracks which subjected the worker during his term of employment to well-nigh total regimentation. Ostensibly to prevent theft, the compounds operated to impede the labor force from organizing, bargaining, striking, or deserting. In 1889 the few gold-mining houses came together to form the Chamber of Mines. "Its major objective was to reduce the mining industry's labor cost." [34] It tried to achieve this by eliminating competition between mines over wages and working conditions, centralizing the control over recruitment of the labor force, and in general establishing a monopolistic policy towards labor. Yet this was not in itself enough. If it controlled, as on export-oriented farms, the labor force which existed, it did not generate a sufficient supply at the wages which mine owners were prepared to pay. Between 1890 and 1910, in fact, the major additions to the gold-mining labor force came from Portuguese East Africa, and between 1902 and 1906 indentured Chinese labor was introduced. This was the old pattern of imported semi-slave labor, seized from beyond the limits of the South African political economy: it was not a proletariat generated by processes within South Africa itself.

Indeed the diamond mines in particular were able to attract a work force without recourse to such measures. From those African areas which had retained their political antonomy came people to buy guns with

[34] Horwitz, *Political Economy,* p. 26.

which to defend themselves against further losses of land or against loss of autonomy. In such areas, already penetrated by the mercantile network, country storekeepers recruited labor among the poorer or landless by advancing goods against prospective mining wages. In such cases the Africans came to the mines or the towns as migrants. Despite class differentiation in these areas, despite their growing connections to the capitalist economy and the consequent impoverishment and underdevelopment, it was in these areas of successful resistance to expropriation of land and loss of sovereignty that Africans found their cultural and economic roots. Africans, Coloureds, or Indians moved to the urban areas from their positions as quasi-slaves or quasi-feudal tenants in the farming sector—railways and harbours, public works, domestic service, transport riding, and petty production provided expanding avenues of employment.

Yet these economic processes, the slow unfolding of the dynamics of the existing political economy, were not sufficient to meet the needs of the new situation.[35] Those non-whites who moved permanently to the towns were competed for by employers and tended to drive up wages, while farmers could not intensify exploitation without losing laborers. The supply of migrant workers from the autonomous African areas was insufficient. In this sector, as in the case of tenants or sharecroppers on white-owned land, the "opportunity cost" of production for subsistence or a market was lower than taking employment in mines or on commercial farms.

The first step towards a solution was taken by completing the process of conquest. In the last quarter of the nineteenth century those African areas which had remained politically autonomous were brought under white rule, either by the exertion of imperial military power or by colonial commandos strengthened by the booming economy. Economically weakened and losing their political autonomy, Africans were now disarmed. Until they could regain their guns, they would be compelled to seek redress within the white-controlled political system. Taxation was imposed, to ensure that no African remained outside the imperatives of the cash economy. Britain, already exerting her hegemony over the Cape Colony and Natal, went to war against the politically independent Orange Free State and Transvaal in 1899 and annexed them in the following year. It seems probable that this extension of British hegemony was stimulated

[35] Because of our inadequate understanding of precolonial "redistributive" economies, the processes within such economies as a result of new external economic and politically coercive pressures are not well understood. One analysis of this, introducing the ideas of "disguised unemployment," "necessary and discretionary income" is made in Arrighi, "Labour Supplies." Clearly the "cultural" assault waged by the missionaries was also important.

by, as much as anything, the need to establish in these areas an administrative system more efficient and powerful than that of the settler republics.[36] Under British hegemony, the four white-ruled republics and most of the recently conquered African areas[37] were constituted into the Union of South Africa. The growing economic interdependence of white capital and coerced non-white labor was crystallised in this political unity. In 1910, Britain returned state power to the alliance of gold and maize.

The major task of this alliance was to increase the supply of non-white labor under conditions which would allow both mine owners and farmers to perpetuate their coercion of the work force. As an early economic historian of South Africa wrote in 1924, "until comparatively recent years the only important labor problem in South Africa was how to secure an adequate supply of labor."[38] In 1911 the Native Labor Regulation Act extended to the mines the criminal sanctions against contract-breaking (strikes) provided elsewhere by the Masters and Servants Acts. Two years later the Native Land Act tackled the problem of a coerced labor supply more directly. "It is possible" writes a recent commentator,

> to regard the 1913 Land Act as being an act of collusion amongst the hirers of farm labor not to give remuneration above a certain level. At the same time as the land legislation was being discussed and passed, the mine owners were working out, not for the first time, an agreement whereby the average wage of blacks on any mine would not exceed a certain maximum, and there is a sense in which the Land Act was, for farmers, what the maximum-permissive-average agreement was for the mining magnates."[39]

As with other measures before and since, it was a major aim of the Land Act to redistribute more evenly the labor supply on white-owned land, and to eliminate the quasi-feudal forms of rent or tribute payment or sharecropping by Africans in favor of either labor tenancy or wage laboring. Its initial application was to the Orange Free State, where farmers wished to convert to maize growing and yet could not intensify the ex-

[36] See Trapido, "Comparative Study of Industrialization," and also G. Blainey, "Lost Causes of the Jameson Raid," *Economic History Review* 18 (1965): 350–366; D. Denoon, " 'Capitalist Influence' and the Transvaal Government during the Crown Colony period, 1900–1906," *Historical Journal* 11 (1968): 301–331.

[37] The areas of Lesotho, Botswana and Swaziland remained under British "protection." However their economies were integrated into that of South Africa. Apart from a white capitalist agricultural sector in Swaziland (and to some extent in Botswana) and some African production of cattle in Botswana and Swaziland, their main export to South Africa was labor, their main revenue a share of customs duties on foreign imports to their countries.

[38] M. H. de Kock, *Economic History of South Africa* (Capetown: 1924), p. 434.

[39] *Oxford History,* vol. 2, p. 128. See also Ibid., pp. 117–8, 127.

ploitation of their work force so long as more favorable opportunities (occupation without labor) were open on other white-owned land. Its enforcement has been gradually extended, along with other measures stiffening criminal sanctions on contract-breaking and inhibiting movement of labor from farms to towns. In consequence, on the farms as well as in the mines, the absolute real wages of the labor force have remained stationary or declined from Union to the present day.[40]

Yet neither farmers nor landowners wanted this transformation of the relations of production in the rural areas to proceed too far. Even if Africans were prevented from sharecropping or rent payment on white-owned land, they still owned land themselves, either as individuals, as groups, through third parties, or in recently conquered areas. Retention of a free market in land, in other words, would have continued the process of class differentiation in the African community between the growing group of market-farmers, potentially competitive with whites, and the vast majority of Africans who would have become permanently landless. Flocking to the towns, such Africans would have increased the pulls away from the rural coerced labor sector, as well as constituting a serious urban political threat to the system of white control.[41] Moreover the mine owners were well satisfied with the system of migrant labor and compounds which had developed in the late nineteenth century, since this allowed them to pay wages at the level appropriate for a single worker, rather than a worker and his family.[42]

Hence the consolidation of the forced labor economy of gold and maize required the abolition of a free market in transfer of land between white and non-white, and restrictions on the permanent urbanization of a potential non-white proletariat. The 1913 Land Act, as amended in 1936, achieved the first of these tasks. The second aspect, though it had half-heartedly characterised earlier policy, was systematised in the Native (Ur-

[40] Among such measures were the Masters and Servants Amendment Act of 1926, the Native (Urban Areas) Amendment Acts of 1930 and 1937, and the Native Service Contract Act of 1932. On the level of real wages see *Oxford History,* vol. 2, pp. 158–162; F. Wilson, *Labour in the South African Gold Mines, 1936–1969* (Cambridge: forthcoming).

[41] The imperatives of social control in white policy-making are stressed by H. J. Simons, *African Women* (London: 1968), p. 42ff; H. J. and R. E. Simons, *Class and Colour in South Africa* (London: 1969), p. 345; P. van den Berghe, *South Africa,* pp. 79, 150–1 etc.; D. Welsh in *Oxford History,* vol. 2, pp. 184–196, *passim.*

[42] Cf *Oxford History,* vol. 2, p. 195; Arrighi, "Labour Supplies," and Rex, *Race Relations,* p. 56: "the compound system in conjunction with the reserves system involves a kind of exploitation unknown to the plantations. For while the plantation owner had a perpetual responsibility for the upkeep of his slave, the mineowner . . . has no responsibility to his worker beyond the nine-month period."

ban Areas) Act of 1923 and its periodic amendments at later times. The premise of this legislation was that "the town is a European area in which there is no place for the redundant Native, who neither works [for the white man] nor serves his or her people"[43] and its instrument was, and remains, the *pass*. All African men from that time, and subsequently all adult Africans, must carry with them at all times a *pass*, containing details of their life history and employment, and hence of their "right" to be where they are. Clearly the pass provides a fundamental instrument of labor regulation, allowing the state to channel and distribute labor between farms and towns, among different capitalist sectors, or—when it is not needed—to remove it from white-controlled sectors of the economy. Moreover in periods of particular rural labor shortage the numerous Africans convicted under the pass laws are directly channeled to jails on white farms where they serve their sentence as convict labor.

Under the Land Act African occupation of territory was restricted to some 13 percent of the area of South Africa, as well as to Swaziland, Lesotho and Botswana which had remained under direct British control. These were the areas, by and large, which because of African resistance had remained autonomous until the late nineteenth century when they were conquered by the British. It was from these areas—the "reserves" as they were known—that migrant labor was to come to the towns. It was to these areas that rent-paying or sharecropping Africans on white-owned land refusing to engage in labor were to go. It was in these areas that the families of migrants were supposed to earn that subsistence that was not paid to the migrant in the mines. It was in these areas that children were to be raised, and old men to die. Thus was the white-controlled state to be spared, in large measure, the welfare costs of housing, pensions, social facilities and amenities for the non-white work force. If during the nineteenth century the tendency of the colonial political economy had been towards the expropriation of African land and the encouragement of class differentiation among the African population, now these processes were halted. What remained of the indigenous African economy was to be frozen in a static form and harnessed to the needs of white development. And not only social services, but social control, were to be exerted through traditional indigenous institutions. The chiefs, whose powers had generally been undermined in the nineteenth century, found their authority resurrected, but in subordination to the administrative arm of the white state. Indeed, the South African Governor-General (now State President) became Supreme Chief of the African population. The corol-

[43] *Report of Native Affairs Commission for 1921,* pp. 25–7. Compare the *Transvaal Local Government Commission* (Stallard Commission) of 1922.

lary was that no Africans, or non-whites as a whole, should be permitted political rights in the central white-controlled institutions, either parliamentary or trade-unionist. The resurrection and consolidation of traditional authority can be traced from the Native Affairs Act (1920) and the Native Administration Act (1927) to the Bantu Authorities Act (1951) and the Promotion of Bantu Self-Government Act (1959). The "reserves" have now become Bantustans; their economic and political functions remain unchanged. Conversely such political rights as non-whites had managed to win during the nineteenth century were gradually whittled away from the 1920's, so that today the South African Parliament contains no direct or indirect representatives of any non-white peoples.

This policy—restrictions on permanent urbanization, territorial separation of land ownership, the use of traditional institutions as providers of "social services" and means of social control—was originally termed "segregation." It was not, as many commentators have argued, a policy produced by the imposition of earlier social attitudes on the new conditions of South African industrialization. Nor were its major proponents the more "backward" of the white rural population. Its major theoreticians and ideologists in the inter-war period—General Smuts, General Hertzog, and Heaton Nicholls—spoke for other groups, essentially for the alliance of gold and maize.[44] Along with other mechanisms of labor coercion, it created and perpetuated the system of migrant labor which has characterized South Africa's road to industrialization. After the Second World War segregation was continued its premises unchanged as *apartheid* or "separate development."

The final achievement of the alliance of gold and maize was the encouragement, through the state, of white capitalist farming at the expense of any potential African peasant production for the market, and in the face of competition from foreign sources. Segregation was one side of the weapon to be used; the other was direct and indirect state subsidization. Already in 1907 one commentator was able to write that "it is probable that during the last twenty years more money per head of the rural population has been devoted to the relief of the farmers in South Africa than in any country in the world," [45] mainly as the result of diversion of surplus

[44] See particularly J. C. Smuts, "Problems in South Africa," *Journal of the African Society* 16 (1917); *Africa and Some World Problems* (Oxford: 1930); "Racial Separation: A View Taken in 1936" [G. Heaton Nicholls], *African Studies* 26 (1967).

[45] F. B. Smith, *Some Observations upon the Probable Effect of the Closer Union of South Africa upon Agriculture* (Pretoria: 1908).

from mining. This policy was intensified after union; between 1910 and 1935 alone, eighty-seven bills relating to the land were enacted by the white parliament. The rating policies of the state-owned railway system favoured agricultural products at the expense of materials needed by the mines. New railway branch lines were constructed largely for the benefit of farmers, particularly maize farmers, who were able to change South Africa's food-importing condition to one of export by the end of the first World War. White farmers were provided with technical assistance and research. Irrigation and land settlement schemes were funded by the state. And, most important of all, the Land Bank established in 1912 provided both short-term loans against crop harvesting and long-term loans for capital improvement. By the inter-war period South Africa was an increasing exporter of maize, dairy products, meat and fruit in addition to the old crops of wool and sugar. In this field the state again came to the assistance of the farmer, controlling the quality of produce, and then protecting him against both external competition and the fluctuations of price in the capitalist world market characteristic of agricultural raw materials. The culmination of this policy was the Marketing Act of 1937, by which the marketing of the bulk of South Africa's farm produce came under the control of a series of producer-controlled boards.

Thus, in a sense, the three economic sectors of nineteenth-century South Africa had by the inter-war period been reduced to two: the white capitalist farming sector with its coerced labor force, and the mining economy with its migrant labor force recruited in the African "reserves." But the processes of development and underdevelopment had continued. Mine owners, capitalist farmers and white workers were reaping the benefits. Those Africans who had retained access to the rural means of production in the nineteenth century were squeezed off white-owned land into the reserves, squeezed out of marketing produce of their own land by the pressures of population, segregation and subsidization of white agriculture. Perhaps by 1900 in some areas, and certainly by the 1920's and 1930's, the African reserves had been reduced from production of a surplus to sub-subsistence. Yet restrictions on permanent urbanization, and the mechanisms of labor-coercion which inhibited African organization and strikes, inhibited the process of proletarianization and struggling for a better standard of living in the urban areas. Real wages for non-whites were, in other words, by and large static or declining in the white-controlled economy; meanwhile the possibilities for supplementing such wages by productive activity in the reserves fell steadily. Indeed while white capitalist agriculture produced vast subsidized surpluses for export, the marketing board policy kept domestic prices high and promoted malnutrition and starvation in the African reserves.

The Mining Economy, Secondary Industrialisation, And the White Worker

The mining of gold, it has been argued by many commentators on South Africa, was the motor of economic transformation and industrialization; the gold-mines were "perhaps the single most important factor determining the rate of economic growth of South Africa then and now."[46] Yet the mine owners themselves were not responsible for this internal structural growth. It was through the state that a part of the mining surplus was diverted to finance commercial agricultural development. Such factors as state-imposed tariffs caused a certain amount of industrial development in support-industry for mining (e.g., explosives) to take place rather than continued importation of foreign products by the mines. And, apart from such support industries for mining, the only manufacturing developments were in "easy import substitution" light industries, probably financed by commercial capital. With such an economy based on mining, export agriculture, and light industry, South Africa remained in the 1920's a colony of international capital.

The fact that many mine owners resided in South Africa itself did give them a certain "national" as well as "international" interest. But by and large their capital was reinvested in mining and not diversified; their interests spread geographically rather than structurally. Between the wars the most notable example was the Anglo-American Corporation, founded by Sir Ernest Oppenheimer. Partly with American capital, Anglo-American gained control of diamond production in South Africa itself, South West Africa, Angola, Tanganyika, and eventually on a world scale. Similarly it was a major investor in the Northern Rhodesian copper mines when these were developed in the late 1920's.[47] As with capital, so with labor: mine owners pressed continually to be allowed to use non-white labor drawn from tropical Africa.

Such economic expansion of mining at the expense of structural change in the South African economy found its political expression. If the "alliance of gold and maize" supported the incorporation of South West Africa as a "mandated colony" of the Union after the first World War, and was pressed for the transfer of the High Commission Territories from British to South African rule,[48] it was predominantly the mining interests

[46] Horwitz, *The Political Economy,* p. 53. Compare de Kock, *Economic History,* p. 238; Houghton, *The South African Economy,* p. 104ff.

[47] See particularly T. Gregory, *Ernest Oppenheimer and the Economic Development of Southern Africa* (Oxford: 1962); Supplement to *Financial Mail* (Johannesburg).

[48] There were also pressures from South Africa towards the annexation of Delagoa Bay and southern Mozambique from Portugal, providing an additional port and control over the labor supply from this area.

that wished for further political expansion. Spurred by his experience in East Africa in World War I, General Smuts was the chief spokesman for such views. "All the highlands of East Africa from the Union to Abyssinia are healthy for Europeans and can be made a great European state or system of states. . . It is one of the richest parts of the world and only wants white brains and capital to become enormously productive" [49] he wrote in 1924 and this remained his policy. "From every previous war South Africa has emerged a greater country and this war will prove no exception" he told departing South African troops in the Second World War, and in the context "greater" clearly was geographic in its meaning.[50]

Such a disinterest in developing South Africa itself was not shared by commercial farmers. The ban on the introduction of mining labor from north of 22S latitude, in force between 1913 and 1933, might well be explained in terms of the farmers' need for mine owners' attention to the creation of a suitable labor force in South Africa itself, and when Smuts's program for expansion was attacked in 1929 as a desire to create "a black Kaffir state extending from the Cape to Egypt," [51] his opponents were deploring his inadequate attention to industrial development in South Africa. For commercial farmers, a national rural bourgeoisie, would benefit from the expanded urban markets for their produce consequent on industrialization. And, as agriculturalists unconcerned about the role of the state in promoting industry, they were able in the 1920's to win the support of two other sections of the white community and to modify and enlarge the scope of the policy of "segregation." [52]

The first of these groups was the organized white working class, especially those in skilled jobs. The "job color bar," division of labor in the form of skilled-white, unskilled-non-white provided a justification for the coercion of non-white labor and was dependent on the forced labor system. As such its overall premises were supported both by the mine owners and the white workers.[53] In the years immediately after the First World War, however, mine owners faced with a falling rate of profit sought to lower their costs by displacing higher-paid whites in borderline occupa-

[49] To Leo Amery, November 1924, quoted in W. K. Hancock, *Smuts; The Fields of Force,* vol. 2 (Cambridge: 1968), p. 223.

[50] J. C. Smuts, *Greater South Africa: Plans for a Better World* (Johannesburg: 1940), Ch. 17.

[51] By General Hertzog: Hancock, *Smuts,* p. 218.

[52] On the nature of the "national interest" of commercial farmers see Arrighi, *Political Economy;* "Labour Supplies" and Simons, *Class and Colour,* p. 347.

[53] This argument is developed in F. R. Johnstone, "Class Conflict and Colour Bars in the South-African Gold-Mining Industry," (mimeo, February 1970), and his forthcoming D.Phil for Oxford University.

tions with lower-paid Africans.[54] White workers, able to organize in trade unions, and with access to state power through political organization and voting, naturally defended their monopoly of skills and level of wages. Denouncing the "semi-slavery system" of coercion of non-white labor practiced by the mine owners, they sometimes advocated total segregation, i.e., a totally white work force on the mines.[55] They recognized correctly that their own relationship to the means of production was different from that of non-white workers. And, believing that mine owners might in time try to use state power to impose similar disabilities on them, they took industrial action, culminating in 1922 in the "Rand revolt." A general strike here escalated into near-insurrection, with the South African government calling out the army to break the resistance of white worker commandos; it was the country's most violent labor struggle up to that time and, perhaps, since. But, in its wake, white workers turned themselves to the state for an entrenchment of their position.

The dissatisfaction of the white working class, which by this time was predominantly Afrikaans-speaking, coincided with the grievances of another largely Afrikaner group. Resistance by African societies, the freezing of the free market in land, the commercialization of agriculture, meant that an increasing number of whites were reduced first to the status of landless *bywoners,* and then displaced from the land to the cities.[56] Characteristically in a colonial economy, jobs did not expand as fast as the demand for them, leading to white unemployment and destitution. In the South African context this was exacerbated by the forced labor system for non-whites which reduced prevailing wages in less skilled jobs below what whites were prepared to accept. Such whites demanded of the state both industrialization to create employment, and an assurance that they would not be paid wages at the level of the forced labor system.

These groups—commercial farmers, organized white workers, and the newly urbanized "poor whites"—were the basis of the Nationalist-Labor Pact government which came to power in 1924. Against the protests of mining capital, but in line with the requirements for development in a colonial economy, this government used state capital (the surplus from mining) to create South Africa's first heavy industry, an iron and steel

[54] However, significantly, the mine owners initially made approaches to the British money market for the raising of the gold price. See de Kock, *Economic History.*

[55] See, for example, Simons, *Class and Colour,* pp. 95, 128–30, 142, 146, 155, 162.

[56] In other words, there was a trend not only of concentration of land ownership in white hands, but of concentration of ownership *within* the white community. Much research is needed on the structure of land ownership within the white community.

plant (ISCOR). Since that time state-industry, or state-capital catalysis of private industry, has been an important lever in South Africa's industrial growth. Of ISCOR itself one commentator has written, "There is hardly a sector in the country's economy which its activities do not permeate and influence to a greater or lesser extent."[57] The state-run Industrial Development Corporation (IDC), founded in 1940 under wartime conditions, has since that time stimulated other industrial "growth poles" —SASOL, for example, producing oil from coal, and laying the basis for petrochemicals, or FOSKOR, producing fertilizers.[58]

Other legislation in the 1920's entrenched the job color bar in mining to the satisfaction of white workers. Over the wider industrial field entry to skilled trades was stringently and racially limited through regulation of apprenticeship, while a structure of collective bargaining between employers and white workers was established which, at least under conditions of economic growth, ensures that the white working class, like white farmers, receives a proportion of the surplus generated by the forced labor economy. As a consequence, industrial peace between white workers and their employers has since reigned on a scale unmatched in any advanced capitalist society. And the final achievement of the period was legislation securing the preferential employment of the "poor whites" at suitable wages: the so-called "civilized labor policy." In the public sector (railways, harbors, ISCOR, postal services, etc.) this was made compulsory, resulting particularly in the displacement of Indians and Coloureds who had moved into such jobs out of the agricultural forced labor sector. In private industry—footwear and clothing, food industries, motor assembly —tariff policy encouraged the employment of "civilized labor."

Much attention has been paid by analysts of South Africa to the "job color bar." It is argued that this, above all, is the product of white racial attitudes. As racist rural whites moved to town, it is claimed, they found themselves in competition with black workers and demanded an entrenchment of their position which, by preventing "least-cost substitution" of labor at the lowest wages, has hindered South Africa's economic growth. This is an absurd argument. The job color bar is the product of two processes (a) the imposition of a system of forced labor on non-whites which, reducing their freedom and bargaining ability, meant that at no time were they directly in competition with white workers (b) the access

[57] A. J. Norval, *A Quarter of a Century of Industrial Progress in South Africa* (Capetown: 1962), p. 31. See also Houghton, *The South African Economy,* pp. 101, 115–6, 122, 195.

[58] On the role of the IDC see, *inter alia,* H. J. van Eck, *Some Apects of the South African Industrial Revolution* (SAIRR, rev ed, 1953); G. S. J. Kuschke, *South Africa: the basic philosophy on which her economy has been built* (IDC: 1966?).

of white workers to state power, a product of the colonial economy of South Africa and of the justification of the forced labor system by the alliance of gold and maize in terms of a racist ideology. In short, the job color bar is merely a special aspect in a total system, a system which has indeed produced South African economic growth. The job color bar is a symptom of the ability of white workers to place themselves on the favorable side of South Africa's unfolding dynamic of development and underdevelopment.

Secondary Industrialisation in a Forced Labor Economy

The degree of state power in the hands of "national" interests rather than international-imperial capital was able to ensure the establishment of an infrastructure for industrialization, and to prevent accumulated capital from being eaten away by inflation or drained out of the country. But the rapid development of manufacturing industry itself, in a situation where the internal market was small and the income distribution grossly skewed, required stimuli from outside the society.[59] The first such stimulus came as a result of the world capitalist depression in 1929. Britain and other countries went off the gold standard and, with initial hesitations South Africa followed suit, resulting in the increase of earnings for her gold exports from 84 shillings per fine oz to 125 shillings and then 140 shillings. Not long after, the outbreak of the Second World War stimulated military manufacture and necessitated import substitution for goods no longer available in wartime trade conditions. Such enforced isolation from foreign markets was encouraged after 1948 by exchange-controls, while another stimulus came through agriculture in the early 1950's as the result of the Korean War induced inflation of raw materials prices. Meanwhile the opening of the Orange Free State gold mines and the discovery of uranium content in the residues of gold-bearing ores gave a fresh life to the mining industry. And, from 1960, South Africa's determination to eliminate her vulnerability to international sanctions and to build up a self-sufficient military machine has provided further stimuli to industry. Since 1933, in fact, the country's rate of economic growth has been steady and high.

Under South African conditions, and with these external stimuli, the rate of capital accumulation is hardly surprising. What the economists euphemistically disguise as "self-financing," "high rates of profit-retention," represents the reinvestment of capital accumulated from the forced labor economy. What available evidence makes harder to discern is the

[59] Compare Arrighi, *Political Economy.*

precise structure of capital control in manufacturing industry. To some extent it has been mining capital, responding to indirect pressures from the state, which has diversified into control of sectors of manufacturing. Particularly in the consumer-goods area—in wholesaling and retailing as well as manufacture—it has been commercial capital which has extended its control, with country storekeepers and emigrés from Hitler's Europe joining the existing merchant class. And state capital has played a crucial role both in totally financing key industries and in providing catalytic finance in others in partnership with private capital. Beyond this, there exist two further important elements in the control of South African industry: foreign capital and agriculturally-based capital.

British capital was already involved in South Africa through commerce and land speculation from the early nineteenth century, and through diamond and gold-mining from the century's end. United States capital partnered South African in the Anglo-American Corporation, and financed motor assembly plants from the 1920's. From after the Second World War such foreign capital moved increasingly into manufacturing industry; between 1945 and 1948, for example, half the capital investment was foreign. Moreover, during the 1950's South Africa received from the World Bank, an international agency of Euro-American capital, more and larger loans than almost any other "developing" country. Until the 1960's the bulk of this foreign capital was British, but in the last decade the contributions from the United States and Western Europe have been increasing rapidly. From the point of view of the investors the major attraction has, of course, been the profits generated by the forced labor economy. Recent estimates suggest a return of some 10 to 15 percent to British capital and 19 percent to United States capital—in both cases higher than the average rate of return on foreign direct investment—though in favorable years the rate has risen as high as 27 percent.[60] For South Africa the advantages have been not so much quantitative as qualitative. If there is debate on the precise significance of foreign capital for rate of economic growth or balance of payments, its contribution to industrial sophistication is undoubted. South African industrialization has depended on employment of more capital-intensive and "modern" methods in a succession of industrial sectors; and in each case, it would appear, it has been foreign capital which has financed the purchasing of the requisite machinery, and foreign firms which have brought the expertise to initiate the handling of such machines. In the 1940's and 1950's this was true in the case of metals-engineering, explosives-chemicals, textiles, food and canning. Backward linkages from assembly, repair, or final processing

[60] See the United Nations document cited in footnote 2.

of semi-finished imports and forward linkages from raw material production made these sectors key growth poles. In the 1960's the new sectors have been production of automobiles and auto accessories, oil prospecting and oil refining—in all of these areas United States corporations have played a key role—and armaments-munitions—where the predominant contribution has been Western European.

In the early stages of industrialization, then, foreign, mining, and commercial capital reaped the greatest benefits. Capital based in agriculture, which had played a major role in guiding the economic structure towards industrialization, found itself unable in a "free market" situation to diversify into manufacturing, commerce, or mining, the commanding heights of the economy. Moreover, as petty commerce and production were abandoned by capital-accumulating whites, their places were taken by Indians and, to a lesser extent, Coloureds, who by operating on small profit margins and working long hours, impeded other aspirant whites from entry to such fields. Hence from the 1930's agriculturally-based capital began to mobilize to gain entry to these areas. Already from the 1920's and earlier rural cooperatives and separate financial institutions for agriculturalists (SANLAM, etc.) had provided means for capital accumulation of the surplus diverted from mining to the farms. Now aspirant rural entrepreneurs began to mobilize those whites whose material position had been entrenched by job color bars and the "civilized labor" policy. In the late nineteenth century Afrikaner nationalism had been the weapon of maize in its formation of an alliance with commercial capital and them mining capital; in the 1920's maize used Afrikaner nationalism to gain the power to lay the infrastructure for industry. Afrikaner nationalism was used to mobilize white savings and consumption patterns in the interest of agricultural entrepreneurs. In 1938 a fund was set up to alleviate the situation of the remaining "poor whites." But when, in the following year, a People's Economic Congress was held to determine the use of the fund, the conference decisions reflected "carefully-prepared schemes, radically different from the simple 'act of salvation' to rescue poor white Afrikaners from poverty . . . on the premise that the main cause of poor-whiteism was the Afrikaners' negligible share in commerce and industry."[61] Save Afrikaans, Buy Afrikaans: these were the initial means by which agriculturally-based capitalists accumulated capital and entered commerce and industry.

The accession of the Nationalist Party to government in 1948, based on a political mobilization of these same groups, was followed by increasing use of state power to assist agriculturally-based entrepreneurs. More

[61] A. Hepple, *Verwoerd* (London: 1967), pp. 60–62.

than ever before, a systematic assault on the economic and political position of Indians and Coloured was launched through the Population Registration Act, the Group Areas Act, and the removal of Coloureds from the common voters role: they were not to be permitted to compete with whites for petty-bourgeois roles in the white-dominated economy.[62] Moreover, by cooperation between agricultural capital and the Industrial Development Corporation, by relocation of industry, through the allocation of building and liquor licenses by political authorities, "national" agricultural capital increased its proportional economic share at the expense of "foreign-connected capital." In 1955 Federale Mynbou made its first forays into the mining industry and, despite efforts by mining and foreign capital to exclude its further participation, acquired a controlling interest in one mining house in 1963.[63] By this latter date foreign-connected mining and industrial capital had well-nigh capitulated; agriculturally-connected entrepreneurs were being invited onto their boards of directors. Indeed some concerns deriving from agricultural capital, such as Anton Rupert's Rembrandt Tobacco Company, had made spectacular advances in Europe and the United States—the firm claims to produce one in every five cigarettes smoked in the capitalist world. This use of self-mobilizing techniques and political power by agricultural Afrikaner capital was analogous to the methods of Italian-Americans and Irish-Americans in the United States. And by the 1960's the goals had been achieved: "verligte" (enlightened) Afrikaner capitalists and their erstwhile "foreign-connected" English and Jewish competitors showed remarkable agreement over the continued dynamics of the South African forced labor economy.

The depression of 1929 had serious effects on both the white commercial and African "reserve" sections of the agricultural economy. If the whites found their remedy through the state, Africans were forced even more imperatively into the forced labor economy. But the rapid expansion of secondary industry, and its changing structure during the Second World War, meant that demand for labor began to give bargaining power to non-whites. Increased capital-intensity, increased mechanization, meant

[62] As a result of pressure from white Natalians, the assault on the Indians was in fact initiated by the Smuts's government in the 1943–8 period.

[63] For some of these points see Trapido, *Comparative Study of Industrialization.* Some research needs to be done on the connections between the opening of a money-market in South Africa as opposed to London by Oppenheimer in 1955–7, the move into the South African field of the American Charles Engelhard (Rand Mines, 1957; American-South African Investment Corporation, 1958), the moves by Federale Mynbou, and the raging controversy among Afrikaners in 1955–8 over the value of foreign capital in the economy.

that the old labor structure of skilled whites and unskilled non-whites began to be replaced by a division between supervisors (white) and semi-skilled machine operators. Increasingly during the wartime years, manufacturers employed in such operative positions non-whites who could be paid lower wages than whites; the segregationist structures of labor control and the restrictions on African movement to the towns were undermined by the needs of industry. Temporarily, indeed, Africans found themselves in a stronger bargaining position and, although strikes in manufacturing industry were banned by a 1942 ordinance which was continued after the war until replaced by legislation in 1953, trade union organizing and collective bargaining among non-whites were more effective than ever before. For the only time in South African history, African wages in the manufacturing sector increased between 1936 and 1948 faster than those of whites.[64]

As in the mining industry in the 1920's, such a situation—in which white workers saw potential or actual deterioration in their material position, in which manufacturing industry was depending on the racial income inequalities of the forced labor economy to substitute non-white for white labor—led to renewed tensions between industrial capital and the white labor force. The white working class, as in the 1920's, looked to the state to provide a statutory entrenchment of its position and hitched its wagon to the force of Afrikaner nationalism being mobilized by agricultural entrepreneurs.[65] Manufacturing capital and the wartime government—for a variety of reasons less dependent than usual on the farming sector of the conventional South African alliance—began tentatively to question the relevance of the interwar structure of labor-coercion to the situation of a booming secondary industry. Did not secondary industry, with its use of semi-skilled labor, require training of workers? Did not trained workers mean that the labor force must be permanent rather than migrant? Must not permanent urbanization of Africans be accepted, and housing and social services oriented to that situation? On the academic peripheries, a few whites went further: if industrialization meant permanent urbanization, did not permanent urbanization mean that political rights would have to be extended to Africans in the central institutions of government, as had happened with industrialization in Europe?[66]

[64] Evidence on this question was drawn together by J. G. B. Maree in an unpublished paper at Sussex University, 1971.

[65] In particular, in crucial trade-unions there was a struggle between Afrikaner nationalist organizers, spearheaded by Albert Hertzog, and those who believed in the illusory possibility of non-racial trade unionism as a "progressive" political force.

[66] This argument, proven empirically false by twenty years of subsequent South African development, has so permeated commentary and analysis on South Africa

Yet such arguments combined wishful thinking by liberals with woolly, short-sighted, or hypocritical argument by manufacturers. Not only would permitting permanent urbanization have slowly undermined the labor-controls and controls on peasant production on which white mining and agriculture relied, but it would in the long run have undermined the position of manufacturers themselves. Their desire for non-white rather than white labor depended on the cheapness of the former, which was dependent on the maintenance of the bans on trade-union organizing, on the labor-pool function performed by the African "reserves," on restricted entry to towns, on the social control and social service functions performed by the maintenance of African "traditional" structures. Nor would it be easy to allow *some* permanent urbanization, *some* relaxation of controls without threatening the whole system. Indeed manufacturing interests were chiefly concerned with continued economic growth and continued profit, and would be content if this could be achieved through elaboration of the existing system.

It was this elaboration, in the context of the new situation of secondary industrialization, which was one major task performed by the Nationalist Government after its accession to power in 1948. *Apartheid,* or separate development, has meant merely tightening the loopholes, ironing out the informalities, eliminating the evasions, modernizing and rationalizing the inter-war structures of "segregationist" labor control. Or, to put it in another way, *apartheid* has meant the extension to the manufacturing economy of the structures of the gold-mining industry. In the towns, all remnants of African land and property ownership have been removed, and a massive building program in so-called "locations" or "townships" means that the African work force is housed in carefully segregated and police-controlled areas that resemble mining compounds on a large scale. All the terms on which Africans could have the right to reside permanently in the towns have been whittled away so that today no African, no matter what his place of birth or that of his parents, no matter where he has lived before, has the right to a permanent residence except in the "reserves"—or, as they are now termed, "Bantustans" or "homelands." Assuming the functions of the mining recruiting organizations, the state has instituted a structure of labor bureaus which are the only means by

---

that it is hard to document its origins and social base. Landmarks in party political thinking were Smuts's speech to the Institute of Race Relations in early 1942, the *Report of the Native Laws Commission* (Fagan Commission) UG 28–1948, the statement of United Party policy in November 1954, and the formation of the Progressive Party in 1959. See, *inter alia,* Hancock, *Smuts,* pp. 481–504; *Oxford History,* vol. 2, pp. 189–191, 198–9; Janet Robertson, *Liberalism in South Africa, 1948–1963* (Oxford: 1971).

which Africans can obtain contracts of employment. The state totally regulates the distribution of labor. In the white-controlled rural areas Africans who had continued to retain some access to the means of production have been evicted. These, and the "surplus" Africans from towns, have been relocated in either the "homelands" or in so-called "resettlement camps" where they can contract out their labor if, when, and where it is needed.[67]

For this reason the state also assumed direct control from 1953 of the non-white educational system which had previously been in the hands of missionaries. A new curriculum was devised with two purposes. Firstly, to provide for the mass of Africans the minimum of educational skills necessary for participation in semi-skilled positions in the forced labor economy. Secondly, to attempt to train a small African elite who would seek their economic and political outlets not within the central white-controlled political economy but in the "homelands." Thus the segregationist structures of social control would be perpetuated and modernized, and since from the late 1950's partly-elected institutions of government have been created in the Bantustans to supplement the rule of chiefs, such an elite could take its place in them.

To protect the white working class, "job reservation" was legislated in 1956. The purpose of this legislation was to provide a systematic classification of the kinds of semi-skilled positions in each industrial sector, and to ensure that white workers received a sufficient allocation of these to secure full employment.[68] Significantly, the legislation itself was much less specific than the entrenchment of the job color bar in mining in the 1920's, indicating a recognition of the need for flexibility and renegotiation of the "level" at which the white versus non-white divide should come. For, given the small numbers of the white work force in conditions of an expanding economy, a rigid demarcation would rapidly produce shortages in the white positions. Indeed in recent years there has been a gradual reclassification, at first covert but now more openly espoused, so that white workers move upwards into more skilled or supervisory posts, while the jobs they vacate are "diluted" into a larger number of less-skilled tasks and filled by non-white workers at lower wages.

[67] The literature on these constantly modified and strengthened labor controls is vast, but A. Hepple, *South Africa: Workers under Apartheid* (International Defence and Aid Fund, 2 Amen Court, London EC4) is a useful introduction. See also C. Desmond, *The Discarded People* (Penguin: 1971) on rural resettlement, and the postscript to the second edition of P. Mayer, *Townsmen or Tribesmen* (Oxford: 1971) for an account of a recent urban resettlement to a compound-like "homeland township."

[68] The 1944 Apprenticeship Act had already ensured that skilled-artisanal work in industry was restricted to whites.

This process of reclassification has often been termed by commentators the "breakdown of job reservation," and is argued to indicate an erosion of racism or *apartheid*. This, of course, is absurd. Like the job color bar in mining, job reservation was a consequence of the forced labor economy, by which the white workers used the state to protect themselves from being supplanted by non-whites whose cheapness as a labor force was conditioned by the state. This reclassification represents simply a means of dynamically modifying the system of racial differentiation in changing economic conditions. Non-whites may indeed move into more jobs, more skilled jobs in manufacturing industry, and may receive marginally increased wages. But the whites move upwards even further. Nor can an attempt to pay equal wages for equal work—as some American and British companies have proclaimed an intention to do—have any greater effect in isolation. This will simply produce greater mechanization and fewer employees—with non-whites rather than whites fired. It is the role of the state in regulating the non-white labor force, the inhibitions on African bargaining power and the differential access to education, which are at the heart of the system of racial differentiation. So long as these institutions exist, the gap between white and non-white wages even in manufacturing industry is likely to increase. And, even more starkly, the gap between white prosperity and the declining real wages, malnutrition, poverty, and starvation of Africans in the mines, on white farms, and in the "reserves," will grow apace.[69]

Development and Underdevelopment in Southern Africa: South Africa as an Imperialist Power

The history of South Africa since the mid-seventeenth century has been essentially expansionist, a part of the absorption of most of the world into the Euro-American capitalist economy. The spreading network of economic relationships has been constantly buttressed by the exertion of political power and the rationale of racialist ideology. State power and ideology have been the means by which white groups within the colonial economy have wrested a share of economic surplus from the metropolis, and wrested it by further exploitation of the indigenous inhabitants. This can be seen in the cattle trade, the development of commercial farming, the entrenchment of the position of white workers in mining, manufacturing and the establishment of secondary industry. In terms of the importation of labor and the export of capital, this economic expansionism began to spread beyond the borders of South Africa from the start of the

[69] See the important article by F. R. Johnstone, "White Prosperity and White Supremacy in South Africa Today," *African Affairs* (April 1970).

twentieth century, and with it an impetus towards political expansion. Resisted at the time by groups concerned with internal structural change, this political and economic expansionism has acquired a new momentum during the 1960's.

This momentum results from the exigencies of continued economic growth in a forced labor economy. The low wages of non-whites make South Africa's domestic market small, so that capital seeking to reinvest must either move itself outside South Africa or develop export markets large enough to produce economies of scale. For minerals and raw materials Europe provided the markets, but in the manufacturing sphere the ever-growing power of Euro-American based multi-national corporations inhibits entry by new producers. In contrast, tropical Africa, with its colonially underdeveloped economies, is South Africa's "natural" outlet.

Although this role which tropical Africa could play for South Africa was recognized as early as 1930, the new orientation dates from the report of the Viljoen Commission of 1958 which argued for the encouragement of "overseas firms that at present export to African territories to establish their factories in the Union, in order to be in close proximity to their markets."[70] The events of Sharpville in 1960 and their national and international repercussions delayed implementation to some extent, but by 1965 to 1966 the South African government was beginning to embark on an "outward-looking" policy: careful cultivation of African allies to destroy the united front of sanctions which newly independent African states had erected against South Africa. In part this policy furthered the interests of foreign capital in South Africa; American businessmen, for example, hope to be in on the ground floor when the political climate eases and South African exports can move freely in Africa.[71] But in large But in large part, this policy has served South African capital.

The current phase of this policy involves the extension of economic, including infrastructural, relationships throughout Southern Africa. Rhodesia, for example, has for some time been a significant importer of South African products. Since UDI in 1965 she has become more dependent on South Africa for goods, finance, and links with the outside world. The Portuguese colonies of Mozambique and Angola were natural candidates for closer ties. Hydroelectric schemes are planned or under construction

[70] *Commission of Enquiry into Policy Relating to the Protection of Industries* (Viljoen Commission), UG 36–1958, para 41. See also, for example, J. Hofmeyr, ed., *Coming of Age* (Capetown: 1930), pp. 100, 109.

[71] Among the immediate stimuli to the outward policy were the forthcoming independence of the High Commission Territories, UDI in Rhodesia, the unfavorable World Court decision on South West Africa in 1966, the successful repression of internal non-white protest.

on the Zambezi (at Cabora Bassa) and the Kunene rivers—with most of the initial power generated to go to South Africa. South African capital, and foreign capital with interests in South Africa, are increasingly involved in exploitation of minerals and natural gas, and prospecting for and producing oil. Such natural gas and oil will be piped to South Africa, while a new road is to link Angola to South West Africa. Investment in mining and infrastructure is also proceeding in the African-ruled former High Commission Territories of Botswana, Lesotho and Swaziland and in Malawi. In Lesotho white South Africans occupy key positions, in, amongst other places, the recently established National Development Corporation, while Malawi has signed a formal trading agreement with South Africa.

The consequences of this South African economic expansionism can be assessed in the light of the history of South Africa itself. Economic growth brought a concentration of industrial activity around limited geographical areas: the Witwatersrand, Durban, Capetown, and Port Elizabeth-East London. Within and outside the formal limits of South Africa, African areas became peripheral satellites of these growth poles, supplying to them labor or primary commodities such as cattle.[72] Within South Africa itself it was the machinery of the state, spurred by the alliance of gold and maize, which instituted the forced labor economy. In the High Commission Territories, Zambia, Mozambique, Malawi, the impetus to labor migration was the British political economy of colonialism. The dynamics of this simultaneous development and underdevelopment have created a situation where South Africa needs outlets for capital and manufactures, while the peripheral areas are dependent on exporting labor, food, or raw materials, and on imports of manufactures and investment goods. Without extension of white rule, without exportation of the full thrust of South Africa's mechanisms of political and ideological coercion, the "satellites" are ripe for plucking.

Even within the political limits of South Africa itself, the current trend is towards decentralization of industry. The Bantustans, pools of unfree labor, are to have manufacturing industry situated adjacent to them in so-called "border areas." In this way the traditional structures continue to reduce "welfare" and "social control" costs to the South African state, the benefits of migrancy are retained, and large concentrations of Africans in major industrial centers are avoided. The state, with its wide powers over wage-determination, has authorized lower wages to the work force in such areas. Significantly, among the first of such border industries was a textile plant jointly financed by the South African I.D.C. and British

[72] See footnote 37.

interests already operating cheap labor plants in Java and India. "They found that their plans fitted in very well with ours" said the chairman of the I.D.C.[73] This pattern will continue in the former High Commission Territories, South West Africa, Angola, Mozambique and Malawi; South African capital will flow to organize primary production, set up facilities for processing food or raw materials or producing inexpensive consumer goods. Capital goods and more sophisticated manufactures will be supplied by South Africa.

In the long run South Africa's plans are more ambitious: the establishment of a common market in Southern Africa presumably involving common decisions on tariffs, investment, currency and so on. Beyond this, South African goods already penetrate the black African boycott through Mauritius and Madagascar, while rumors circulate of the possibility of trading agreements with the Ivory Coast, Gabon, Ghana, Senegal, or Kenya. In the words of former Prime Minister Strijdom, South Africa's aims are "what we believe God has put us here for—our influence to spread right through Africa."[74] Clearly such economic expansion, given South Africa's current economic, political and military predominance, would place economic change in African countries under South African control and perpetuate the development of the white South African center and the underdevelopment of the African peripheries. Moreover, any threats to South African hegemony would be countered diplomatically or militarily. Already South African troops have operated in Rhodesia and, sporadically, in Mozambique and Angola. Already South African air bases in the Caprivi strip and projected in Malawi give her strike power over most of tropical Africa. Already Zambia, striving to escape from the Southern African system, has been subjected to covert South African manipulation and overt border incursions and sabotage. Already white South African mercenaries have operated in the Congo to suppress an anti-imperialist movement. South Africa intends to dominate Africa's southern parts, "to the same, if not a greater extent, than the United States enjoys pre-eminence in the Americas," as a recent South African writer puts it.[75]

[73] Van Eck, *South African Industrial Revolution*, pp. 19–28.

[74] Quoted by S. Patterson, *The Last Trek* (London: 1957), p. 128. Compare Prime Minister Vorster, November 1968: "We are of Africa and our destiny lies in Africa . . . It is our challenge and we dare not fail in our mission."

[75] Quoted by S. Gervasi, "South Africa's Economic Expansionism," *Sechaba* (Official Organ of the African National Congress South Africa, 49 Rathbone Street, London WC1) 5 (June 1971). On South African expansion see also the United Nations document cited in footnote 2 and R. Molteno, *Africa and South Africa* (The Africa Bureau, 2 Arundel Street, London WC2R 3DA: 1971).

Conclusion

The exploitation of the indigenous peoples of South Africa and imported bondsmen began with the establishment of a colony of white settlement in the latter part of the seventeenth century. Situated on a "frontier" of the expansion of European mercantile capitalism, the colonists were already imbued with an ideology of racial superiority and deployed superior military power. Between this time and the late nineteenth century the colonial economic relationships, reinforced by political coercion and racist ideology, spread to embrace almost all the peoples of South Africa. Unequal trade and the harnessing of non-white labor created a surplus. Moreover the colonial (white) ruling class alliance was able to deploy its resources to retain a share of the surplus in local, rather than metropolitan hands. Increasing white supremacist control brought increasing white privilege; increasing white privilege spurred further white control.

The establishment of full white control occurred only at the end of the nineteenth century, with the imperatives of the new imperialist investment in mining and those of the emerging white commercial farmers. British political-military power, deployed to create a unified and efficient administration in South Africa, was the means to control. Within the single South African state, white control used political devices to secure a non-white labor supply and to distribute it to the requirements of mines, farms, and secondary industry, while perpetuating the African "reserves" as a labor pool in which traditional institutions could minimize the costs of social welfare and social control of workers for the white state. Political power and racial ideology (Afrikaner nationalism) was similarly used in the struggle to divert the mining surplus from metropolitan appropriation to develop white farming, to secure material privileges for white workers, and to establish the infrastructure and "growth poles" for the transformation of South Africa into an industrial economy. Meanwhile South African economic ties extended outwards into African colonies through the importation of migrant labor and the export of mining capital. As before, white control of the coerced non-white labor force increased white privilege. "The energy of the enormous labor pool gradually changed South Africa. The whites became rich and the Africans remained poor. The meaning of white supremacy today is to be found not only in the ability of one race to control other races but also in the incredible differences of wealth and opportunity which separate the races." [76] The patterns of power, ideology and privilege characteristic of a colonial society of conquest amplify those class differentiations which coincide with the system

[76] UN, *Industrialization,* p. 26.

of racial differentiation and suppress those within each "racial" community.

In each phase of South Africa's development the pattern of racial attitudes—of "race relations"—has acted on and been acted on by the existing balance of political and economic power, and the exigencies of economic growth and white control. Today, with an expanding industrial economy needing markets and outlets for investment, and in a changing international political climate, South Africa seeks to transform the internal patterns of development and underdevelopment and to extend these to embrace the former colonies of Southern Africa. Hence the ideology, too, is undergoing change. It might be described, as Heribert Adam writes, as "racialism without racism":

> What is now practised is a system of racially defined discrimination and exploitation without, however, justifying it with the traditional ideology of race inferiority. . . The underprivileged ought no longer to be regarded as inferior, but solely as different. The tendency towards greater rationality in the implementation of domination is also reflected in the official ideology, which now focuses on cultural and social differences. The idea of inherent inferiority was, after all . . . fictitious and easily shattered by examples to the contrary. In contrast, reference to the cultural pluralism of the different population groups has a real basis, especially since ethnocentrism is promoted by the forced separation of Apartheid policy. The results of the imposed separatism no longer need an ideological justification; their mere existence demonstrates their correctness.[77]

White privilege and prosperity increases, non-white poverty and underdevelopment intensifies and spreads, but the form of racial attitudes changes. This, perhaps, is the final confirmation that South African society is not explicable in terms of white racial attitudes, or the impediments they have exerted on "natural" forces of economic change.

What of the changing of the system? Clearly the ending of white supremacy implies an end to white control and to white privileges—a political and a social transformation. Clearly the major contradiction in the society is between white capital and its coerced non-white labor force, and clearly, as South Africa expands economically this contradiction spreads through Southern Africa. It has not been possible in this essay to discuss the historical forms of non-white opposition to the South African system. Perhaps the dominant theme of this opposition, as is natural in a society defined by colonial conquest, has been African nationalism. Yet the content of this nationalism, the focus of its struggle, the allies it

[77] H. Adam, ed., *South Africa: Sociological Perspectives* (London: 1971), p. 79.

has sought, have been various; and its apprehension, it could perhaps be said, has always been partial or too vague. Sometimes the focus has been on the extension of democratic political rights within the white society, seeking allies among "democratic" sections of the white electorate. Yet this has ignored the centrality of white control to the perpetuation of white privilege. Sometimes the focus has been on the formation of non-white or non-racial trade unions, perhaps allied with the white working class, and able to turn from wage demands to a general strike. Yet this has ignored those structures of political power which have placed white and non-white workers in different relations to the means of production, and which have deliberately prevented the formation of a concentrated, stable proletariat conscious of the contradiction between the social character and individual ownership of the means of production.[78] Sometimes the focus has been on land, on its repurchase in the market or its reclamation from white ownership. Yet it is doubtful whether either on white-owned farms or in the Bantustans there are landlords and peasants, or that expropriation and redivision of land in either area could secure "base areas" which the population would fight for and extend, as occurred in China and Vietnam. At times, as with the I.C.U. in the 1920's and the African National Congress in the 1950's, several elements have combined, yet without the means for sustaining the momentum through a period of severe repression.

What has been clear since the early 1960's is that the African nationalist liberation movement in South Africa intends to take up again the arms that were laid down in the 1880's. And, with armed struggle in progress at various stages in Rhodesia and South West Africa, and South Africans themselves participating in guerrilla activity and sabotage, the opposition to white colonial rule has been generalized to the whole of Southern Africa. As yet one cannot say, however, what modes of political and social transformation will be involved in the struggle of South Africa's non-white proletariat, moving between Bantustans and industry, scattered over white farms, coerced and controlled by the state and traditional institutions. Yet it may be that the very cultural tradition which Africans preserved in their resistance of the nineteenth century, and which has been frozen, used, and manipulated by the system of white control, will prove the most powerful lever of hegemony. The most overt current signs of African protest in South Africa lie in the emergence in the urban areas of a "black power" consciousness, and in the growing assertiveness of black political leaders—spurred by their followers—in the Bantustans.

[78] See K. Marx and F. Engels, *Communist Manifesto.*

Insofar as these forces, responding to the structure of white control, can integrate politics and culture with a social content and strategies of struggle, they might emerge as the death-knell of white privilege.

Postscript.

This essay was originally completed in late 1971, and was then circulated in draft form to a number of people. Were I to rewrite it now, I would change it in the light of theoretical criticism it has received, of research then in progress and now completed, and of subsequent events. However because it has already been cited and commented upon in its original form, I have thought it better to leave it substantively as it is. For criticism see, for example, H. Wolpe, "Capitalism and cheap labour-power: from segregation to apartheid" *Economy and Society,* I, 4 (1972) ; N. Bromberger in A. Leftwich (ed) *South Africa: Economic Growth and Political Change* (1973) ; M. Lipton, "White Farming: A Case Study of Social Change in South Africa" *Journal of Commonwealth and Comparative Politics,* I, 1, March 1974. For more recent formulations of my own, see M. Legassick, "South Africa: Capital Accumulation and Violence" *Economy and Society,* III, 3, (1974) ; "Legislation, Ideology, and Economy in post-1948 South Africa," *Journal of Southern African Studies,* I, 1, October 1974. The concluding sections of this essay should also take account of: the Ovambo strike in Namibia in 1972; the wave of black workers strikes in South Africa in early 1973; the Portuguese coup in 1974 and its effects on transfer of power to liberation movements in Mozambique and (more problematically), Angola; the negotiations towards negotiations over "Rhodesia" in late 1974–early 1975, spearheaded by Vorster and Kaunda. It is as yet unclear to what extent these series of events represent a sharpening of the contradictions within South Africa itself, or to what extent it is possible in the existing situation of the world economy for South Africa to stabilise its relationships with its periphery, make minor concessions internally, and continue with the development of underdevelopment throughout Southern Africa, backed by multi-national corporations.